PUBLIC SPEAKING
and CRITICAL LISTENING

PUBLIC SPEAKING
and CRITICAL LISTENING

Gary Cronkhite
University of California, Davis

The Benjamin/Cummings Publishing Company, Inc.
Menlo Park, California • Reading Massachusetts
London • Amsterdam • Don Mills, Ontario • Sydney

Sponsoring Editor: Larry J. Wilson
Production Editor: Pat Sorensen
Cover Design: Sharron O'Neil
Book Design: Donna Davis
Artist: Sharron O'Neil

ISBN 0-8053-1901-8
ABCDEFGHIJ-HA-798

The Benjamin/Cummings Publishing Company, Inc.
2727 Sand Hill Road
Menlo Park, California 94025

PREFACE

This is a textbook designed for use in introductory college-level courses in public speaking. It will be especially useful to professors who wish to give their students explicit instruction and practice in critical listening and who wish to instill in their students a sense of ethical responsibility without making pronouncements about rhetorical morality. This text provides a synthesis of humanistic and empirical approaches to the study of public deliberation and combines theoretical foundations with specific practical suggestions. I feel that this approach best ensures understanding and ability that can be generalized beyond the classroom.

Public Speaking and Critical Listening

I believe speech students ought to receive instruction in critical listening that is as explicit as that they receive in public speaking. Students function as both speakers and listeners, more often the latter than the former. The classroom provides an excellent opportunity for students to practice the critical listening skills they will need to function as discriminating adults.

Much of critical listening is already provided by instruction in public speaking if what is learned about the one is generalized to the other. However, the principles of critical listening are not always simply the mirror image of those of public speaking. Self-analysis while listening and analysis of speaker motivation are as important as audience analysis.

This book frequently addresses students directly in their roles as listeners, advising them of specific ways to avoid being duped by clever speakers and, conversely, of specific ways to avoid *rejecting* meritorious proposals merely because their advocates are inept or irritating.

Ethical Rationale versus Moralistic Edicts

Ever since I gave up the ministry I have been disinclined to issue moralistic edicts. On the other hand, I have been dissatisfied with the school which holds that speech is basically amoral, capable of being used for good or evil, so that teachers of speech communication are absolved from any responsibility to deal with ethical matters.

A critical listening approach has ethical implications, as I have noted, since one good way to keep speakers ethical is to keep listeners critical. Additionally, students are likely to use the same basic ethical criteria to guide their speech behavior that they use in choosing among other behavioral alternatives. Thus this book suggests an ethical rationale that goes beyond merely "helping the buyer beware" and still stops short of religious conversion. That rationale is this: Since objective public deliberation is crucial in the evolution of ideas, and the evolution of ideas is crucial to the survival of humanity, any device that reduces the objectivity of awareness of any participant in public deliberation tends to dilute the quality of ideological evolution and poses a threat to the survival of the human species. With one reservation, the suggestion that there may be cases when *immediate* awareness constitutes a "clear and present danger," that rationale is maintained throughout the book and forms the basis for the conclusion.

This rationale applies to listeners as well as speakers. Speakers have some obvious techniques available for reducing listener awareness, of course. But listeners are not entirely innocent victims. They choose speakers to whom they will attend, and they choose and encourage speakers to use certain types of appeals. To a considerable extent listeners shape public discourse and contribute to its quality, so they bear no small responsibility when ideological evolution goes awry. Thus, I have attempted to advance and maintain a clear ethical rationale which applies to both speaking and listening.

Humanism and Empiricism

I am persuaded that the individual who exclusively espouses one method of inquiry is condemned to suffer the presence of numerous tantalizing questions he or she can neither ask nor answer. Professors who present their students with the fruits of a single method of inquiry visit their own affliction upon them as well; they lure them into the prison they have constructed for themselves.

Because I believe so strongly in the pragmatic principle of suiting the method of inquiry to the question to seek appropriate answers, I do not hesitate to invoke the name of Martin Buber as well as that of Martin Fishbein, of Fritz Perls as well as Fritz Heider, of George Campbell and Donald Campbell, of Kenneth Burke and Kenneth Boulding, Donald Byrne and Eric Berne, Toulmin and Tolman, or of any other theorists whose ideas seem relevant and useful. In this book I have made mention of syllogisms and statistics, of reasoning and reinforcement, of ego-defense and ego-involvement, frequently in what may appear to be embarrassing proximity. I hope you approve of such academic promiscuity. If not, at least consider yourself forewarned.

Theory in Practice

I believe the ideal textbook in speech communication should demonstrate the wisdom of the observation that there is nothing so practical as a good theory. Striving toward that ideal, I have tried to provide a framework of sound theory from which to derive practical suggestions for speakers and listeners. The line from theory to practice is easier to trace in some cases than in others. Some advice is not derived from any existing theory, of course. I have tried to present that theory which *does* appear to have practical application, avoid that which does not, and offer any specific advice that seems to make sense on the basis of either theory or direct observation. One consequence is that the *depth* of theoretical foundation for specific advice varies from topic to topic.

People and Messages

Probably the most extensive theoretical development occurs early in the book and deals with interpersonal differences: differences in demographic characteristics, personality, reference persons and groups, cultural assumptions, beliefs, values plans, and policies. The extent of that development is premeditated and predicated on the belief that the first and most essential task of speakers and listeners is to understand one another and themselves. A speaker who fails to understand the listeners' motivations as well as his or her own will seldom succeed in producing a speech that successfully melds those motivations, and even if the student does inadvertently produce a successful speech he or she will not understand why it happened. On the basis of such understanding, effective speakers choose their topics, their methods of explanation and amplification, the motives to which they appeal, the types of reasoning they use, the information they present, the speech structure and sequence, the language, and even the physical environment and manner of presentation. Listeners who do not understand their own motivations as well as those of the speaker will be hard put to decide whether they should concentrate on comprehending material which is intended to be informative and will in fact be useful to them or should also concentrate on deciding whether to accept or reject what the speaker offers, in which case it will be especially important for them to know what motivates the speaker to offer the proposal as well as motivations the listeners themselves may harbor that might lead them into uncritical acceptance or rejection of that proposal.

In short, I believe *understanding people* provides the bases for all the decisions speakers and listeners make in the process of public deliberation, and that is why I have made the *analysis of interpersonal differences* both prominent and extensive.

Structure and Sequence

Despite its importance, you may feel that extensive analysis of interpersonal differences is more than your students can profitably absorb early in the course. If so, there is certainly nothing to prevent you from interspersing those chapters throughout the course as you feel students are ready to return to interpersonal analysis. The only section of Part I that may be prerequisite to understanding succeeding chapters appears to be the description of the Image: Belief–Value–Plan model, which appears at the beginning of the chapter dealing with opinions and policies.

For that matter, you may want to treat the chapters dealing with explanation, amplification, and research as a unit relating to informative speeches, followed by the chapters that deal with persuasive appeals, reasoning, and evidence. Or you may believe that novice speakers need to be introduced first to matters of delivery, or that speech structure is a more natural place to begin.

There are a number of possible ways to organize a textbook for an introductory course in public speaking. One way is to cover topics in the sequence in which I believe novice speakers need to learn about them. However, there is no substantial agreement as to what that natural sequence *is*. A novice speaker must know something about understanding listeners, methods of explanation, finding information, organization, and delivery but, which comes first?

My compromise has been to provide some basic principles in the first chapter to carry students through their earliest speeches. After that, the material follows the sequence in which one ordinarily proceeds in preparing a speech. That sequence is essentially a classical pattern based on the five canons of rhetorical theory: invention, disposition, style, memory, and delivery, with treatment of memory appearing as part of the final chapter on delivery. In more contemporary terminology, the sequence is analysis of people; analysis, amplification, and support of the thesis or central idea; structuring and sequencing the material; expressing the message in language; and delivering the speech.

Illustrative Speeches

Speeches are included at the end of most chapters as illustrations of concepts developed in the chapters and as specimens for analysis in general class discussion or as group or individual projects. Introductory comments are also provided. However, three matters deserve mention at this point.

First, not all the speeches are offered as examples of "good" speeches for students to emulate. I have made a particular point of choosing some speeches that contain fallacious reasoning and questionable appeals to motives in order to provide students practice in recognizing such devices. Further, some speeches may be effective examples of the concept they were chosen to illustrate, but may be inadequate in other respects. In fact, some speeches have been chosen because they are exaggerated examples of the concepts they illustrate, which makes it easier for students to recognize the concept but especially important that they be cautioned not to use them as patterns for their own efforts.

Second, it is obviously impossible and probably undesirable to find speeches exemplifying a single concept. Consequently, a speech that appears as an example for one chapter may well be useful to illustrate concepts covered elsewhere.

Third, speeches have not been included for all chapters simply because they are not always useful. The process of research can hardly be exemplified in a speech, and delivery cannot be effectively exemplified in a printed text

Questions for Self-evaluation

Two lists of questions are developed throughout the book—one for the evaluation of speaking competencies and another for evaluation of listening competencies. The questions appear at the ends of the parts to which they relate, and they are compiled into two comprehensive lists in the Conclusion.

A sample speech rating form developed on the basis of the checklist for speakers appears at the end of the text. No numerical scale is provided. That is quite intentional; it allows for the use of different point systems depending upon the professor and the specific assignment. Of particular importance is the fact that it allows different *weights* to be given to different aspects of preparation and performance. The rating form can also be used by students as they listen to speeches as a device for sharpening their critical listening abilities.

Gary Cronkhite

CONTENTS

CHAPTER ONE

Introduction: Theory and Practice

The focus of this book is upon public deliberation, which contains two aspects. The first of these aspects in public speaking—that is, that part of the process of public deliberation in which a speaker tries to inform or persuade an audience in some way. The second aspect of public deliberation is listening—listeners participate in the process of public deliberation to gather information or to make some decision that a speaker is urging upon them.

It is important to consider both of these aspects—the point of view of the speaker and the point of view of the listener. One must learn to participate in the process of public deliberation from both points of view. Sometimes one is a speaker; sometimes one is a listener. People probably listen more frequently, and for that reason, if for no other, something ought to be said about how to conduct oneself in that role.

It is also important to view the process of public deliberation as it fits into the process of human communication in general. We think of public deliberation as something that occurs occasionally in which we participate as either speaker or listener. It is more difficult to recognize how important public deliberation is in the larger social context.

Social change usually takes place by some combination of various types of human communication. Sometimes its purposes are achieved by deliberation in a public context. Sometimes its purposes are achieved in face-to-face interaction between two participants or a small group of participants. Public deliberation usually arises out of other types of communication, and it usually results in other types of communication; that is, public deliberation cannot be studied as an isolated phenomenon.

Public deliberation is a particular type of communication that occurs when a clearly identifiable speaker addresses a number of listeners. Exactly when communication becomes public deliberation instead of some other kind of communication is not always clear. For instance, imagine two men who meet on a street corner. They are presently involved in a strike against a particular company, and they begin discussing the strike. One becomes fairly emotional about what he's saying and begins to speak in a louder voice. This attracts a couple of other people who join in the discussion. As the group grows larger, one of the speakers begins to urge the other members of the group to march on the factory and seek an audience with the president of the company. The others gather around to listen to his arguments. Now the question is, at what point does this become public deliberation and stop being some other form of communication: dyadic two-person communication or small group communication? It is difficult to draw the line. Probably the major distinction is when the turn-taking stops.

In a two-person discussion the general pattern is that one person speaks, then the other responds; the first person speaks again, and the other responds. This process can also take place in a small group. One person after another speaks, and although small group communication is sometimes monopolized by one speaker, the potential exists for other members of the group to break in and express their opinions. When all pretense of turn-taking is abandoned and one person begins to produce an extended monologue with the others responding to him or her in some way, perhaps verbally, but more likely nonverbally, the phenomenon becomes public deliberation rather than small group communication.

By taking this course you have indicated that public deliberation is the sort of thing that you want to study, that you want to study specifically how to present yourself before an audience and the best way to go about the process of making critical decisions when you are the member of an audience. What you want to study is human communication. But public deliberation is a particular type of human communication, one in which there is an identifiable speaker and an identifiable group of listeners, and one in which the speaker presents a monologue that is somewhat extended and uninterrupted.

THE FUNCTIONS OF PUBLIC DELIBERATION

I would like to think about the functions of public deliberation in two ways: (a) how public deliberation functions in society in general in what has been called the "evolution of ideas" and (b) some types of functions that public deliberation performs.

Public Deliberation and the Evolution of Ideas

Donald Campbell, a psychologist-philosopher from Northwestern University, has described the process of ideological evolution. Evolution, in general, requires three things: variety, selection and retention.[1] To see why these three are necessary, suppose we imagine what might happen if atmospheric pollution continues to increase gradually over the next three centuries. First, if there is too little variety among human respiratory systems, the human race will soon become extinct. There must be enough human beings with large lung capacities, less need for oxygen, and high tolerance for pollutants for the species to survive. If everyone were nearly the same in all these characteristics, they would all die off before evolution had any chance to save the species.

Second, there will have to be a selection mechanism. In biological evolution that selection mechanism is very harsh. Unfit organisms either die or fail to reproduce. In our example, as atmospheric pollution increases we will expect more of those with small lung capacities to die at an early age or to be less capable of reproduction. But variety and selection, by themselves, still would not save the species—people would just die off slowly. Although those with large lung capacities would disappear last, the number of human beings would just slowly dwindle.

But that does not take into account what Campbell calls the "retention or propagation mechanism." Notice that in each succeeding generation a greater proportion of those with large lung capacity will be reproducing and thus transmitting large lung capacity as a genetic characteristic to their offspring. In effect, by continuing to pollute the atmosphere, we will be selectively breeding a new type of human being with large lungs, reduced need for oxygen, and increased tolerance for pollutants. It is all a race, of course. Atmospheric pollution may increase so rapidly that this evolutionary process cannot keep up with it, and we will join the dinosaurs, the sabre tooth tigers, and the dodo birds.

That kind of evolution is strictly biological. Fortunately, we also have on our side *ideological evolution—the evolution of ideas*. If we can make public policy evolve fast enough, we can stop pollution before it stops us. The problem is that the evolution of ideas works in ways very much like biological evolution. Public policy is overrun with ideological dinosaurs, dodos, and sterile cuckoos. The evolution of ideas also requires variety, selection, and retention. If we do not have a variety of ideas and plans available to us, we may suddenly find ourselves facing a time whose idea has not yet come. The evolution of ideas requires that we encourage free thinking. If we allow censorship of ideas by those in power now, we may find ourselves sharing a common tomb later when the ideas that are powerful now are no longer equal to the challenge of a new age. Freedom of speech is not just an academic sacred cow; it is a very practical necessity for survival.

But if we have a variety of ideas, we are also going to need a reliable means of selecting those we need at any particular time. We cannot allow every weird idea that happens along to be put into practice. In biological evolution, many—in fact, most—mutations are ill-adapted and frequently do not survive on their own. The same is probably true of ideological evolution. Without some means of selection we would soon be overrun with ideological mutations.

By selection of ideas, I do not mean "censorship." There is a vast difference between killing an idea and merely refusing to adopt it. An idea that seems to be a wild mutation today may be exactly what we need tomorrow. Death is not the selection mechanism in the evolution of ideas. An idea is selected when it is accepted by those who are capable of retaining and propagating it. In ideological evolution retention is the process of weaving a selected idea into the fabric of society, institutionalizing it by expressing it in laws, customs, and conventions, and defending it against attack.

To return to the pollution example, if this process of ideological evolution progresses rapidly enough, we may never have to face the harsher prospect of biological evolution. At the very worst, we may be able to buy time so that humanity can evolve biologically instead of becoming extinct. To do that we need to encourage free-thinking people to produce a variety of ideas—even somewhat radical ideas—for dealing with pollution. We need a gigantic worldwide brainstorming session. At the same time we must evaluate critically each of the ideas in order to select those that are likely to succeed, and we must institutionalize as public policy those that are selected. If this evolution of ideas proceeds rapidly enough, we may find and adopt a means of dealing with pollution in time to preserve ourselves.

Now it seems obvious that public deliberation is a necessary part of all three processes. It is in public deliberation that the necessary variety of ideas occurs. In free, uncensored public deliberation the public may be exposed to a wide variety of ideas, some of which will certainly not be useful to them, some of which may not be useful to them at the moment but will become useful later, and, of course, some of which will be useful at the time they're expressed. Without public speaking, however, this process would proceed very slowly because the necessary variety of ideas—even though they might be expressed by one person to another or in small groups—would not have much chance of reaching the population in general.

The second step in ideological evolution—that is, the selection of ideas—occurs by a process of *critical* public deliberation and *debate* in which we all participate. We *listen* to political speeches in favor of certain candidates. We *listen* to political speeches that favor certain propositions. We watch commercials. And in the end each of us operates as a part of the selector mechanism by voting for a candidate, for one side or the other of a proposition, and by buying certain products and refusing to buy others.

Finally, it is generally by a process of public deliberation that the selected ideas are publicized, institutionalized, and retained. I have written about that before, referring to the function of communication in general in this process of evolution.

The functioning of this selector mechanism depends upon the use of communication. Of course, communication is involved in all three processes. Mutant ideas are carried like seeds on the winds of communication. The retention-propagation system uses communication as a selective herbicide to destroy the ideological mutation and as a fertilizer to maintain the health of the ideological strains that have been chosen for preservation. But at the heart of the entire process is the selector mechanism and the discipline which ministers to its health—communication.[2]

That is what this book is about—a wide variety of influences may prevent you from making objective, reliable decisions in response to public deliberation. That is important because each one of us functions day by day as a part of this selection mechanism, making thousands of seemingly trivial decisions each day in response to thousands of seemingly trivial messages. But in the long run, as the years and generations pass, it is these trivial decisions that are going to determine the quality of the ideas that survive this evolutionary process. No single dinosaur at any one time ever felt a specific chill that alerted it to the slow advance of the Ice Age, and no one of us is likely to make one single decision that will assure the survival of critical thinking or even noticeably alter the course of ideological evolution. Yet humanity may well stand or fall, survive or perish, on the overall quality of its public deliberation.

Specific Functions of Public Deliberation

Suppose we become a little more specific about the functions that communication in general and public deliberation in particular serve in this process of ideological evolution. The functions that communication serves are different for each situation, of course. Trying to summarize them is bound to be difficult. In this book, however, I'm going to focus on three general functions: First, the dissemination of information; second, the facilitation of cooperation; and third, self-actualization.

The dissemination of information   In a book titled *Teaching as a Subversive Activity*, Postman and Weingartner report that Hemingway once said, "In order to be a great writer, a person must have a built-in shock-proof crap detector." They go on to say, "It seems to us that Hemingway identified an essential survival strategy and the central function of the schools in today's world. We have in mind a new education that sets out to cultivate just such people—experts at crap detecting."[3]

Now if that should be the central function of the schools in general—and I believe it should—it is an even more central function of the study of public deliberation. We're bombarded with propaganda almost every minute of every day through every means politicians and businessmen and others can devise. All too frequently they are assisted by college courses and professors who teach them how to sell themselves, their ideas, and their wares more effectively. More subtly, they are assisted by a system of education that rewards students who learn to accept what is told them by their professors and textbooks. As Postman and Weingartner point out, the medium is the message in education, too. And while a student may or may not remember the content of a course, the typical classroom activity, or medium, he's absorbing information, and information is hard to distinguish from propaganda.

Somewhere, in some course, someone ought to actively teach the critical evaluation of propaganda. That is why, in this book, I am trying to teach public deliberation as a process that includes not only the functions performed by the speaker but the functions performed by listeners. Speakers must learn to present their information effectively, but effectively in the sense of being accurate. Listeners, on the other hand, must learn to receive that information, evaluate it critically, and make decisions on the basis of the information they consider reliable without being affected by irrelevant psychological considerations.

Obviously, it is of considerable advantage to an individual to learn to detect unreliable communication. It is also advantageous to a society for its members to develop that ability. Otherwise, particular individuals or groups can use communication to advance their own interests at the expense of society. Free enterprise is especially dependent on the consumer's ability to evaluate advertising critically and to make practical decisions about what to buy. Democracy is equally dependent upon the voter's ability to critically evaluate political propaganda and make practical decisions about how to vote. *The quality of life in a free society is a rather direct reflection of its members' critical listening abilities and the abilities and motivations of its public speakers to present information accurately.*

We get much of our information about the world by listening to public speakers. College classes that use the lecture format constitute one example very close to you. Teachers are especially likely to use public speaking as a means of giving information to a large group. I hardly need to tell you that some do it well, but others do it very poorly. I am sure you have spent a good many hours sitting in lecture halls wishing the professor knew as much about how to communicate in public as he or she knew about the content of the course.

Students are also called upon to speak in public. You may give reports in classes or speak to your fraternity, sorority, club, dorm council, or student association. Sometimes the purpose of your speech is to provide information. The university where I teach has a tradition of holding concerts and public forums on the quad at noon. Speakers there explain yoga, karate, or skiing, or they speak on controversial issues, elections, ballot initiatives, student association decisions, or issues being considered by the city council that might affect students. Your university may handle it differently, but it propably has some form of public discussion of matters of general interest and significance.

Graduation is not going to mark the end of your involvement in public deliberation. Whatever profession you choose, you will be speaking in public—at least if you are successful. If you teach, public speaking and information dissemination will be a major part of your job.

In other professions you may give sales presentations, financial reports, and convention papers. The occasions on which you give such speeches are likely to be very important to your career. Speaking to a large number of people is an opportunity to have unusual impact if you can make your speech serve this function of providing reliable information for your listeners.

Facilitation of cooperation   All of this discussion may sound as if I am arguing that the use of public speaking to influence others is never justifiable. I do not believe that. The human race probably would not have survived so long and certainly not so well if it had not been for the second function of communication—facilitating cooperation. The building you live in would never have been built if it had not been for carefully coordinated cooperation, including specialization and division of labor. If you were not busy finding shelter or food, you would probably be busy protecting yourself from others if it were not for carefully coordinated social agreements which make the need for violent defense something of a rarity. All of this cooperation would be impossible if it were not for communication, and it certainly would not be so widespread if it were not for public deliberation. We deliberate about the need to cooperate and ways to cooperate, we use public deliberation to coordinate the activities of the participants, and we use it to persuade others to join us. Everything that makes up what we call "civilization" depends upon cooperation, and cooperation of any complexity and flexibility depends upon communication and, to some extent, public deliberation.

The real problem in a public-speaking situation is that the public speaker may be attempting to get his audience to cooperate with him in *his* own best interests rather than in *their* own best interests. To accomplish that, he may try to deceive them, or he may take advantage of certain psychological characteristics that he knows they have in order either to deceive them or to get them to cooperate with him to their disadvantage. Thinking of any given public speech in the greater context of public deliberation and public deliberation, in turn, in the larger context of the evolution of ideas makes it more likely that a public speaker will depend upon *accurate presentation* of information, *careful reasoning,* and *appeals to actual needs and motives* of his or her listeners rather than upon deception and appeals to unconscious, irrelevant motives. Furthermore, if listeners can be trained to understand the means by which deception is practiced, if they can be trained to identify reasoning fallacies, and if they can become aware of their own subconscious, psychological motives, they will be better equipped to deal with public speakers who may, in fact, wish to mislead them.

Self-actualization   The essence of this third function is that people use communication to practice self-disclosure and to learn to trust others, to empathize with the feelings and motives of others, and to improve their own self-understanding.

Self-disclosure and trust are both necessary as bases for the cooperation-facilitation function, of course. But they also seem to be rewarding in their own right in that people seem to have a need for intimate interaction with one another. Intimate interaction certainly requires that we trust those with whom we are interacting. In fact, to some extent, it requires that we reveal things about ourselves that other people could not know without communication. *The practice of self-disclosure and trust, in turn, teaches one to empathize with others;* that is, one comes to know what the feelings and motives of others are likely to be. This, in turn, allows one to better understand oneself. Especially in the area of subjective experiences and feelings, it is necessary to communicate with others in order to confirm one's own internal feelings, thus gaining self-confidence. It allows one to anchor one's own feelings because it provides a means of discovering when they drift too far. It is important to know what others believe your own abilities are, especially in the area of personal aspirations, so that if your own opinion of yourself is too high or too low you will be able to revise it and make it more realistic. Sometimes communication provides an outlet for the expression of emotions before they reach an explosive level. In short, communication provides the means for social transaction that improves an individual's mental health, which, in turn, improves the quality of his or her social transaction.

Many authors talk about how communication in general serves the function of self-actualization. It may seem a little strange to think of public deliberation as serving that function since we usually think of self-actualization being accomplished by intimate, face-to-face communication between two people or, at most, among very few people who know one another well. Public deliberation is hardly intimate, and the participants cannot know one another very well. Yet there have been times when large groups of people, faced with a common threat to their self-images or to their personal welfare, have gained confidence from charismatic speakers who have redefined those self-images. Such speakers have essentially performed the function of self-actualization for the members of their groups. The speakers of the American Revolution performed that function for the colonists, redefining their self-images so they came to consider themselves members of an independent republic capable of creating a new nation. In more modern times Winston Churchill and Franklin Roosevelt galvanized their respective nations by adding new dimension to the self-images of their listeners. John Kennedy was on his way to doing that for Americans once again when he was assassinated. Martin Luther King, Malcolm X, and a number of others did it for blacks.

Germaine Greer, Gloria Steinem, and a host of others are enhancing the self-images of women. Caesar Chavez is doing it for Chicano farm laborers in the West. Numerous public speakers are performing the function of self-actualization for citizens of the third-world nations. Protestant and Catholic factions in Northern Ireland are waiting for someone to help them align their self-images so they can stop shooting one another and build a unified nation. As the United States moves into its third century, Americans are waiting for a leader to tell them how to repair their self-images, which have been so badly damaged by the Vietnam debacle, the Nixon Administration, the economic and energy crises, and the revelation of foreign meddling and domestic violations of cherished civil rights by two of the most respected American institutions: the FBI and the CIA. These are instances of self-actualization and the need for it on a mass scale, but self-actualization nonetheless. The major tool for such self-actualization is public deliberation.

AN INTRODUCTION TO THE PRACTICE OF PUBLIC SPEAKING

Speakers ordinarily think first of the audience and, second, of the arguments and available evidence. Then they begin to gather evidence and put it into some organizational pattern. They give some thought to the language they are going to use—both before and during the speech— and, of course, to the delivery of the speech. But since you cannot read this entire book at once before you deliver your first speech, or at least you are very unlikely to, I would like to discuss some of the basic things you must know before you deliver your first speech in class.

Choosing and Analyzing a Topic

Your earliest speeches are probably going to be informative in nature, which means that you will be trying to explain something to your listeners as clearly as possible, and your purpose will be to get them to understand what you have to say. The topic of your speech has to be determined by some intersection of your own interests and those of your listeners.

For example, suppose you are an agriculture major, and you want to explain some aspect of agriculture in your first speech. You must keep in mind that students in class who are not agriculture majors are going to perceive information about agriculture differently than you intend. You are going to have to overcome this problem, not only for a speech on agriculture, but also if you explain some aspect of electrical engineering, business administration, English literature, psychology, or other subject. It would probably be a good idea to give some thought to what your audience interests and perceptions may be before you even choose your specific topic. Certainly you want to give some thought to it before you write your introduction.

It is not just your listeners' *perceptions* and *interests* you will have to know about. Their perceptions and interests are based on their *beliefs* and *values*. Knowing their beliefs and values will help you understand why their perceptions are different from yours and what you can do about it. So how do you find out about their perceptions and the beliefs and values on which these perceptions are based? Probably the best way is to *ask them* before you plan your speech. Now trust me in this—the other people in the class are just as worried about their speeches as you are about yours. How about getting three or four of them together after class and making a deal with them? The deal is that you will listen to what they plan to talk about and react to it if they will do the same for you. That is *not* cheating; it is a good approach to audience analysis. But be careful who you choose to be part of the group. If you are an agriculture major, it is not going to help much to get other agriculture majors together. Their perceptions, beliefs, and values are probably going to be too much like your own. You should find three or four other students who are very different from you so that you can get the widest sampling of reactions possible. But you won't help each other much if you all sit around and congratulate one another on your choice of topics, the brilliance and clarity of your explanation, and the interesting material and examples you are going to use. You want to be mutually supportive, but you also want to get a good idea of how the rest of the class is going to respond, so be honest with one another—constructively and helpfully honest.

Now suppose you really want to talk about the expense involved in turning a calf into marketable beef. The other people in your group respond with something like, "Oh my God! Not another speech about cows!" What to do? Find out why they respond that way. Don't argue with them; don't give them a sermon about why they should be interested in cows. You don't want to convince them at this point. You just want to find out why other people may be bored or antagonistic when they hear your topic. You also want to find out the conditions under which they might become interested, what you can do to make them interested. You may discover that the only time they care about raising a calf is when they go to the store to buy meat. That gives you something to work with. You have discovered that when they hear someone talk about agriculture, they turn off and start thinking about skiing or sex. That is because they believe agriculture is not related to anything they value. Your job is to make them believe that argiculture *is* related to something they value—

namely, money—so they will be attentive. So you may decide to begin your speech with something like this:

> Three years ago you could still buy some grades of hamburger for 59¢. Today when you go down to Dick's Market, you'll be lucky if you can touch raw hamburger for less than $1.00. That really adds up! If you eat a pound of hamburger or some other kind of meat every day, you'll be paying over thirty dollars a month now instead of about eighteen dollars a month three years ago. Or if you eat in the dorm, it means you're eating a lot more "mystery meat," or rice, or "Hamburger Helper" and a lot less real hamburger than you would have three years ago. What I want to do in the next three minutes is tell you why you're paying so much for meat so you'll at least know who to be mad at and what to do about it. For a project last year in Future Farmers of America, I raised a calf for market. Now I originally bought the calf for . . .

If it were successful, such an introduction would cause your listeners to listen attentively because you have made them believe that attentive listening will result in something they value.

In this example the speaker already knew generally what he wanted to talk about. You may not have found a topic for your speech yet. For most students, determining the topic is the most difficult part of giving a speech. The first place to look for a topic is not in the library; *it is among the things that you value*. One possibility to consider is your *major*. Spend some time thinking about things you know as a result of your major that might interest the other students in your speech class. What especially interesting courses have you taken as part of your major? For that matter, what especially interesting elective courses have you taken? What kinds of things did you learn that made those courses interesting? Is there something that you learned that might make an interesting speech topic?

Another area to consider is *hobbies, sports,* and *special activities,* especially if they are unusual in some way. If you are a skier attending the University of Colorado or a surfer attending the University of Hawaii, it will be difficult to tell most of your classmates anything they do not already know about those sports. But if you are a skier attending the University of Hawaii or a surfer attending the University of Colorado, you have a ready-made topic.

If you are working as well as going to school, your *job* may offer some possibilities. If you have a part-time job as a radio announcer, explain to the class how you keep all the records, news, and commercials straight. If you work as a computer programmer, explain something about how computers work and how you communicate with them. If you are a salesperson, tell a little about the line you sell and how you go about making a sale, or describe some of the strange people you encounter. Your precollege and family background may yield something of interest. Is your father a judge? A doctor? A pilot? A rancher? An oilfield worker? A minister? How did his job or your mother's job make your life a little different from what the other members of your class may have experienced? Where were you raised? If you lived in a large city and most of your classmates did not, or if you lived on a farm or a ranch and most of your classmates did not, they might enjoy hearing about it. If your parents have traveled and you have lived in Paris, Tripoli, and Turkey or if your father taught at the College of the Virgin Islands, in Mexico, or on a Navajo Reservation, or if you are a Southerner attending a Northern college, or vice versa, do not overlook those sources of interesting topics.

What interesting experiences did you have in high school or elementary school? Did your home ever burn, or was it burglarized? If so, a description of such a personal experience would make a great lead-in to a speech about fire safety or home security. Were you ever arrested? If so and if you are willing to talk about it, that could lead you very neatly to the topic of your legal rights if you are stopped by the police.

What about topics of current interest, especially topics that are in the news at the moment? Do you have inside information about such a topic? Or can you get any extra information by doing some research? Is the city where your college is located considering some changes that will affect students? Is the student association considering some interesting proposals? Is the state legislature or the board of regents considering a tuition increase?

What you are doing as you search for a topic is sifting through your mental *"image"* as described in the fourth chapter of this book. Public speaking is really a speaker's means of broadcasting part of his or her mental image when an audience considers that part of that image important enough to be broadcast—for example, when they feel they may want to adopt that part of a speaker's image. What you are doing as you prepare a speech is considering how your mental image corresponds to those of your listeners. You are "giving them a piece of your mind."[4]

Narrowing the Topic

You have selected a general topic area that you want to use for your speech. The best favor you can do yourself before beginning your research is to decide as specifically as possible what it is that you're going to look for, specifically what you're going to say in that speech. Otherwise, you may spend hours of unnecessary time searching about aimlessly, wandering through books and periodicals in the library, and stumbling about in your mind like a person lost in the fog.

Now the process of learning about your listeners will probably have given you some ideas about how to become more specific. At the same time, you ought to ask yourself what it is in particular that interests you about the general topic area. Can you settle on something that interests both you and your listeners? You may begin to survey the available supporting material. This initial survey should also help you narrow your topic because you may find that some types of information just are not available or are very difficult to get.

Thesis

Now somewhere within that general area that represents the convergence of your interests, the interests of your listeners, and the available material lies your specific *thesis*. Contrary to popular opinion, a thesis is not just something that candidates for a master's degree have to write. The thesis of your speech is *the* major point of your speech, condensed into a single sentence. In fact, you can think of the word *thesis* as standing for *THE Speech In a Sentence.*

The more quickly you settle on that single sentence summary of your speech, the less time you will waste reading and copying material that will eventually turn out to be useless to you. For an example of a thesis and its development, you might look at the speech outline in Chapter 9, "Structure and Sequence." The thesis of that proposed speech is, "Approaching the corner correctly, choosing the best line, and steering with the accelerator are necessary to drift a sports car through a simple corner at maximum speed without wiping out."

Before settling on that thesis, I started by recognizing that I am interested in the general topic area of automobiles. Then I began to narrow that area by thinking about what it is that especially interests me. I decided it is not designing automobiles, or riding in them, or selling them, or fixing them; it is driving them. I decided the part of driving that interests me the most is cornering, so I decided to build an outline of a speech based on that specific thesis.

Once you have selected a thesis that specific, the task of locating material is much easier. You know much more precisely what you are looking for. If I were to have developed a speech about cornering a sports car, I could look for magazine articles and books on cornering rather than looking at automobile repair manuals and histories of automobile development, all of which would eventually prove to be totally useless. But you have to exercise a really strong will to avoid digressing, even after you have selected a thesis. You have to be absolutely ruthless. For instance, I know I am also interested in what it is about sports cars that makes them corner well. In developing my speech I would be very tempted to toss in some material about weight distribution, center of gravity, roll center, suspension design, steering geometry, tire width, tread design, radial-ply versus bias-ply tires, and on and on, none of which would relate directly to my specific thesis. You will be tempted, too. Resist it! If you do not, the point of your speech will become fuzzy in your own mind, and your audience may lose the point entirely.

Statement of Purpose

Another device that may help you focus your speech is the *statement of purpose*. Try to describe in a single sentence what you want to accomplish in your speech, what you want your audience to understand, be able to do, accept, or be willing to do. The statement of purpose is not the same as the thesis, and it is no substitute for a thesis, but it performs some of the same functions. It helps you focus your mind on exactly what you want to do in your speech.

Major Divisions

Notice that the thesis statement in this example includes a statement of the *major divisions* of the speech, which is nice if you can do it. Sometimes you can, and sometimes you cannot. Whether you get them into your thesis statement or not, you should work as rapidly as possible toward deciding what your major divisions will be. That would be one more aid to you in deciding what material is directly related to your thesis and purpose and what material should be omitted. In the example given, I decided to divide the explanation according to three things a driver has to do in sequence as he or she moves into a corner. Your thesis may also be most easily divided chronologically if it is a description of a process or a sequence of events, or it may be obviously divisible spatially if it is a description of an object or a location. If it cannot be divided chronologically or spatially, you will have to resort to something else, especially if your speech is persuasive.

Analyzing for a persuasive speech when your thesis must be not only understood but also accepted by your audience is a somewhat different matter. What you have to do is list the major reasons why your listeners should accept your thesis. These are your major arguments, each of which will require supporting material. Each argument will *appeal* to one or more of your listeners' *motives*, and each will take the form of, or be supported by, one of the forms of *reasoning*.

Gathering Information

Now that you have your general topic, your specific thesis, your statement of purpose, and some idea of what your major divisions are going to be, your next problem is to try to find information on your topic. If you've really chosen a topic that interests you, the chances are that you are going to know something about it. The best thing you can do at this point is to sit down and list what you know. Think of where you encountered your information; it may give you an idea of where to look for more. Did you get it from newspaper or magazine articles, from someone who seemed to know a lot about it, from one of your professors in a lecture, or from a television program? Be especially alert for possible resource persons who might know a great deal about your topic and who might be willing to share either their information or places to locate further information.

The college library is, of course, very helpful. You will probably find that encyclopedias, annual almanacs such as *Information Please,* or *The Statistical Abstract of the United States,* all of which are located in the reference room of the library, will be especially helpful in locating material. Check the *Reader's Guide to Periodical Literature* for magazine sources. It's probably a good idea to begin with the latest volume, work back, and check all the terms you can imagine that might relate to your topic. Try to build a list of those terms as you go along. If you have chosen a topic on which there is some scholarly research, you'll soon realize that scholarly journals are not indexed in the *Reader's Guide to Periodical Literature.* To find those, you'll have to go to the publication that indexes other publications in that discipline. The best thing to do is ask one of the professors in the department under which your topic falls just what those major indexes are. Start with the most recent articles again and work back, because you can pick up footnotes and bibliographies of previous articles from the most recent articles.

As you probably know, books are indexed in the card catalog in your library. The best thing to do is record the call numbers of specific books you're interested in, but look at other books in that area of the library because you might encounter a book there that would also be useful.

In these early explanatory speeches, as in any speech for that matter, there may be certain materials you can bring to class that will help clarify your explanation. If so, it might be a good idea to look at the section dealing with audio/visual materials that appears in Chapter 8, "Search and Research." Remember that audio/visual materials must be large enough to be seen or loud enough to be heard. They should be pretested to determine that they are in working order, or if they are such visual aids as posters, you should be sure that they will not fall down or blow away. You should probably clear them with your instructor to make sure they are acceptable before bringing them to class. Probably the best rule is to pretest them in the actual room in which you will be giving the speech or in a room that is very similar to make sure that they are going to come off as well as you imagine.

Organizing Your Speech

You have already analyzed your speech topic in that you have settled on a central idea or thesis; you have decided on a central purpose; and you have divided your thesis into two, three, or four major divisions. Organization consists primarily of indicating to your audience how your speech has been analyzed and keeping them informed at all times about where you are in the speech, how what you are saying now relates to what has gone before, and how it relates to what is yet to come.

The first device you have to carry much of the burden is the *introduction*. There are a number of things that have to be done in an introduction, one of which is to try to get the *attention* of the audience and make them like and respect you. This is sometimes called the "attention step," and it is one to which you should devote some thought. Avoid an overly dramatic device to get listener attention, but use one that will make them realize that what you are going to say is relevant to them and to their interests. Don't be afraid to reveal a few things about yourself—in particular, about how you became interested in this topic—at the very beginning of the speech. It will not only help increase their interest in what you have to say, but it will function to make them identify with you, like you better, respect you more, and consequently, be more willing to listen to what is to come.

The second major function of the introduction—at least in an explanatory speech—is to indicate the overall organization of your speech. This is the point at which you tell your audience not only what your general topic is—that is, not only what you are going to talk about—but specifically what you are going to say—that is, your central idea or thesis at this point. You may follow the thesis with a statement of purpose if you wish, but your purpose may be obvious from your thesis statement.

Next, tell your audience how you are going to proceed through the speech. The easiest way to do that is to tell them that your speech is going to be divided into two, three, or four parts and then simply to explain to them what the major divisions of your speech will be; or you can indicate that the order of your speech will be chronological, spatial, or some other type of organizational pattern. An introduction serves a number of other functions, and those are discussed in more detail later.

Now, at this point, you need some *transition* to indicate to your listeners that you are moving from the introduction into the first major point. The awkward way to do that is simply to say, "Now to move to my first major point." I hope you can be more creative than that, but creative or not, you must indicate that you are making a move. You will need another transition at the end of your first major point that may—if you do it well—simultaneously summarize what you have said and indicate that you are moving into a second major division. The same thing then will be true after each of your major points. After your last major division, you have to indicate that you are concluding. Another awkward, obvious way to do that is to say, "in conclusion." Again, I hope you will use a more interesting and subtle transition to indicate that you are concluding your speech.

conclusion

✓
1

The *conclusion* of a speech serves a number of purposes. The first of those is to summarize what you have said. You have probably heard the old statement that what you do in a speech is to first tell them what you are going to tell them, then tell them, and then tell them what you have told them. That is not a bad way for a beginning speaker to think about organization in a speech, although it is certainly more complicated than that. At any rate, one function of the conclusion is to remind the listeners

✓
2

of what has been said in the hopes that they will carry it with them after they leave. It also allows them another chance to organize the material in their own minds. A second function is to bring the speech to a *climax of attention and interest.* Although you want to pay considerable attention to maintaining audience interest throughout the speech, the introduction and the conclusion are two points at which you have to pay particular attention to attention. In an explanatory speech those two functions of conclusions may be all you want to deal with. However, remember that if you give a persuasive speech, or rather, *when* you give a persuasive speech, there really ought to be a third concluding step, which is to make a specific kind of action appeal. Of course, such an appeal is not possible in all persuasive messages because some ask only for an opinion change. But it enhances a speaker's image as well as the possibility of getting the audience to actually do something to make some specific appeal for overt action.

Sequence of Material

I have not said much about the *order* in which you present your material. Primarily what I've talked about is how you indicate to your audience what that order is. There are a number of considerations that determine the order in which material is presented, some of which apply to informative speeches and some of which apply to persuasive speeches. They are listed in Chapter 9, "Structure and Sequence." But let me give you a brief preview of them.

First, let's consider the arrangement of the material in informative speeches. If you describe a process, obviously you describe it in chronological order from the beginning to the end. If you describe an object or a room, a building or something of that sort—something that occupies space—then it may be best—probably will be best—to describe it spatially from top to bottom, from bottom to top, from left to right, right to left, front to back, inside toward the outside, or outside toward the inside, or some other spatial order. If neither of those patterns fits what you will be explaining, then you will have to analyze your material by asking yourself in what order it might be most reasonably presented.

Let's review some of the possible considerations. First, explanation of some parts of the material is going to depend upon your explanation of other parts; obviously you want to explain those parts first that are necessary to the understanding of later parts. Second, the audience may already have some knowledge of your topic, and it may be possible to take advantage of the knowledge that the audience already has. In that case you may want to begin with what they already know and work toward what they don't know. Third, the most difficult explanation ought to come when your listeners are best able to cope with it, which is probably near the beginning of the speech, but after they have had a short period of time in which to adjust to you and to focus their attention on what you have to say. Fourth, the attention of the audience is likely to fall off in places, and you ought to put the most interesting parts of your explanation at those points. Finally, the first and last parts of the speech are those that are better remembered, all else being equal. Consequently, it seems reasonable that if you had some particularly important information that you want the listeners to remember, that information ought to come either first or last. This problem of ordering or sequencing the material is discussed in much more detail in Chapter 9, which suggests patterns for organization.

Responding to the Audience

Delivery is the final element with which beginning speakers are customarily concerned. They are sometimes worried about how they are going to look and sound as they actually present the speech to an audience.

There are probably two things that will do the most to reduce the anxiety you may feel as you stand in front of an audience. The first thing is to be acquainted with your listeners. Obviously, that is not always possible, but in a speech class it should be. Try to get your instructor to give you an opportunity to get acquainted with the other members of the class, and if you do not have that opportunity during the first few class meetings, try to arrive early and stay late and talk to other people in the class. Having a few friends in your first audience will make you feel a great deal more comfortable than you would if you were speaking to a group of complete strangers. The second way to reduce that feeling of anxiety is to forget about yourself. As you deliver that speech, your mind should not be on what you look like or what you sound like but, rather, on what you have to say to that audience and how you can best get them to understand it.

For example, imagine a student—we'll call her Paula Sanford—who wants to explain to her class some aspects of computer programming. She is a major in computer science, and she works part time at the computer center. She knows quite a bit about programming, which will help her feel a great deal more at ease with her audience. One problem is that she does not know just how much her audience knows about computer programming. She does not want to start at too elementary a level because the class will get bored. She does not want to begin at too high a level because the class will become confused. She has to find out how much of what she knows is available only to her and how much of it is available also to the audience.

Something else bothers her. She knows that people frequently have misconceptions about computers, that they view computers as extremely intelligent, for example, or that they imagine computers as having minds of their own, and she is afraid some of her listeners have had previous experiences with computers that may interfere with their listening to and understanding her message. Many people have had frustrating experiences with bank computers, for example. Bank clerks are fond of telling customers that their accounts are figured by a computer, and computers "never make mistakes." Others may have had the frustrating experience of being billed by a computer for amounts they did not owe. Have you ever tried to explain to a computer by letter that it has not credited your account with the payment you made two months before? It just keeps on sending out threatening letters. Such experiences or misconceptions about computers might interfere with some of the audience's listening, and Paula should find out about it. The best way to do that may be to talk to some of them.

Suppose we go now to the speech itself. Paula wants to begin by explaining the differences among control cards, data cards, and program cards. She has two means of explaining: verbal and nonverbal. The verbal means is self-explanatory, I think. She may produce two types of nonverbal explanation. She may bring some simple, typical examples of the three types of cards and display them on a screen by means of an opaque projector, prepare transparencies for an overhead projector, or take time to draw them on the chalkboard. These are nonverbal cues of one sort: audiovisual materials. Her vocal inflections, facial expressions, gestures, posture, and the distance she maintains between herself and her listeners are another type of nonverbal cue. The listeners are observing the verbal and nonverbal cues Paula is producing. They are also producing some nonverbal cues of their own. Suppose Paula says, "This card is the 'number-of-cases' card. It has the characters capital N, capital OF, capital CASES punched into the control field and the number 225 punched in the specification field." Then she starts to move to an explanation of the next card. But Roger and Derek have slightly puzzled expressions on their faces. They glance sideways at one another, and each sees that his own lack of understanding is shared by the other. They both shrug their shoulders and raise their eyebrows. The puzzled expressions spread through the audience, and the members reinforce one another's reaction. Paula notices this and, thinking back about what she has said, realizes she has not told them what she means by a *field*, let alone a *control field* and a *specification field*, nor has she told them what she means by a *character* or a *case*. So she backs up and provides more explanation until their expressions tell her they understand.

When Paula noticed the puzzled expressions on the faces of her listeners, she was using *feedback* to detect the presence of semantic *noise*. She identified the location of the noise when she realized she had failed to adequately explain several terms. She was trying to transmit too much information in too few words. The term *control field* for instance, was a form of shorthand she was accustomed to using in place of the longer explanation that was unnecessary when she was talking with her friends in the computer center. But she was packing too much information into too few words for this audience. Had any of those words been omitted, the chance of her audience guessing what they were would have been near zero, whereas her computer science colleagues could have easily guessed. She had created an information overload. When she recognized the problem, she went back and supplied more *redundancy*. For those familiar with the terms, that redundancy would have been unnecessary, boring, and perhaps, condescending, but for her audience it was very helpful.

Please notice that Paula appears to have lost all concern for what she looks like or what she sounds like. She has focused her concern instead on what she wants to explain to the audience, on whether or not the audience is comprehending, and on how best to get them to comprehend. This kind of *sensitivity* to an audience, the "empathy" that I will discuss in the next chapters, is a great help in avoiding excessive anxiety in the public-speaking situation. If you concentrate on putting yourself in the place of the listener and if you use your time trying to figure out how best to explain to them, you simply will not have time to be concerned about how you look or sound, and you will probably forget all about being nervous. *The best way to avoid speech anxiety is to concentrate on the task at hand, and the task at hand is to get that explanation across to that audience in the best way possible.*

Such a statement suggests that there may be nothing to be said about delivery, that instead of worrying about delivery, you ought to concentrate entirely on what you have to say. Beginning speakers usually do some things that are a product of their nervousness and that you really should avoid. First, you should neither read nor memorize your speech since reading your speech will not allow you to look directly at your audience and memorizing your speech will make it appear that you are sort of gazing off into space, searching behind your eyeballs for what it is that you are going to say. You should speak to your audience in a direct, friendly, conversational manner; you should look at them, talk with them, and be as spontaneous as possible—use some lively, animated, meaningful movements, occasionally walking and gesturing. But you want to avoid pacing about the room, shifting from one foot to another, swaying back and forth, or swinging. You also want to stand erect, put your weight more or less on both feet, try to avoid distracting and repetitive mannerisms, and try to keep your notes from being too obtrusive and distracting. But you can see that thinking about all those things as you speak is going to drive you into a state of near panic. That's why I advise that you think about how to explain your topic to your audience; most of those delivery problems will probably disappear as your anxiety disappears.

SUMMARY

The process of public deliberation includes public speaking and listening. It occurs when a clearly identifiable speaker addresses a number of listeners. Public deliberation serves a crucial general function in the evolution of ideas by serving the more specific functions of disseminating information, facilitating cooperation, and sometimes enhancing self-actualization. In describing the process of public deliberation, this book will use the chronological order of matters that must be considered in preparing a speech: analyzing the people involved; analyzing the topic; methods of explaining, persuading, and reasoning; finding information; organizing the message; and expressing the message in language and delivery. In the meantime, however, since you will be delivering your first speech before you read all that, you can begin by reviewing a few basic principles.

ILLUSTRATIVE SPEECHES

This chapter has attempted to accomplish two purposes: to describe the crucial function of public address in the evolution of ideas, which constitutes humanity's best chance for survival, and to give some initial, practical directions to students preparing to deliver their first speech in a course in public deliberation. Both purposes are "introductory"—one at a somewhat philosophical level, the other at an intensely practical level. They do, however, require different illustrative speeches.

   Martin Luther King's speech "I Have a Dream," delivered on August 28, 1963, during a rally of more than 200,000 people in Washington, D.C., shows such a sense of history and such a view toward future change that it seems to exemplify the spirit of ideological evolution as well as any single speech I can imagine. Read it for the infectious sense of evolutionary but inevitable social change that it conveys. Influenced by this and many other speeches, as well as all the other events of those months, the American electorate chose Lyndon Johnson as president over Barry Goldwater in November 1964. It was an election in which Americans did indeed have "a choice, not an echo," in domestic social affairs, at least.

The second speech, "Are They Really 'Unteachable'?" was delivered in a speech class at the University of Kansas by Carolyn Kay Geiman, who was a sophomore at the time. The speech is presented here to illustrate some means of securing listener attention and promoting comprehension and retention when explaining a concept. To be sure, Ms. Geiman's purpose goes beyond explanation—she obviously feels a need to persuade her listeners as well.

Is the topic one you would expect to be inherently interesting to students in a speech class? Is the general topic narrowed to a specific thesis or central idea? Is there a statement of that central idea as well as a statement of purpose? Does the speech have clear major divisions? Are they stated in the introduction? Do you think the order in which the material is presented is a good one? Do the transitions clearly indicate the direction in which the speech is moving? Does Ms. Geiman give the sources of her information? What are some of the things she does to maintain attention and interest? Does her conclusion include a summary? Does it bring attention and interest to a peak at the end, or does the speech just seem to die?

You will probably see fairly quickly that the introduction does *not* state the major divisions. Yet the speech *has* major divisions, and they proceed in reasonable order. What Ms. Geiman has done is to make the transitions do the work of the statement of major divisions, so that the speech organization is quite clear. With that exception, I think the speech follows rather closely the basic principles suggested in this chapter. What do you think? On the other hand, can you find some things the speaker does that are not included among the recommendations? Are they effective?

I Have a Dream*
Martin Luther King, Jr.

Five score years ago, a great American, in whose symbolic shadow we stand today, signed the Emancipation Proclamation. This momentous decree came as a great beacon of light of hope to millions of Negro slaves

---

*From *Rhetoric of Racial Revolt*, ed. Roy L. Hill (Denver, Colorado: Golden Bell Press, 1964), pp. 371-375. Reprinted by permission of Golden Bell Press.

who had been seared in the flames of withering injustice. It came as a joyous daybreak to end the long night of their captivity.

But one hundred years later, the Negro still is not free. One hundred years later, the life of the Negro is still sadly crippled by the manacles of segregation and the chains of discrimination.

One hundred years later, the Negro lives on a lonely island of poverty in the midst of a vast ocean of material prosperity. One hundred years later, the Negro is still languished in the corners of American society and finds himself an exile in his own land. So we have come here today to dramatize a shameful condition.

In a sense we have come to our nation's capital to cash a check. When the architects of our republic wrote the magnificent words of the Constitution and the Declaration of Independence, they were signing a promissory note to which every American was to fall heir. This note was a promise that all men, yes, black men as well as white men, would be granted the unalienable rights of life, liberty, and the pursuit of happiness.

It is obvious today that America has defaulted on this promissory note insofar as her citizens of color are concerned. Instead of honoring this sacred obligation, America has given the Negro people a bad check which has come back marked "insufficient funds."

But we refuse to believe that the bank of justice is bankrupt. We refuse to believe that there are insufficient funds in the great vaults of opportunity of this nation. So we have come to cash this check—a check that will give us upon demand the riches of freedom and the security of justice.

We have also come to this hallowed spot to remind America of the fierce urgency of now. This is no time to engage in the luxury of cooling off or to take the tranquilizing drug of gradualism. Now is the time to make real the promises of democracy. Now is the time to rise from the dark and desolate valley of segregation to the sunlit path of racial justice. Now is the time to lift our nation from the quick sands of racial injustice to the solid rock of brotherhood. Now is the time to make justice a reality for all of God's children.

It would be fatal for the nation to overlook the urgency of the movement and to underestimate the determination of the Negro. This sweltering summer of the Negro's legitimate discontent will not pass until there is an invigorating autumn of freedom and equality. 1963 is not an end but a beginning. Those who hope that the Negro needed to blow off steam and will now be content will have a rude awakening if the nation returns to business as usual.

There will be neither rest nor tranquility in America until the Negro is granted his citizenship rights. The whirlwinds of revolt will continue to shake the foundations of our nation until the bright day of justice emerges.

But there is something that I must say to my people who stand on the warm threshold which leads into the palace of justice. In the process of gaining our rightful place we must not be guilty of wrongful deeds.

Let us not seek to satisfy our thirst for freedom by drinking from the cup of bitterness and hatred. We must forever conduct our struggle on the high plane of dignity and discipline. We must not allow our creative protest to degenerate into physical violence. Again and again we must rise to the majestic heights of meeting physical force with soul force.

The marvelous new militancy which has engulfed the Negro community must not lead us to a distrust of all white people, for many of our white brothers, as evidenced by their presence here today, have come to realize that their destiny is tied up with our destiny and they have come to realize that their freedom is inextricably bound to our freedom. This offense we share mounted to storm the battlements of injustice must be carried forth by a bi-racial army. We cannot walk alone.

And as we walk, we must make the pledge that we shall always march ahead. We cannot turn back. There are those who are asking the devotees of civil rights, "When will you be satisfied?" We can never be satisfied as long as the Negro is the victim of the unspeakable horrors of police brutality.

We can never be satisfied as long as our bodies, heavy with the fatigue of travel, cannot gain lodging in the motels of the highways and the hotels of the cities. We cannot be satisfied as long as the Negro's basic mobility is from a smaller ghetto to a larger one.

We can never be satisfied as long as our children are stripped of their selfhood and robbed of their dignity by signs stating "for whites only." We cannot be satisfied as long as a Negro in Mississippi cannot vote and a Negro in New York believes he has nothing for which to vote. No, we are not satisfied, and we will not be satisfied until justice rolls down like waters and righteousness like a mighty stream.

I am not unmindful that some of you have come here out of excessive trials and tribulations. Some of you have come fresh from narrow jail cells. Some of you have come from areas where your quest for freedom left you battered by the storms of persecution and staggered by the winds of police brutality. You have been the veterans of creative suffering. Continue to work with the faith that unearned suffering is redemptive.

Go back to Mississippi; go back to Alabama; go back to South Carolina; go back to Georgia; go back to Louisiana; go back to the slums and ghettos of the Northern cities, knowing that somehow this situation can and will be changed. Let us not wallow in the valley of despair.

So I say to you, my friends, that even though we must face the difficulties of today and tomorrow, I still have a dream. It is a dream deeply rooted in the American dream that one day this nation will rise up and live out the true meaning of its creed—we hold these truths to be self evident, that all men are created equal.

I have a dream that one day on the red hills of Georgia, sons of former slaves and sons of former slave-owners will be able to sit down together at the table of brotherhood.

I have a dream that one day even the state of Mississippi, a state sweltering with the heat of injustice, sweltering with the heat of oppression, will be transformed into an oasis of freedom and justice.

I have a dream my four little children will one day live in a nation where they will not be judged by the color of their skin but by content of their character. I have a dream today!

I have a dream that one day, down in Alabama, with its vicious racists, with its governor having his lips dripping with the words of interposition and nullification, that one day, right there in Alabama, little black boys and black girls will be able to join hands with little white boys and white girls as sisters and brothers. I have a dream today!

I have a dream that one day every valley shall be exalted, every hill and mountain shall be made low, the rough places shall be made plain, and the crooked places shall be made straight and the glory of the Lord will be revealed and all flesh shall see it together.

This is our hope. This is the faith that I go back to the South with.

With this faith we will be able to hew out of the mountain of despair a stone of hope. With this faith we will be able to transform the jangling discords of our nation into a beautiful symphony of brotherhood.

With this faith we will be able to work together, to pray together, to struggle together, to go to jail together, to stand up for freedom together, knowing that we will be free one day. This will be the day when all of God's children will be able to sing with new meaning—"my country 'tis of thee; sweet land of liberty; of thee I sing; land where my fathers died, land of the pilgrim's pride; from every mountain side, let freedom ring"— and if America is to be a great nation, this must become true.

So let freedom ring from the prodigious hilltops of New Hampshire.

Let freedom ring from the mighty mountains of New York.

Let freedom ring from the heightening Alleghenies of Pennsylvania.

Let freedom ring from the snow-capped Rockies of Colorado.

Let freedom ring from the curvaceous slopes of California.

But not only that.

Let freedom ring from Stone Mountain of Georgia.

Let freedom ring from Lookout Mountain of Tennessee.

Let freedom ring from every hill and molehill of Mississippi, from every mountainside, let freedom ring.

And when we allow freedom to ring, when we let it ring from every village and hamlet, from every state and city, we will be able to speed up that day when all of God's children—black men and white men, Jews and Gentiles, Catholics and Protestants—will be able to join hands and to sing in the words of the old Negro spiritual. "Free at last, free at last; thank God Almighty, we are free at last."

Are They Really "Uteachable"?*
Carolyn Kay Geiman

In Charles Schulz's popular cartoon depiction of happiness, one of his definitions has special significance for the American school system. The drawing shows Linus, with his eyes closed in a state of supreme bliss, a broad smile across two-thirds of his face and holding a report card upon which is a big bold "A." The caption reads: "Happiness is finding out you're not so dumb after all." For once, happiness is not defined as a function of material possessions, yet even this happiness is practically unattainable for the "unteachables" of the city slums. Are these children intellectually inferior? Are they unable to learn? Are they not worth the time and the effort to teach? Unfortunately, too many people have answered "yes" to these questions and promptly dismissed the issue.

If we base our answers on the results of IQ tests, "yes" answers may seem justified. In the largest American metropolitan areas, the students in the top school of the wealthiest suburbs have an average IQ of 120; those in the bottom school of the worst slums have an average IQ of 85. Valid factual proof, right?

In a city-wide group testing program in the New York City schools, IQ scores showed a lower and slower rate of increase with grade advancement in the large, low socio-economic districts than in the median for the city as a whole. In the third grade, there was a ten-point difference in IQ's; in the sixth grade, a seventeen-point difference; and in the eighth grade, a twenty-point difference. Valid factual proof again, right?

No, wrong! The fallacy of these "facts" lies in the IQ test itself. The very fact that IQ test results vary over a given span of time indicates, as many educators today are realizing, that these are in truth tests of cultural experience and not of native ability. These children of the slums are underdeveloped culturally, but are not innately unintelligent, and this deficiency can and should be corrected.

Horace Mann Bond, Dean of the School of Education at Atlanta University, in his lecture entitled "The Search for Talent," points out that the almost universal reliance upon the results of standardized testing is allowing an enormous leakage of human resources in our society. The results of such tests, he argues, tend to follow the lines of social class and cultural opportunity and thus tend to mask the real intellectual ability of children in slum areas. There are two specific problems which limit the educational development of these children. The first is that many of them arrive at school-age possessing very little skill in communication as a result of the stifling environment of the slum. Secondly, children in slum areas, and often their parents as well, show little interest in education.

Let's take a look at the culturally deprived child and his environment. First of all, what he calls home may be one poorly-lit room on the sixth

*Reprinted by permission of Carolyn Geiman Wilson.

floor of a large apartment building—a room which he shares with eleven
other people. On either side loom identical buildings. The noise and filth
are inescapable. Look around. There are no pencils, no paper, no books,
maybe a few scattered toys. To gain even a semblance of privacy in the
midst of the clatter, he must train himself to shut out the noise so that he
hears only what he wants to hear. He has learned to communicate by
pulling or pointing, by grunts or groans. In the "living unit," which can
hardly be called a home, a question such as, "How are we going to eat?"
is valid, but there is no time for questions like "Where do the stars come
from?" or "What causes rain?" When the child talks baby talk, his
parents are either too harrassed or not articulate enough themselves to
correct him. This child may not even know that things have names, that
he himself is a somebody with a name. He may seem to have trouble
looking at things, but the fault lies not in his eyes, but in his experiences.
He can't see differences in size, shape, color, and texture because he
hasn't been taught to look for them. So what happens when he starts to
school? He is branded as "unteachable" by teachers who cannot or will
not understand this background or its effect on the child.

Dr. Martin Deutsch, the Director of the Institution for Developmental
Studies of New York Medical College's Department of Psychiatry,
became interested in the plight of the culturally deprived child in the
public schools and studied the problem for five years. Following his
theory that "intelligence is not inherited, but a dynamic process that can
be stunted or stimulated by experience," he inaugurated the first
scientific and concerted attempt by any public school system to confront
the problem of the education of the poor pre-school age child. Ninety-six
four year olds in New York City were given the advantage of this
progressive program. Let's see what methods were used.

First, each child was taught that he had a name of his own, that he was
somebody special, a unique person. Every work of art was signed.
Parents were urged to make a fuss over the child's work, even if it was
poorly done. "If a child doesn't feel pride, he can't learn."

Secondly, each child was urged to express his thoughts and wishes in
words. Teachers were instructed not to respond to tuggings at their skirts
or mumbled noises. The formation of a thought into a complete
sentence, with subject, verb, and predicate was lauded as a major
accomplishment.

Rhoda was one of the subjects of this experiment. In the classroom she
stands, "clutching her favorite toys—a Negro doll and a toy baby bottle.
The only game she knows is caring for the baby—bathing it, feeding it,
rocking it. Fatherless Rhoda lives with her mother, who bore her at
fifteen, her thirty-eight year old grandmother, two younger sisters, and
eight uncles and aunts ranging in age from two months to ten years.
After eleven weeks in school, Rhoda still hasn't spoken or smiled. Scowl-
ing fiercely now, she reaches out for some wax grapes and puts them in a

frying pan on the stove." Hearing a noise behind her, the teacher turned around to discover Rhoda struggling with a pan. She heard Rhoda speak her first whole sentence: "Dem goddam peaches is burnin'." It's poor English, it's profane, but it is a complete thought, and this is a major achievement. Rhoda was rewarded with a big hug from her teacher, not scolded for her profanity.

Projects such as this one indicate that with care, understanding, and attention children in slum areas can be helped in mastering the basic skill of communication so vital to their educational process. What then of the indifference so prevalent in slum areas? Frank Reissman, a noted educator who has spent much of the last twenty years dealing with problems in the education of underprivileged children, is quick to point out that a distinction must be made in talking about indifference to education. Children and parents in slum areas, he says, are apathetic, and even antagonistic, not toward education, but rather toward the school system which writes them off as hopeless. Parents see the teacher as a middle-class citizen uninterested in their or their children's problems. The children, who sense their rejection strongly, begin to simply tune the teacher out. The results of this neglect are that the streets that used to be their playgrounds become their hangouts. They roam the streets. They join the ranks of the unemployed. Instead of becoming constructive citizens of the community, they become anti-social and rebellious. But this need not be. Dr. Reissman points out that time and time again projects in our major cities have established that interest in the schools can be achieved simply by demonstrating the school's interest in the underprivileged child. Parents called in for conferences, not because Johnny played hookey, but because the teacher wanted to discuss his progress have responded gratefully. Children treated with respect and interest have blossomed.

When we understand that these two major stumbling blocks to the educational progress of the underprivileged child can be eliminated— that they can be encouraged to communicate and that apathy and antagonism can be conquered—we realize that we need not write these children off as a lost cause. We need not lose these valuable human resources. We can help the "unteachables" to discover the magic of learning and achieving. We can help them to understand Schulz's definition: "Happiness is finding out you're not so dumb after all."

Chapter One References

1 Donald T. Campbell, "Ethnocentric and Other Altruistic Motives," in *Nebraska Symposium on Motivation*, ed. D. Levine (Lincoln: University of Nebraska Press, 1965), pp. 306-307.

2 Gary Cronkhite, "Rhetoric, Communication, and Psychoepistemology," in *Rhetoric: A Tradition in Transition*, ed. Walter Fisher (East Lansing: Michigan State University Press, 1974), p. 268.

3 Neil Postman and Charles Weingartner, *Teaching as a Subversive Activity* (New York: Dell, 1969), ch. 1.

4 John Vohs and Gerald Mohrmann, *Audiences, Messages, Speakers* (New York: Harcourt, Brace, 1975), p. 49.

CHAPTER ONE
QUESTIONS FOR SELF-EVALUATION

Speaking Objectives

Topic analysis
1. Do you have a clear purpose in mind; that is, do you know specifically what you want your listeners to learn, be able to do, or believe, or what actions you want them to take?
2. Do you have a clear, unified central idea (thesis) that is adapted to that purpose?
3. Is your central idea narrowed so that you can do it justice in the time you have available?
4. Is your central idea important, significant, and interesting to your listeners?
5. Is your central idea adapted to this assignment or occasion?
6. Is your central idea adapted to your own knowledge and interests?
7. Is adequate information available to explain or support your central idea?
8. Have you analyzed your central idea into divisions that are appropriate to the material, significant to you and your listeners, roughly proportionate to one another?

Listening Objectives

Preparing for reception and retention
1. Are you sitting where you can clearly see and hear the speaker?
2. Are you physically comfortable, mentally relaxed, and yet alert?
3. Are you ready to concentrate on the speech rather than reminisce, daydream, or plan future activities?

4. Are there distractions in the physical environment that you can eliminate or minimize?
5. Is there anything about the speech topic or about the speaker's prior reputation or immediate appearance that might cause you to prematurely dismiss the topic and/or the speaker?
6. Are you prepared to temporarily suspend your own preconceptions or counterarguments until you have given the speaker a fair hearing?

PART ONE

Audiences and Speakers

The first place to look for means of explaining and persuading is in the minds of listeners. The first place to look for the means of understanding and critically evaluating speeches is in the minds of speakers. But since in the process of public deliberation those who assume roles as speakers at one time invariably serve as listeners at another, understanding public deliberation as an exchange of public speaking and critical listening requires an understanding of people.

The major obstacle to understanding people is that they are so different—the human race is a mottled collection of individuals who differ in personal characteristics, personality, and in what they believe, value, and plan. Thus, the key to understanding people, if there is such a key, must lie in understanding how they differ. But as we enumerate the differences among individuals, there occurs a feeling that we have been here before. Can it be—dare we suggest—that people differ in ways that are similar?

Indeed, that appears to be the case, which raises the possibility of using these girders of similarity to build bridges of empathy on the bedrock of communication—or bridges of communication on the bedrock of empathy—to span the chasms that separate us from one another.

Thus, in studying public deliberation we inevitably become interested in studying people. Not, however, in the limited sense of "audience analysis," in which public speakers are interested in understanding audiences for much the same reasons wolves are interested in understanding sheep. Our interest must be based on a more sophisticated rationale. We must come to understand that we are forever players in the game of public deliberation. That game is not played using the "platoon system" of modern football. There is not an offensive platoon of public speakers, no defensive platoon of critical listeners. In fact, if we can transcend our own immediate and egocentric concerns, we are engaged in a long-term game based on cooperation rather than competition—a cooperative attempt to improve the quality of ideological evolution by improving the quality of public deliberation.

Even at a competitive level, however, it makes good sense to avoid placing disproportionate emphasis on either public speaking or critical listening. Football players on offense profit from their experience playing defense and vice versa because they have a *better idea of what their opponents are trying to do. Affirmative debaters can better anticipate negative arguments if they themselves have spent some time supporting the negative position. You can do a better job as public speaker or critical listener, respectively, if you have experienced and come to understand the respective problems of critical listeners and public speakers. This is true whether you are playing the game of public deliberation competitively or cooperatively.*

So let us begin our study of the game by trying to improve our understanding of the ways people differ as they perform their roles as speakers and listeners.

CHAPTER TWO

Interpersonal Differences and Empathy

The central task in any form of communication involving human beings is the bridging of interpersonal differences. This is the essence of any form of human communication. Although the bridging of interpersonal differences seems to have been most emphasized by those dealing with interpersonal communication and especially with intimate types of interpersonal communication, it is no less important in the format of public deliberation.

Long before they actually stand up to deliver a speech, public speakers' first task is one of identifying the differences between themselves and their listeners, and bridging those differences by bringing themselves to actually feel and to think as their listeners feel and think. The task of listeners is to identify the differences between themselves and a speaker and to work toward a real understanding of how the speaker feels and thinks, not necessarily to adopt the speaker's feeling and thoughts but rather to understand the speaker's position so fully and at such a personal level that it is possible to decide whether or not to adopt the speaker's position. Speakers who perform their task well will be much more able to speak to the true needs and desires of their listeners. Listeners who perform their task well will be less likely to be hoodwinked by a clever, conniving speaker and will be less likely to misinterpret the intent of a sincere speaker.

EMPATHY: A BRIDGE OVER INTERPERSONAL DIFFERENCES

The typical approach to public speaking has been a very manipulative one generally described from the speaker's point of view by people who seem to be primarily in sympathy with the speaker's purpose of informing or persuading listeners. The concept of empathy as a bridge over interpersonal differences has been advanced by those who have been more concerned with communication between two people in face-to-face exchanges. In this chapter I will try to wed the public-speaking format with the kind of sensitivity, empathy, and concern ordinarily developed in interpersonal communication.

The Speaker-Oriented Approach

The approach used in most textbooks in public speaking and certainly most textbooks in persuasion can be characterized as speaker-oriented. Authors of such textbooks seem to conceive of themselves as coaches who look over speakers' shoulders while they fire messages at listeners and who explain how speakers can more effectively hit their targets. Those adopting the speaker-oriented approach talk about interpersonal differences, of course, but they generally discuss such differences in terms of audience analysis. Speakers have been encouraged to understand their listeners in the more than 2,000 years since Aristotle wrote his *Rhetoric*; but they have been encouraged to do so in order to more effectively transmit information they consider to be important or to more effectively bring the listeners to do what they, the speakers, want them to do.

One of the results of this approach has been the extended treatment of a concept labeled general persuasability. *General persuasability* is the tendency of the listener to be influenced regardless of who the speaker is, regardless of what position the speaker takes on what topic, and regardless of the kinds of arguments or appeals the speaker uses. For example, in a 1969 textbook,[1] I discussed general persuasability in detail by listing the kinds of people who were most likely and least likely to be influenced. At that time the evidence seemed to indicate that younger people were more likely to be influenced than those of greater maturity, that women were more likely to be influenced than were men, that individuals low in self-esteem were easier to influence, and that people who were especially aggressive were less likely to be influenced. Since that time, I have come to the conclusion that such information is of very limited use to speakers because, after all, they cannot change their listeners from one group to another in order to make them more persuadable. Furthermore, I have become more interested in public speaking and in persuasion from the point of view of the listener. I have come to the conclusion as I noted in the first chapter that it is time those of us teaching public deliberation spend at least as much time teaching listeners how to make critical decisions in response to communication as we spend teaching speakers how to inform and influence listeners.

You will undoubtedly do more listening in your lifetime in the public deliberation format than you do speaking. Even in this speech course in which you are presently enrolled you will spend more time listening to the other class members than you will spend delivering speeches to them. Hopefully that time will not be wasted; that is, I hope you listen to the other members of your class instead of studying for other classes or doodling. I hope you will practice the skills of critical listening that are at least of equal importance to those in public speaking. Your professor obviously shares this point of view because he or she has chosen to use this textbook, which takes the point of view that critical listening skills are at least as important as public speaking skills.

But the primacy of the public speaker as an informer and persuader still prevails in our society. In view of the kinds of public speaking you encounter, especially in the political arena, and in view of the influence attempts that you constantly encounter in advertising, it may be very difficult to adopt a view of public deliberation as a cooperative enterprise in which speaker and listener try to achieve mutual empathy.

The Advent of Communication as Dialogue

Donald Bryant wrote a very influential article many years ago titled "Rhetoric—Its Function and Its Scope" in which he characterized the speaker-oriented approach to public speaking.[2] He listed a number of public speakers' intentions in that article, intentions that included the creating of opinion, the promulgating of ideas, information, attitudes and attitude change, adaptation, manipulation, wielding, subverting, circumventing, and the like, all of which amount to the imposition of opinions on another. Bryant was describing public speaking. He was not necessarily advocating these intentions. But it is certainly instructive to constrast the intentions he lists with those described by writers who have been interested in interpersonal dialogue.

Writers interested in interpersonal dialogue and intimate communication have described a mutual unfolding of knowledge and feeling—a mutual sharing of information and opinions. In a sense, their position has been that we ought to outlaw opinion transplants, and they have described the intimate sort of communication to be contrasted with the intimidating communication that too frequently characterizes public speaking. For example, Martin Buber writes of what he calls dialogic which he characterizes as thinking between "I" and "Thou."[3] Allen Clark has described Buber's approach to persuasion as including not only the "coming to actuality" of results but also the "coming to be" of the persons involved.[4] In other words, Buber is more concerned with the development of the people involved in a communication exchange than he is with the speaker's purpose of achieving certain results. Carl Rogers has written in much the same vein about the importance of communication in achieving self-disclosure, a revealing of oneself to others by means of which individuals can develop interpersonal trust.[5] Kierkegaard has written about edifying discourse, meaning the type of discourse that stimulates listeners to discover themselves.[6] Kierkegaard's edifying discourse does not achieve its results by lecture, argument, or persuasion but rather by indirection and ambiguity so that if listeners are to learn anything, they have to discover it themselves. The purpose of such discourse is not for clarification, acceptance, or emotional arousal, but rather to stimulate listeners to *independent* activity.

Most of the writers who have discussed this type of communication have emphasized the concept of empathy as an important means of improving such communication. *Empathy—the ability to feel and understand what another person is feeling and thinking—is probably the most valuable asset a communicator can acquire.* Empathy is both a cause and an effect of successful communication. In fact, cause and effect in this case blend so completely that in a broad sense we can say that empathy *is* communication. If one is able to empathize with another, the two are better able to communicate. If they are better able to communicate, they are better able to empathize. Kenneth Burke calls this "identification through consubstantiality."[7] He says there is a natural divisiveness among people that is prompted by interpersonal differences such as those we are discussing. Identification, communication, and persuasion, which all seem to blend into one in Burke's description, help to bridge this natural divisiveness. One person persuades another by talking the other's language and by identifying his or her own needs and goals with those of the other so the two become consubstantial, which means literally a part of the same substance. It seems to me that this is the real importance of interpersonal differences in communication. When you differ from another person in age, sex, intelligence, educational level, race, socioeconomic status, and various personality characteristics, it is more difficult for the two of you to achieve empathy or identification. You can achieve it, but you will both have to work at it. You will have more difficulty in feeling and understanding each other's feelings and thoughts. You will be more likely to suspect one another of having different beliefs, values, needs, and goals, which may lead you to distrust and dislike one another.

Empathy has been described in a variety of ways. The description I like best is this: If I truly empathize with another person and the other person cries, I taste salt. When the other person is exposed to danger, the hairs rise on the back of my neck, and I feel goosebumps on my arms. When the other person experiences something unexpectedly pleasant, I may cry tears of joy.

Rogers has pointed out that this kind of empathy is not going to develop unless one abandons a hyperactive concern with one's own self-concept and a paranoid protection of that self-concept. The manic impressive person whose idea of an ideal reincarnation would be to return as himself or herself is not going to develop that kind of empathy. The kind of person who is so ego-defensive that he or she must know everything and must be best at everything is not going to develop that kind of empathy.

What is important here is to realize that my perceptions of you and my perceptions of the ways you perceive me are likely to be those that will enhance my own self-concept. For example, I am more likely to perceive you as intelligent because you are reading my book, and I am likely to believe that you perceive me to be intelligent as a result of your reading. Those perceptions may or may not be accurate, but they enhance my own self-concept so I am more likely to adopt them. Furthermore, to the extent that we believe one another to be intelligent and sensitive and the like, we will each expect the other to agree with our own perceptions of the world. Thus, we will be likely to exaggerate our agreements and minimize our disagreements. If two people see one another as basically different, they are more likely to dislike one another, exaggerating their disagreements and minimizing their similarities. All of that can hinder real empathy because it can cause us to misperceive one another. Real empathy consists of recognizing and understanding our actual similarities and differences, of realizing that they need not threaten our respective self-concepts. Empathy is achieved by a process of illumination.

Goffman has written about similar problems. He describes how people present themselves in interpersonal encounters, how they choose their clothes, their friends, the books they read, the opinions they express, their interests, the ways they behave and the ways they communicate so as to enhance not only the images they present to others but also the ways they conceive of themselves.[8] Such contrived images can interfere with the perceptions of ourselves and others, which is the basis of empathy.

Berne has expressed it in terms of the games people play in their inter-personal relationships as they alternately adopt the postures or strategies of the immature Child, the authoritarian Parent, or the mature Adult.[9] He describes such games as Man-talk, Morning After, Ain't It Awful, and Rapo, among others. Each is a transactional strategy for dealing with reality and other people, much like Goffman's interaction rituals. All these writers deal basically with the ways in which we protect and conceal our self-concepts from one another and from ourselves, sabotaging self-actualization, empathy, and social transaction in the process. They all recommend development of mutual trust and self-disclosure in some form or another, to a greater or lesser degree, as an antidote. They are joined by many other writers including Maslow,[10] Jourard,[11] and Fromm.[12] The idea is that we must learn to recognize and accept interpersonal differences and then learn to trust one another to the point that we can use communication to disclose our true selves.

Reconciling Dialogue with Public Speaking

Now, all this may be fine for the kind of communication in which one person is speaking directly to another in a fairly intimate sort of encounter, but how does it apply to the situation in which one individual is delivering a public speech to a large audience and in which the individual intends to present certain information to the listeners or intends to change their opinions or their actions? Everett Lee Hunt has suggested a definition of rhetoric (that is, in fact, a term usually applied to public speaking) as *the study of men persuading men to make free choices.*[13] Kierkegaard has suggested that it may be the art of using power to make men free.[14] It is fairly closely related to Kierkegaard's definition of a belief, which he says is the product of a volitional act in which one chooses to risk asserting a particular position even though he realizes that its truth is objectively uncertain.[15] It is also closely related to Kierkegaard's notion of edifying discourse.

From all this we can say that in order for public speaking to be reconciled with these notions of self-actualization through dialogue, *public speakers must recognize that listeners are free to choose,* they must not do anything that would restrict listeners' freedom of choice or anything that would restrict listeners' responsibility for their own actions. Rather, speakers must stimulate listeners to make free choices; and speakers and listeners must understand that the propositions speakers advance are not Truth but are propositions speakers choose to advance with the realization that they might be wrong. In short, neither speakers nor listeners should take speakers too seriously. If speakers take themselves too seriously and do not admit that they might be wrong, they cut off the possibility that they may grow and learn in the future, the possibility that they will become better persons as they unravel the plot of life by experiencing its story, as Heidegger puts it.[16] Even with all these cautions, it is quite certain that a public speech in which the speaker intends to inform or persuade the listener is not going to be the kind of edifying discourse of which Kierkegaard speaks, and it is never going to achieve the concentration upon personal development that can be achieved in a face-to-face encounter between two people. Most of the writers who deal with dialogue, however, recognize that they are dealing with a particular form of communication and that there is a parallel form of communication in which the intentions of informing and persuading are primary and not really objectionable. What I am trying to achieve is not mimicry of dialogue in the public speaking situation, but rather an application of the concepts of empathy, sensitivity, and concern to a situation that has been too frequently characterized by manipulation.

It is important to apply some of the concepts and models developed by writers concerned with the interpersonal encounter as we concern ourselves with public deliberation. It is important, for example, to consider how speakers' and listeners' self-concepts may interfere with the making of critical decisions in public deliberation. It is also important to think about how speakers' and listeners' ego defensiveness may sabotage public deliberation and how the development of trust may be enhanced by means of self-disclosure, especially by the speaker, who has the greatest opportunity for self-disclosure. Furthermore, we can take advantage of some of the models developed in the context of interpersonal encounter as we attempt to analyze public deliberation.

Stewart's Model

Stewart's model is one in which I am particularly interested.[17] Stewart analyzes a dyadic or two-person situation in terms of interpersonal perception. His model, he says, is transactional in the sense that he assumes individuals change as a function of the communication in which they are involved. His transactional paradigm specifies the perceptual relationships involved in a two-person communication. In Stewart's terms "my → me" represents my self-image and "my → you" represents my perceptions of you. The perceptual relationships involved can be represented in this way:

$$my \rightarrow me$$
$$my \rightarrow you$$
$$your \rightarrow you$$
$$your \rightarrow me$$

In addition, I have some perception of your perception of me and you have a perception of my perception of you, and so on; thus:

$$my \rightarrow your \rightarrow me$$
$$my \rightarrow your \rightarrow you$$
$$your \rightarrow my \rightarrow me$$
$$your \rightarrow my \rightarrow you$$

It is possible to extend Stewart's basic paradigm to include other elements. For example, it has been suggested that each of us has a different perception of our relationships, so we can add the following perceptual relationships.

$$my \rightarrow us$$
$$your \rightarrow us$$
$$my \rightarrow your \rightarrow us$$
$$your \rightarrow my \rightarrow us$$

We can extend the paradigm beyond the two-person situation by adding "him_1, him_2,. . .," and "her_1, her_2,. . .," and we can add other objects, events, concepts, and ideas as "it_1, it_2,. . . ." This makes it possible to represent an infinite variety of relationships, and it serves to remind us of the incredible complexity of the perceptions involved in a communication exchange.

Consider the problems we could cause if we complicated the model further by representing *messages* as perceptual relations enclosed in parentheses, so that

$$my \ (my \rightarrow your \rightarrow me) \ you$$

represents my attempt to describe to you my perception of your perception of me. Besides being fun to play with, this model seems useful in that it serves as a reminder of the tremendous complexity of the simplest perceptions we try to communicate.

Now suppose we translate Stewart's model into the terms of public deliberation. There are a number of things the speaker may want to consider that can be diagrammed in this way.

speaker → speaker
speaker → audience
audience → speaker
audience → audience

That is, it may be useful to you to consider your perception of yourself and of the audience and the listeners' perceptions of themselves and of you. Furthermore, you may want to give some thought to how the audience thinks you perceive yourself and how the audience thinks you perceive them.

audience → speaker → speaker
audience → speaker → audience

Finally, you and your audience may perceive the relationships between you differently, and you and your audience may each have mistaken impressions of how the other perceives that relationship.

audience → relationship
speaker → relationship
audience → speaker → relationship
speaker → audience → relationship

Recall Paula who was giving the speech on computer programming. Paula may consider herself an expert on computer programming, so she perceives her relationship to her listeners as one of teacher to students, and she may believe her listeners perceive the relationship in that way, too. In actual fact, however, if the listeners know nothing of Paula's expertise, they may think she read a magazine article on computer programming the night before. Consequently, when she begins to talk to them as teacher to student, they may get the impression that she sees herself as superior to them and may react very unfavorably. Paula might avoid all that by consciously considering her own perception of her relationship to the audience, the ways her perception might affect her behavior toward them, and their possible reactions.

The Johari Window

Another model that has been treated extensively by those interested in interpersonal communication is the model of Johari's window.[18] Johari's window consists of a chart that looks very much like a window pane. It is a square divided into four smaller squares.

Known to speaker and audience	Known to audience only
Known to speaker only	Not known to speaker or audience

We can translate this model into the public-speaking situation by dividing the larger square into four smaller squares: material known to both speaker and listeners, material known to speaker only, material known to listeners only, and material known to neither. Then as you think about the problems you have to overcome as a speaker trying to transmit information to listeners, you can concentrate on each of the four smaller squares. You can try to identify information you and your listeners have in common, information you have that your listeners do not have, and then you can begin to try to determine what information your listeners might have that you do not have. If you are successful, of course, that information will move to another square since both you and your listeners will be aware of it. We could expand on Johari's window in a way that would make it a little more consistent with reality by thinking of a window covered by a venetian blind in which some of the slats of the blind are more open than others. Thus, we could represent what the speaker knows by a diagram such as this:

And we could represent what listeners know by a diagram such as this:

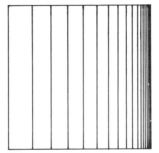

This way of conceptualizing knowledge takes into account the fact that information is generally neither known nor unknown, but rather that we are more or less aware of various items of information. Now if we take these two windows representing the information awareness of speaker and listeners and superimpose one on the other, we get the following model:

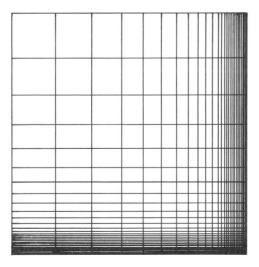

This allows us to conceptualize information of which the speaker may be more aware and the listener less aware, rather than being trapped into conceiving of information as either known or unknown to speaker and listener. I think that this is a much more realistic picture, and I think that we can extend this model even further. In the next chapter I will talk about how people process information and how they make decisions, and I will introduce three concepts that I will label beliefs, values, and plans. I do not think we have to go into those very deeply at this point, but I would like to make the initial distinction among these three concepts.

People *believe* that things exist or do not exist or that one thing is somehow related to something else, that one event causes another or is similar to another. In addition, people have different *values* in the sense that they place different values on the objects, events, people, and ideas that they recognize. Furthermore, people have *plans* for dealing with the objects, events, and ideas in their environments. Thus, I may believe that a fairly heavy snowfall is necessary for skiing. Therefore, if I value skiing highly, I probably will also value heavy snowfall. However, if I place a very small value on skiing and a very high value on warm weather, I will probably value heavy snowfall considerably less. Given this belief and given that I value skiing highly, I may plan to live in a climate in which there is heavy snowfall. These ideas will be covered more extensively in the next chapter. But suppose we combine those notions with the Johari's window model. We could build a picture of speaker and listener beliefs by means of this model so that we could identify beliefs shared by speaker and listeners, beliefs the speaker accepts but the listeners do not, beliefs listeners accept but the speaker does not, and beliefs accepted by neither speaker nor listeners. Having such a picture of related speaker and listener beliefs could be very important in public deliberation. We could then build another window to represent shared speaker and listener values, values that the speakers have but the listeners do not, values that the listeners have but the speaker does not, and values held by neither speaker nor listener.

BELIEFS	VALUES	PLANS

Accepted by speaker	Accepted by speaker	Accepted by speaker

	Yes	No			Yes	No			Yes	No
Accepted by audience — Yes			Accepted by audience — Yes			Accepted by audience — Yes		
Accepted by audience — No			Accepted by audience — No			Accepted by audience — No		

Finally, we could build a window that would represent the plans of the speaker and the listeners so that we could identify plans shared by speaker and listeners, plans the speaker has but the listeners do not, plans the listeners have but the speaker does not, and plans entertained by neither speaker nor listeners. This would give us a fairly good start in analyzing a particular instance of public deliberation.

Transactional Analysis

A third model that has been extensively developed by those interested in interpersonal communication is the one described by Berne, particularly in his book *Games People Play*. I simply do not have space to describe this model of transactional analysis very extensively, so I will leave it to you to read Berne's book or some other description of transactional analysis if you are really interested in developing the concept.

I have already described three of the basic notions that Berne advances, which are that people can relate to one another or adopt the roles of immature Child, authoritarian Parent, or mature Adult. Speakers relate to listeners in much the same way, and, in fact, we might extend this model to the point of describing the games people play in public deliberation. A speaker may perceive his or her role as that of the authoritarian parent and may perceive the listeners as immature children, in which case the speech will taken on certain characteristics as a result of these perceptions and role expectations. If the speaker perceives himself or herself as the authoritarian parent, but the listeners do not, the resulting public deliberation is going to be considerably handicapped. On the other hand, a speaker may (infrequently) take the role of an immature child, demanding or pleading for considerations from listener-parents who have the power to grant or deny such considerations. Again, this may result in very unsatisfactory public deliberation, especially if the listeners do not share the speaker's perceptions. The healthiest kind of public deliberation results, I think, when speaker and listeners perceive one another as mature adults trying to achieve mutual satisfaction of all their needs insofar as that is possible. If they adopt this posture of adult-to-adult communication, they will not be as likely to fall into heavily one-sided dependency relationships or relationships that acquire acquiescence to authority, both of which characterize public deliberation all too frequently.

If they perceive themselves as free, responsible adults capable of making their own decisions and taking the responsibility for them, if they recognize that both speakers and listeners are capable of being wrong, they will be less likely to play some of the destructive games in public deliberation that are analogous to the destructive games Berne describes as occurring in interpersonal communication. For example, Berne's interpersonal communication game of Rapo occurs in public deliberation when listeners feel that the speaker is trying to take advantage of them or when the speaker feels that his or her purpose is to take advantage of the listeners, if at all possible.

Another game I mentioned earlier—Ain't It Awful—has its parallel in public deliberation when speakers simply assist their listeners in lamenting some horrible conditions that exist in the world without offering any serious workable proposals for changing those conditions. I think the possibilities are practically endless, and I will not try to enumerate them, but I hope the point is made. Speakers and listeners alike adopt the role of authoritarian parent, immature child, and mature adult, and public deliberation is handicapped or enhanced by the extent to which their roles mesh and by the extent to which their roles reflect the maturity necessary to deal with the problems encountererd in public deliberation.

A General Model

I would like to describe a model or framework we can use in thinking about interpersonal perception and then relate that to public deliberation.

Imagine that Joan and Marsha have just moved into a new apartment building. They have moved into different wings of the building, and their apartments are situated so that they face one another across the courtyard. Both have large picture windows in their living rooms. Joan becomes uncomfortable that Marsha can so easily see everything that happens in her living room, so she asks around to find something to do about it.

She feels that draperies or venetian blinds for such a window would be too expensive, the sun would fade the drapes, and the venetian blinds might not provide all the privacy she wants. But she has seen vans and station wagons with a reflective film on their windows which allows the person inside to see out but prevents those outside from seeing in. She has seen the same sort of thing on the windows of office buildings. She remembers that one of the brand names for the one-way reflective film is "Mylar."

She locates a dealer and arranges to have Mylar applied to the outside of her picture window. She chooses a type of Mylar that is not merely reflective; it has a tropical scene on the reflective side.

When Marsha sees this, she decides that Joan may be staring into her living room from behind that opaque window. So Marsha reciprocates by having her own picture window coated with one-way reflective film with a mountain scene.

Joan doesn't especially care for the scene Marsha has chosen, but what bothers her more is that people are always coming and going and seem to be enjoying themselves at Marsha's apartment, which distracts Joan from her studying. One day it dawns on Joan that she could shut all this out by having a Mylar coating applied to the *inside* of her window, and she could choose whatever scene she wanted to see.

Now, if Marsha were to reciprocate by applying a reflective film to the inside of *her* window, the two women would have created a situation in which they have reciprocally limited their own accessibility to others and the access they have to the outside world.

People can do the same by altering the "windows" of perception by which they relate to others: they can refuse to disclose their true selves, presenting tranquil scenes to hide the turmoil or disorder within; they can choose how they want others and the outside world in general to appear, constructing scenes that make them feel comfortable and secure. Then, when two people try to communicate, each faces a barrier he himself has created and one the other has created, as pictured in Figure 2-1.

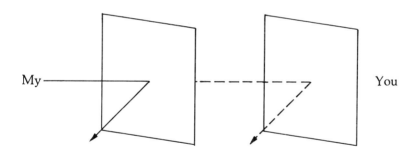

FIGURE 2-1
Double Barriers to Interpersonal Communication

I am labeling this the MYLAR model of interpersonal communication, MYLAR standing for "Myself-Yourself Limited-Access Reciprocity." The situation pictured in Figure 2-1 is that in which both parties are playing immature and destructive communication games, one by perceiving what he/she wants to perceive and the other by presenting a false picture of himself or herself, refusing to self-disclose.

But this model is not as useful as it might be. In reality, people are generally selective as to what they are willing to reveal about themselves and selective as to what they will perceive accurately. Suppose we exchange the apartment with a single picture window for a mansion with many rooms and many windows facing in many directions. Some windows may face in directions in which the owner does not want to see; the interiors of those windows will be heavily coated. Other windows face in directions in which the owner wishes to perceive more accurately; the interiors of those windows will be coated with a thin film or not coated at all.

From the other direction, some rooms will be entirely open to view from outside, whereas other rooms will have all their windows with heavy reflective coatings on the outside. Many rooms will be open to view through windows facing toward some people but not toward others.

Finally, the rooms will differ in their accessibility to the owner. There are some rooms in which the owner will spend a great deal of time. Others were locked or nailed shut so securely so long ago that the owner never goes there and may, in fact, have forgotten of their existence. Most of the rooms are used by the owner occasionally depending on his or her mood or purpose; they vary in their accessibility.

This picture of human perception and cognition, which I will entitle the MYLAR Mansion, is so metaphorical that it will be of little use in research, of course. But that is not its purpose. Hopefully, it will be helpful in thinking about how people regulate their own thoughts, their perceptions of others, and their disclosures of themselves to others.

There will always be some aspects of our private selves that we refuse to disclose; there will always be some aspects of the outside world that we will fail to perceive accurately; and there will probably be parts of our inner selves to which even our own access is restricted. Some such restrictions are normal, healthy, and probably even necessary.

But too many restrictions on perception, cognition, and self-disclosure can create problems not only in two-person communication, but also in public speaking and critical listening. Speakers who do not trust their listeners and are not confident of themselves will try to conceal their own beliefs, values, and plans out of fear their listeners will think them less believable if those beliefs, values, and plans are revealed. The listeners, on the other hand, may fear persuasion, which I once heard defined thusly: "Persuasion is that which, if you wake up without your beliefs, there has been a speaker around with." Listeners who do not trust speakers may conceal their belief files, their value vaults, and the blueprints of their plans on the assumption that unprincipled speakers would use them to their own advantage. The result is that, in the absence of reliable information about one another, mutually suspicious speakers and listeners rely instead on stereotypes based on age, sex, race, culture, educational level, socioeconomic status, behaviors they associate with certain personality types, or those with whom each observes the other associating. From these stereotypes, speakers and listeners may try to infer the others' beliefs, values, and plans.

On the other hand, if speakers and listeners are not fully aware of their *own* beliefs, values, and plans, they will be poorly equipped to construct responsible speeches or to listen critically. To a considerable extent, one's age, sex, race, culture, educational level, socioeconomic status, personality characteristics, and associates *do* affect what one believes, values, and plans, and sometimes in ways detrimental to one's role in public deliberation. Thus, it is important to be self-analytic, to increase one's awareness of the ways in which one's personal characteristics, personality, and associates may affect one's opinions and policies and thus the extent to which one's speaking is responsible and one's listening is critical.

PERSONAL CHARACTERISTICS

The empathy and self-awareness so important in public deliberation are not likely to be achieved merely by understanding that they are important. Beyond that one needs some information regarding the kinds of interpersonal differences to be bridged by empathy or the kinds of characteristics to be aware of in oneself. One needs some familiarity with the kinds of personal characteristics, personality characteristics, and interpersonal associations that are important in public deliberation. The remainder of this chapter will consider personal characteristics, whereas the next chapter will deal with personality characteristics and interpersonal associations.

Age

Commencement speakers who want to do more than fill their time and collect their fees may feel they are at a disadvantage simply because they are older than their listeners. Student representatives speaking before college administrators or faculty may feel similarly disadvantaged because they are younger. If such speakers indicate that they expect their listeners to be fair and open-minded, they are more likely to be. Furthermore, speakers in such situations can help bridge the age difference by emphasizing ways in which they and their listeners are similar, especially the interests, concerns, and motives they have in common. That is not to suggest that anyone should compromise principles for the sake of effect. It is to suggest that, especially when the age difference is great, one should make the most of those similarities and common concerns that do exist.

On the other hand, listeners ought to be aware of age differences between themselves and speakers and seriously explore the possibility that the age difference alone is predisposing them to distrust and disagree with a speaker and thus is putting them in danger of making an uncritical decision.

Sex

Communication between the sexes has some natural, built-in advantages, which hardly need to be elaborated. However, there are a number of sex-related problems in public deliberation, most of which have been imposed by society. After all, there is not that much difference between the actual physical needs and goals of men and women. Most of these social differences are vestigial in the sense that they are left over from less civilized days when the generally greater physical aggressiveness and strength of the male was more of an advantage than a disadvantage. These social differences seem now to be about as useful as other vestigial characteristics, such as the tail bone and the appendix. But they still exist, and they still hamper public deliberation, so we still have to deal with them.

What seems to have developed is the extension or transformation of the physical strength of the male into a general social and economic dominance as well, without any rational grounds for the extension. All of that has been discussed and is being discussed at length elsewhere. What is important for our purposes is that speakers and listeners of opposite sex may unwittingly adopt socially sterotyped roles that hinder public deliberation. Sometimes everyone involved plays the game, so that speakers and listeners act out socially prescribed roles without ever really coming to terms with their respective needs and goals; they feign a divisiveness that need not exist. Sometimes one of the communicators assumes that the social roles are in effect, while the other will reject the roles, which can be very destructive to communication. A male speaker may be so accustomed to playing the dominant role that even when he tries to shed it his speech reveals his assumption of superiority. The woman who rejects that assumption will be offended, and the male speaker may never know what went wrong. Similarly, a woman speaker may be so accustomed to assuming that the man is going to take care of her or that males are more knowledgeable or capable that her speech projects helplessness quite unintentionally, even while she protests her inequality at a conscious level. The liberated male listener may then decide that this woman is really a helpless ninny or that she is using her helplessness when that is to her advantage and using her equality when that seems more beneficial. Neither interpretation is very flattering, and either one is going to sabotage public deliberation.

The third problem is a rather pervasive tendency by both men and women to give a man more credit for knowing what he is talking about unless there is some reason to believe otherwise. That is simply irrational and has led to all manner of foolish decisions. Fortunately, there is some evidence that among college-educated people at least this prejudice against female speakers is beginning to decline, and we can only hope that it will shortly be eradicated. In the meantime, however, it is important for listeners to realize that assigning greater credibility to male speakers is a real threat to the acquisition of reliable information and to the making of critical decisions.

Culture

Speakers and listeners who operate exclusively within a single culture come to tacitly accept certain beliefs, values, and policies as truisms because they are never questioned within that culture. This is important in public deliberation for two reasons: first, because such unquestioned cultural assumptions can lead to uncritical decisions and, second, because those who do listen to or speak to those of other cultures will be seriously handicapped by those unquestioned assumptions. A third reason why it is important to understand the cultural assumptions of others is more general: By understanding people of other cultures and communicating with them, one can form a better picture of one's own culture and hence a better understanding of oneself.

Americans argue about many things, of course. But the beliefs, values, and patterns of behavior (plans and policies) most typical of our culture are those that are least controversial. They are "truisms" that are assumed and accepted without question. Because they are not questioned by others within our culture, we often accept them as *facts about the world* rather than mere culturally bound opinions.

For example, Americans in general seem to cherish certain *beliefs* regarding human nature, the physical world, and the supernatural. Regarding human nature, Americans seem to assume that people are basically rational, or at least should be; that humans are some mixture of good and evil in that they are either good but corruptible or evil but capable of being rehabilitated. Regarding the physical world, they believe that fate is just and hard work will be justly rewarded, whereas laziness will be justly punished; that progress requires human domination of nature by means of science and technology; that practical, concrete knowledge is to be preferred to abstract knowledge, although they are a little more tolerant of *scientific* abstractions. Regarding the supernatural, Americans adopt a peculiar approach: Although they generally place great emphasis on the ability of humans to better themselves and to control nature by their own industry and ingenuity, thus putting humankind at the center of a basically orderly, mechanistic, and comprehensible universe, most Americans also believe that a single all-knowing and all-powerful God is at the center of the universe, dispensing rewards and punishments at his/her discretion. The apparent contradiction seems to be reconciled by two beliefs: God rewards a person's industry and ingenuity, just as the owner of a firm might be expected to reward a junior partner, and the orderly, lawful nature of the universe is evidence that it was created by God, although he may have used evolution as one of his tools.

Furthermore, Americans *value* individuality; they value youth above age; they value equality of opportunity between the sexes and among racial groups; and they value doing more than merely being. Regarding the family, Americans prefer an individualistic, democratic, open, mobile orientation rather than an authoritarian family structure based on family lineage and the age and sex of siblings. Regarding social structures and relationships Americans are less likely to value social obligations, rules, and group loyalty; they do value directness and, most of all, informality.

Of course, "typical" Americans are about as hard to find as are "typical" Japanese, Argentines, and Ukranians. Few Americans explicitly accept all these beliefs and values or the plans and policies they support. But many of the institutions and procedures we tacitly accept—and many of the arguments speakers advance and the criteria by which listeners judge those arguments—would make little sense were it not for such cultural assumptions. Even those beliefs and values most frequently violated—for example, racial and sexual equality—will be paid lip service or touted as ideals, and speakers who openly oppose them are going to be rejected by most American audiences.

Race

Since many different races live together in American culture, speakers and listeners of different races confront one another more frequently than do speakers and listeners of different cultures. In fact, different races are *forced* to deal with one another to some extent because they live near one another and are part of the same culture, whereas people usually engage in intercultural communication because they want to. In fact, visiting another culture is usually a privilege for which one pays; but interacting with another racial group within one's own country is not usually highly valued. The intercultural differences are considered exotic; the interracial differences are at best common and at worst irritating.

Furthermore, different racial groups within a culture naturally share many of the same assumptions, behaviors, symbols, and the like, which only serve to emphasize the differences. Different racial and ethnic characteristics, including different skin colors, accents, and customs, provide a variety of cues for group formation. All of this is complicated by the fact that these "groups" inevitably compete for limited jobs, money, and other resources. Theoretically, the *groups* don't compete, *individuals* compete with one another. But, in fact, those in power are likely to give preference to those of their own ethnic or racial groups. Frequently, they do not realize they are doing so; it is just that those of their own groups also coincidentally have many characteristics they consider valuable.

People of one racial or ethnic group tend to form *stereotyped* images of other groups. Stereotypes are not *necessarily* derogatory. But racial stereotypes are dangerous because they are so likely to be used to justify exploitation of those of other groups and because these stereotypical *beliefs* about other groups tend to involve *values* as well—values that are too frequently negative. Negative valuation of a racial stereotype becomes *prejudice*, and prejudice tends to lead to plans and policies for *discrimination*.

Many of the policies that constitute racial discrimination are advocated or opposed by speakers in public deliberation. Furthermore, anytime speakers differ from their listeners in race, the actual physical differences are exaggerated by stereotyping, prejudice, and discrimination. Consequently, racial differences form a threat to critical public deliberation which is particularly difficult to overcome and requires an unusual amount of empathy.

Certain personality types are especially likely to stereotype, as pointed out in the next chapter. Sometimes racial stereotypes are socially learned, and sometimes they serve ego needs. They may serve, or be served by, different reference groups. They may be represented in language differences, and they may be the result of actual intercultural differences in beliefs, values, and plans. Whatever its causes, interracial stereotyping is the sworn enemy of empathy and successful public deliberation. But the racist is also a stereotype, an object for understanding and empathy, an individual, who as a speaker, needs to be understood by listeners, and an individual who as a listener needs to be understood by a speaker.

Formal Education

It is probably most useful to consider the kinds of experiences that may conspire to make the formally educated person different from the person who has less formal education. First, the vocabulary of the person who chooses to remain in school is likely to differ from that of the person who leaves school. The educated vocabulary may or may not be more extensive. It will, however, be different. The college professor talking to a group of longshoremen will have at least as much difficulty with vocabulary as the longshoremen in the opposite situation. The misguided notion that the academic vocabulary is more extensive or correct is probably due to the fact that college professors teach speech and English, but longshoremen generally do not. Until educators abandon the provincial conviction that their vocabularies are somehow superior, their brand of public speaking will continue to be well adapted to the academic community, and uniquely poorly adapted to other communities.

Second, much of the experience provided by education is experience in dealing with abstractions. Thus, the educated person is probably better equipped to deal with involved abstract arguments, which is often what is meant by logical argument. However, an involved abstract argument can be less logical than one that is simple and concrete, and it is certainly more difficult to evaluate. This may make the educated person unusually susceptible to erroneous reasoning. That person may be a pushover for any argument that sounds complicated.

Further, the more education people have, the more pressure they feel to have an opinion on any subject, and they may be too inclined to adopt neat packages of opinions and justifications. Consider, for example, a person arguing that the members of a craft union should admit more blacks to membership. That person's reasoning and evidence will have to be unimpeachable; it will probably have to be less impeachable, in fact, than if he or she were arguing the same proposition with the members of the American Association of University Professors, which, by the way, might be no less segregated.

Third, it should be obvious that the educated person will have areas of specific knowledge different from those of the less educated person. His or her general knowledge may be greater or less than that of the person having less formal education. Certainly, education alone does not guarantee general knowledge. There will be certain areas in which an educated person has greater knowledge depending upon the direction his or her formal education has taken. Similarly, the less educated person will have certain areas of greater knowledge depending on the direction his or her nonacademic experiences take. A speaker had best know what his listeners know, whether their knowledge is academic or nonacademic. If listeners' knowledge is extensive in the area, a speaker will have an easier job in that he or she can assume much of what would otherwise have to be explained. But the job will also be more difficult in that the information must be completely accurate and documented, and the inferences must be carefully reasoned. The speaker will also run a greater risk of boring listeners by telling them things they already know.

Fourth, educated people can be expected to be more committed to, and interested in, anything academic, whereas uneducated people may have some degree of antiintellectual bias. Certainly, research and theory in choice behavior would lead one to that prediction. If a person has made a choice as significant as that between leaving school and remaining and has committed time and money as completely as one usually must to either of those alternatives, that person is likely to seek justification for the choice and be more favorable toward the alternative chosen and less favorable toward the one rejected. However, some reservations are in order. For example, teachers would probably agree strongly that there is a need for more educational television programs. Persuading them to watch such programs, however, may be about as easy as persuading a bus driver to take a vacation trip. Uneducated people, too, often have a strangely ambivalent attitude toward education. They may make tremendous sacrifices to send their children to college on the assumption that one must have a college education to get ahead. But they may remain suspicious, even antagonistic, toward what is taught.

Finally, the different experiences of educated and less educated persons create a gap. The educated person talking with less educated persons has at least two problems to overcome. They will be watching closely for indications that the educated person considers himself or herself superior to them, and they will be suspicious that education may have produced motives that they do not share and that may or may not be in their own best interests. If a speaker can satisfy listeners on those two points, they will probably respect his or her education and be more likely to believe the speech. Such a speaker would be well advised to avoid any suggestion of deliberately choosing simple language and over-simplifying explanations as a condescension to the stupidity of the listeners. He will avoid technical jargon, of course, but can still use standard American English. He may simplify the explanation, but he can do so by using illustrations with which the listeners are familiar, rather than by treating them as if they were children. If he can handle it, some humorous deprecation of himself or his educational experiences or of education in general may be helpful. Above all, he should try to be relaxed, natural, and friendly.

Such a person will take the time to remind his listeners of motives, interests, and opinions they have in common in order to assure them that he is interested in their welfare. The less educated person conversing with those who are educated has two somewhat different problems: to overcome his own insecurity and to convince the listeners that he is well informed. To overcome insecurity, one should remember that if the topic has been narrowed adequately and researched carefully, he or she should be the leading expert on that topic. To assure the listeners of his credibility, it may be best to tell them just that: While you feel somewhat overwhelmed at the prospect of speaking to such a distinguished audience, you also feel that because you have done some careful research on this topic, you believe that you have some specific information which will be useful to them.

Socioeconomic Status

Again, when a person has a much higher or much lower socioeconomic status than that of his listeners, there may be a serious lack of identification between them. High-status speakers talking to those of low status will have problems very similar to those of educated people talking to those who are less educated. Such listeners will be quick to see that speakers are trying to adopt their slang or dialect and will probably interpret this as condescension. They will also suspect speakers of trying to exploit them unless a speaker can give good evidence of being interested in their welfare. The speaker of low status speaking to those of high status has less critical problems. There may be some tendency on the part of the listeners to think, "If you're so smart, why ain't you rich," but that problem will probably not be too serious unless his or her socioeconomic status is extremely low. In that case, there may be an additional problem. One may also be suspected of being lazy. A speaker in such a position should be aware of such tendencies and should subtly introduce evidence that he or she is neither stupid nor lazy. Under certain circumstances some high-status listeners may suspect that poor speakers are trying to exploit them to get something for nothing. Speakers will need to emphasize whatever motives and interests they share with the listeners in order to minimize the differences that exist.

It may also be useful to consider the different concerns and opinions that may be created by the different experiences of those in the middle and upper classes. For example, young people should be especially aware that there are many older persons in the middle and upper classes who have risen from the poverty and insecurity of the depression to their present positions of relative affluence and security. It is easy for such persons to attribute the increase in their personal fortunes to their own industry and ingenuity and to become quite impatient with the poor. One should be aware of this rather pervasive economic viewpoint, for it is relevant to a wide variety of topics, and one is likely to encounter it often. This may also account, to some extent, for the preeminence of the economic-security motive among the middle class. It is interesting that economic security has become such a god-term for the middle class, whereas it seems somewhat less important to the upper and lower classes. The security motive generally is not high in the hierarchy for an upper class audience because they have achieved security. Security is simply lower in the hierarchy for a lower class audience because matters of mere survival are of more immediate concern.

Et Cetera

Obviously it would be possible to continue this discussion at some length by dealing with matters such as religion and geographic location. However, with an understanding of the general approach, you should be prepared to continue the analysis to whatever extent seems profitable. Ultimately, the individual must use his or her own judgment to discern the characteristics that predominate among the listeners and to devise means for adapting to those characteristics. Generally, one should ask at least the following questions and add others of his or her own:

1. What general characteristics of these listeners can interfere with our public deliberation, and how can I overcome the effects of these characteristics?
2. What characteristics and motives of these listeners make our public deliberation on this topic especially difficult, and what can I do to overcome the effects of those characteristics and motives?
3. In what ways do I differ from these listeners that might make them feel a lack of identification with me or a dislike for me or might make them doubt my credibility or distrust my motives, and what can I do to overcome these differences?

With careful study, observation, and practice, one can develop the sensitivity and imagination to answer those questions in ways that will enhance public deliberation.

SUMMARY

The first job of speakers and listeners is to identify the differences that separate them and to attempt to bridge those differences by means of empathy. The typical approach to the teaching of public speaking has been to concentrate on providing speakers with techniques for affecting listeners. In the area of interpersonal dialogue, however, the emphasis has been upon *empathy,* the ability to feel and understand what others are feeling and thinking, developed through a process of mutual trust and self-disclosure. Although public deliberation is not, and never can be, interpersonal dialogue, empathy can be a useful tool for both the public speaker and the critical listener. Some of the models for developing empathy that are especially useful in public deliberation are Stewart's "my → you" model, Johari's window, and Berne's transactional analysis, in this case modified to include games people play in public deliberation. A model can be described to represent the ways people manipulate perception and thus hamper empathy.

In addition, it is important for both speakers and listeners to give some thought to specific demographic differences that may separate them, such as age, sex, race, educational level, socioeconomic status, and the like.

ILLUSTRATIVE SPEECH

The need for speakers to practice empathy in order to bridge differences between themselves and their listeners is present in most (if not all) speaking situations. For purposes of illustration, however, I have chosen a speech delivered in a situation in which that need was especially compelling.

The speech that follows was delivered by Senator John F. Kennedy on September 12, 1960, less than two months before he defeated Richard M. Nixon in that year's presidential election. The famous Kennedy–Nixon debates were televised during this campaign. One of the issues not directly confronted in those debates was the question of whether Kennedy, as a Catholic, would be able to make the decisions he would confront as president without being influenced by his religion. Many Protestants believed that the Catholic Church held so much power over its members that a Catholic president would face a conflict of interest in administering certain laws that might be interpreted as opposed to Catholic doctrine.

This speech deals directly with that issue. The listeners who were physically present were members of the Greater Houston Ministerial Association. Note, however, that it was obviously intended for—and, in fact, reached—a much larger audience, consisting of all those potential voters who had doubts about his ability to maintain our traditional and constitutional separation of church and state if he were elected.

I say it was "obviously" intended for the larger audience because Kennedy certainly had no obligation to accept the speaking invitation from this particular group. Certainly, their support was not crucial to his election, especially since Texas is a traditionally Democratic state. We must speculate that he chose this occasion to address the religious issue because he felt this group epitomized those who were concerned about that issue. Not only was the group composed of ministers, but they were *Southern* ministers. Protestantism, and especially *conservative* or "fundamental" Protestantism, predominates in the South, and it was among conservative Protestants that religious opposition to his candidacy ran highest.

Thus, Kennedy had to empathize not only with the immediate audience but also with a much larger audience whom they represented. Note how he begins by emphasizing their areas of agreement—the Communist menace; anti-American sentiment abroad; the need for space exploration; and problems of poverty, hunger, lack of housing, agricultural economics, poor education, and poor medical care. And note especially his implication not only that it is irresponsible to obscure such issues with the religious question, but also that his listeners would not be so irresponsible as to do so.

He also begins to encourage his listeners to empathize by imagining those of their own religions in similar positions. His use of the word *Baptist* is especially important, since that denomination is unusually strong in the South, and his reference to the Quaker religion is especially interesting, since Nixon proclaimed himself a Quaker.

As you continue this analysis, see how many examples you can find of Kennedy's attempts to empathize with his listeners and cause them to identify with him—that is, to see themselves as similar to him. Hopefully, the questions for speakers and listeners that appear at the end of Part One will provide some guidance in your search.

Church and State
John F. Kennedy

I am grateful for your generous invitation to state my views.

While the so-called religious issue is necessarily and properly the chief topic here tonight, I want to emphasize from the outset that I believe that we have far more critical issues in the 1960 election: the spread of Communist influence, until it now festers only ninety miles off the coast of Florida—the humiliating treatment of our President and Vice-President by those who no longer respect our power—the hungry children I saw in West Virginia, the old people who cannot pay their doctor's bills, the families forced to give up their farms—an America with too many slums, with too few schools, and too late to the moon and outer space.

These are the real issues which should decide this campaign. And they are not religious issues—for war and hunger and ignorance and despair know no religious barrier.

But because I am a Catholic, and no Catholic has ever been elected President, the real issues in this campaign have been obscured—perhaps deliberately in some quarters less responsible than this. So it is apparently necessary for me to state once again—not what kind of church I believe in, for that should be important only to me, but what kind of America I believe in.

I believe in an America where the separation of church and state is absolute—where no Catholic prelate would tell the President (should he be a Catholic) how to act and no Protestant minister would tell his parishioners for whom to vote—where no church or church school is granted any public funds or political preference—and where no man is denied public office merely because his religion differs from the President who might appoint him or the people who might elect him.

I believe in an America that is officially neither Catholic, Protestant nor Jewish—where no public official either requests or accepts instructions on public policy from the Pope, the National Council of Churches or any other ecclesiastical source—where no religious body seeks to impose its will directly or indirectly upon the general populace or the public acts of its officials—and where religious liberty is so indivisible that an act against one church is treated as an act against all.

For while this year it may be a Catholic against whom the finger of suspicion is pointed, in other years it has been, and may someday be again, a Jew—or a Quaker—or a Unitarian—or a Baptist. It was Virginia's harassment of Baptist preachers, for example, that led to Jefferson's statute of religious freedom. Today, I may be the victim—but tomorrow it may be you—until the whole fabric of our harmonious society is ripped apart at a time of great national peril.

Finally, I believe in an America where religious intolerance will someday end—where all men and all churches are treated as equal—where every man has the same right to attend or not to attend the church of his choice—where there is no Catholic vote, no anti-Catholic vote, no bloc voting of any kind—and where Catholics, Protestants and Jews, both the lay and the pastoral level, will refrain from those attitudes of disdain and division which have so often marred their works in the past, and promote instead the American ideal of brotherhood.

That is the kind of America in which I believe. And it represents the kind of Presidency in which I believe—a great office that must be neither humbled by making it the instrument of any religious group, nor tarnished by arbitrarily witholding it, its occupancy, from the members of any religious group. I believe in a President whose views on religion are his own private affair, neither imposed upon him by the nation nor imposed by the nation upon him as a condition to holding that office.

I would not look with favor upon a President working to subvert the First Amendment's guarantees of religious liberty (nor would our system of checks and balances permit him to do so). And neither do I look with favor upon those who would work to subvert Article VI of the Consitution by requiring a religious test—even by indirection—for if they disagree with that safeguard, they should be openly working to repeal it.

I want a Chief Executive whose public acts are responsible to all and obligated to none—who can attend any ceremony, service or dinner his office may appropriately require him to fulfill—and whose fulfillment of his Presidential office is not limited or conditioned by any religious oath, ritual or obligation.

This is the kind of America I believe in—and this is the kind of America I fought for in the South Pacific and the kind my brother died for in Europe. No one suggested then that we might have a "divided loyalty," that we did "not believe in liberty" or that we belonged to a disloyal group that threatened "the freedoms for which our forefathers died."

And in fact this is the kind of America for which our forefathers did die when they fled here to escape religious test oaths, that denied office to members of less favored churches, when they fought for the Constitution, the Bill of Rights, the Virginia Statute of Religious Freedom—and when they fought at the shrine I visited today—the Alamo. For side by side with Bowie and Crockett died Fuentes and McCafferty and Bailey and Bebillio and Carey—but no one knows whether they were Catholics or not. For there was no religious test there.

I ask you tonight to follow in that tradition, to judge me on the basis of fourteen years in the Congress—on my declared stands against an ambassador to the Vatican, against unconstitutional aid to parochial schools, and against any boycott of the public schools (which I attended myself)—instead of judging me on the basis of these pamphlets and publications we have all seen that carefully select quotations out of context from the statements of Catholic Church leaders, usually in other countries, frequently in other centuries, and rarely relevant to any situation here—and always omitting, of course, that statement of the American bishops in 1948 which strongly endorsed church–state separation.

I do not consider these other quotations binding upon my public acts—why should you? But let me say, with respect to other countries, that I am wholly opposed to the state being used by any religious group, Catholic or Protestant, to compel, prohibit or persecute the free exercise of any other religion. And that goes for any persecution at any time, by anyone, in any country.

And I hope that you and I condemn with equal fervor those nations which deny their Presidency to Protestants and those which deny it to Catholics. And rather than cite the misdeeds of those who differ, I would also cite the record of the Catholic Church in such nations as France and

Ireland—and the independence of such statesmen as de Gaulle and Adenauer.

But let me stress again that these are my views—for, contrary to common newspaper usage, I am not the Catholic candidate for President. I am the Democratic Party's candidate for President, who happens also to be a Catholic.

I do not speak for my church on public matters—and the church does not speak for me.

Whatever issue may come before me as President, if I should be elected—on birth control, divorce, censorship, gambling, or any other subject—I will make my decision in accordance with these views, in accordance with what my conscience tells me to be in the national interest, and without regard to outside religious pressure or dictate. And no power or threat of punishment could cause me to decide otherwise.

But if the time should ever come—and I do not concede any conflict to be remotely possible—when my office would require me to either violate my conscience, or violate the national interest, then I would resign the office, and I hope any other conscientious public servant would do likewise.

But I do not intend to apologize for these views to my critics of either Catholic or Protestant faith, nor do I intend to disavow either my views or my church in order to win this election. If I should lose on the real issues, I shall return to my seat in the Senate, satisfied that I tried my best and was fairly judged.

But if this election is decided on the basis that 40,000,000 Americans lost their chance of being President on the day they were baptized, then it is the whole nation that will be the loser in the eyes of Catholics and non-Catholics around the world, in the eyes of history, and in the eyes of our own people.

But if, on the other hand, I should win this election, I shall devote every effort of mind and spirit to fulfilling the oath of the Presidency—practically identical, I might add, with the oath I have taken for fourteen years in Congress. For, without reservation, I can, and I quote, "solemnly swear that I will faithfully execute the office of President of the United States and will to the best of my ability preserve, protect and defend the Constitution, so help me God."

Chapter Two References

1 Gary Cronkhite, *Persuasion: Speech and Behavioral Change* (Indianapolis: Bobbs-Merrill, 1969).

2 Donald Bryant, "Rhetoric: Its Functions and Its Scope," *Quarterly Journal of Speech* (1953), 401–424.

3 Martin Buber, *I and Thou*, second ed., tr. Ronald Gregor Smith (New York: Charles Scribner's Sons, 1958).

4 Allen Clark, "Martin Buber, Dialogue, and the Philosophy of Rhetoric," in *Philosophers on Rhetoric*, ed. Donald

G. Douglas (Skokie, Ill.: National Text-book, 1973), pp. 225–242.

5 Carl Rogers, *On Becoming a Person* (Boston: Houghton Mifflin, 1961).

6 Sören Kierkegaard, *Concluding Unscientific Postscript to the "Philosophical Fragments,"* tr. David F. Swenson and Walter Lowrie, ed. Walter Lowrie (Princeton, N.J.: Princeton University Press, 1944), p. 182.

7 Kenneth Burke, *A Rhetoric of Motives* (Berkeley: University of California Press, 1969).

8 Erving Goffman, *The Presentation of Self in Everyday Life* (New York: Doubleday, 1959).

9 Eric Berne, *Games People Play* (New York: Grove, 1964).

10 Abraham Maslow, *Toward a Psychology of Being* (Princeton, N.J.: Van Nostrand-Reinhold, 1962).

11 Sidney M. Jourard, *The Transparent Self* (Princeton, N.J.: Van Nostrand-Reinhold, 1964).

12 Eric Fromm, *The Sane Society* (New York: Rinehard, 1955).

13 Everett Lee Hunt, "Rhetoric as a Humane Study," *Quarterly Journal of Speech* (1955), 114.

14 Sören Kierkegaard, *The Journals of Sören Kierkegaard,* ed. and tr. Alexander Dru (London: Oxford University Press, 1938), p. 180.

15 Sören Kierkegaard, *Philosophical Fragments,* tr. David E. Swenson (Princeton, N.J.: Princeton University Press, 1936), pp. 67–69.

16 Martin Heidegger, "On the Essence of Truth," in *Existence and Being,* tr. Werner Brock (Chicago: Henry Regnery, 1949), pp. 321–350.

17 John Stewart, ed., *Bridges Not Walls* (Reading, Mass.: Addison-Wesley, 1973), editor's introduction.

18 Joseph Luft, *Of Human Interaction* (Palo Alto, Calif.: National Press, 1969), pp. 6 and 13.

CHAPTER THREE

Personality Characteristics and Reference Persons

In this chapter we will continue the consideration of characteristics of speakers and listeners that are important in public deliberation. In Chapter Two I dealt with demographic characteristics that are either directly observable or can be inferred from observation. The personality characteristics of others and the reference persons and groups who influence their beliefs, values, and plans are not directly observable and may be difficult to infer from observation, so they must be used a bit differently. The purpose of this chapter is to describe them and the ways in which they are useful.

PERSONALITY CHARACTERISTICS

It is not really very useful for speakers to try to analyze their listeners in terms of personality characteristics. It is useful for speakers to have some understanding of the modes of thinking that characterize certain personality characteristics so that they can try to put themselves in the place of, or feel empathy with, people who have those characteristics, even though they may not know which specific listeners have which characteristics. It is certainly advantageous for listeners to know about the effects of personality characteristics so that they may be able to determine which of their own personality characteristics may be operating in a given situation to handicap them in their task of making a critical decision.

By a personality characteristic, I mean a characteristic mode of response that remains fairly consistent from one situation to another. I cannot begin to do justice to the wide variety of personality characteristics that is treated in the literature of social psychology. However, I would like to choose a few that seem to be especially related to public deliberation.

Authoritarianism and Dogmatism

These two characteristics are discussed together because dogmatism appears to be a more general extension of authoritarianism. Both characteristics seem to be collections of symptoms, which makes them rather difficult to define. An authoritarian individual, as described by Adorno, is one who tends to use beliefs for the purpose of ego defense and is especially likely to be influenced by what that individual considers to be an authority.[1] Rokeach objected to the F-scale, the test of authoritarianism, on the grounds that it measured authoritarianism only among those on the extreme right of the political spectrum, whereas the symptoms it is supposed to measure may be equally characteristic of left-wing radicals. He defined open-mindedness, the opposite of dogmatism, as "the extent to which the person can receive, evaluate, and act on relevant information received from outside on its own intrinsic merits, unencumbered by irrelevant factors in the situation arising from within the person or from the outside."[2] Obviously that should be of interest to those engaged in public deliberation. Suppose we consider, then, some of the symptoms of dogmatic individuals that are especially relevant to public deliberation.

For one thing, dogmatic persons tend to maintain strong central beliefs that are highly resistant to change. These are generally religious, political, or philosophical values; beliefs about the nature of personal worth; and beliefs about the nature of authority. Dogmatic individuals, for example, are expected to agree strongly with statements such as: "It is better to be a dead hero than a live coward"; "The main thing in life is for a person to want to do something important"; and "Man on his own is a helpless and miserable creature." It is interesting that most studies have found that dogmatic persons are especially easy to persuade. This is probably because these studies have used messages designed to change what Rokeach has termed "peripheral" beliefs; dogmatic persons seem to be willing to sacrifice these peripheral beliefs in order to maintain those beliefs that are more central.

A second characteristic of dogmatic persons is that they tend to overlook the relevance of one of their beliefs to another, which allows them to maintain two contradictory beliefs simultaneously. Two test items with which dogmatic persons will agree are: "Even though freedom of speech for all groups is a worthwhile goal, it is unfortunately necessary to restrict the freedom of certain political groups"; and "The highest form of government is a democracy, and the highest form of democracy is a government run by those who are most intelligent." Rokeach has reported remarkable belief change when people are made aware of such inconsistencies in a subtle way, so that they do not feel the need to defend the contradictions.

A third characteristic of dogmatic persons is their tendency to organize the world into two primary categories: things they accept and things they reject. This is evidenced by their tendency to agree with statements such as: "Of all the different philosophies that exist in this world, there is probably only one that is correct"; "To compromise with our political opponents is dangerous because it usually leads to the betrayal of our own side"; and "There are two kinds of people in this world—those who are for the truth and those who are against the truth."

Furthermore, it is especially difficult for dogmatic listeners to accept a person but reject something that person says, or vice versa. Dogmatic persons rely heavily on the opinions of those they consider to be authorities. Such people agree, for instance, that "It is often desirable to reserve judgment about what's going on until one has had a chance to hear the opinions of those one respects," and "In this complicated world of ours the only way we can know what's going on is to rely on leaders or experts who can be trusted." Dogmatic persons would like to find someone who would tell them how to solve personal problems. On the other hand, dogmatic listeners are quick to reject someone who disagrees with them on an important issue; one test item with which such a person will be likely to agree is the statement, "My blood boils whenever a person stubbornly refuses to admit he's wrong."

I worked one summer as one of a crew of four men charged with the job of building a road through a mountain pass in which the snow had only recently melted. With concerted and collective ingenuity the crew succeeded in miring the only available truck and the only available bulldozer in one of the many available mudholes. Trying to pull one with the other made both sink deeper. After the winch cable was fastened to a very sturdy tree, the bulldozer pulled itself onto solid ground using its own power and was then used to pull the truck free. This is mentioned not because it was an unusually brilliant or original solution, but rather because a person talking to those who are highly dogmatic is in a very similar situation. If the speaker and the proposition are both somewhat suspect, the speaker coming out in favor of that proposition will only reaffirm the listeners' suspicion of both. Instead, one must find stable central beliefs of the listeners with which he agrees and use those common beliefs to gain firmer terra for himself; once he is on solid ground, he is in a better position to advance the proposition. Dogmatic listeners will be especially likely to accept a speaker who agrees with some of their strong central beliefs, and once they have accepted that speaker, they will be especially likely to accept the arguments. Open-minded listeners may not respond as favorably to such treatment, but neither will they take offense as long as the approach is not obvious and insincere. A speaker is well advised, both ethically and pragmatically, to choose central beliefs with which he or she actually agrees. Listeners are well advised to consider what effect their own dogmatism may have on *response* to communication.

Three words of caution seem appropriate. First, there is a tendency to think of dogmatic persons as less intelligent than open-minded persons. There is no research evidence that intelligence provides any guard against dogmatism. Second, *it is tempting to consider those who agree with us as being open-minded*. The reverse is more likely, since dogmatic individuals seem to be generally more easily persuaded. Finally, the fact that individuals take extreme positions on any one issue does not necessarily indicate that they are dogmatic as defined here; they may simply believe that they are right. Individuals may be suspected of being dogmatic if they take extreme positions on *many* issues; change many of their less consequential opinions often and especially in response to the influence of persons believed to be authorities; refuse to consider the possibility of being wrong in certain central beliefs; fail to see how their beliefs relate to one another; and reject other persons to the extent that they reject what those others say.

Dominance, Leadership, Need to Influence, and Mach IV

The terms *dominance, leadership,* and *need to influence* seem to be self-explanatory. Mach IV and Mach V are not. They are short for *Machiavellianism,* and are two forms of a test designed to determine the extent to which an individual desires to manipulate others. These traits are considered together not because they are identical but because people who are dominant, often leaders, high in need to influence others, or "Machiavellian" pose special problems in communication situations.

Such persons are easier to identify than some of those previously discussed. Persons who are in positions of leadership are likely to be there because their need to influence is unusually strong, and the need to influence is likely to be unusually strong because they are in positions of leadership. Furthermore, persons in professions that require close interpersonal relationships, such as psychiatry and sales, have been demonstrated to have especially high scores on Mach IV and V. Finally, men on the average seem to be more Machiavellian than are women; as Christie and Geis put it, "Aside from Lucretia Borgia, most of Machiavelli's observations were of males (his titles suggest this: *The Prince* rather than *The Princess; The Discourses* rather than *The Gossip*)." Forgive them, they were writing several years ago.[3]

It is possible, of course, to fight Machiavelli with Machiavelli. If a speaker knows that his or her listeners are more interested in influencing than in being influenced, he or she may use that knowledge by indicating that the listeners have, indeed, been influential. This may be done by dwelling upon matters on which both agree or by demonstrating a willingness to change opinions in response to reasonable arguments. A subtle speaker may allow the listener to take credit for "discovering" the speaker's own arguments and propositions. Thus, "inductive" organization leading from data to the formation of conclusions may be more effective with highly manipulative people than is an organizational pattern in which the conclusions are stated and then supported. Manipulative people are especially susceptible to one form of the "bandwagon" device in which the proposed plan is presented as a new one that is likely to be accepted by others. This gives the manipulative person the "opportunity" to be among the early advocates of something that is likely to prove popular. Whether such manipulation is justified even as a defense against manipulation is a decision you will have to make. Beware of such techniques if you are a "high Mach" yourself.

"Interpersonal trust" seems self-explanatory. It is another component of the conglomerate of symptoms Rokeach has termed "dogmatism." Christie and Geis have been puzzled by the fact that their measurement of desire to manipulate others bears no demonstrable relationship to measures of authoritarianism and dogmatism, but it is significantly related to "anomic disenchantment," a species of interpersonal distrust. They have concluded that there are two types of interpersonal distrust, one of which is characteristic of highly authoritarian and dogmatic persons, includes an apathetic response and moralistic judgment, and amounts to saying "People are no damn good, *but they should be.*" The other, characteristic of the Machiavellian individual, is neither apathetic nor moralistic, and it amounts to saying "People are no damn good, *so why not take advantage of them?*"

The distinction seems to be useful in public deliberation. In either case a speaker may have the problem of convincing people who are characteristically distrustful that he or she is a trustworthy person. The one type of interpersonal distrust, however, seems to be most characteristic of older persons and those of low socioeconomic status, in particular. Such people will probably be more responsive to a speaker who says, in effect, "People are not to be trusted, but one should be able to trust. I trust you and would like you to trust me because I have your interests at heart." The untrusting opportunist, on the other hand, may be more responsive to a speaker who says, "Granted that people in general cannot be trusted, but you can trust me in this specific case because my goals are the same as yours."

In both cases, however, as in most situations, the listener's responsiveness depends upon a speaker's ability to demonstrate that their interests, attitudes, and intentions are *really* similar.

Personality Characteristics and Psychological States

There are many personality characteristics that relate to public deliberation, characteristics that may separate speakers from their listeners or may cause listeners to make uncritical decisions. I cannot begin to survey those that may become important in some speech situation, so I hope you have absorbed enough of the approach to apply it in circumstances you encounter.

You may, for example, find yourself or your listeners in a state of low self-esteem or insecurity at some time. In that case, you will want to understand that people low in self-esteem seem to be unusually susceptible to persuasion. But some of the same conditions that produce low self-esteem in some listeners—especially frustration and threat—may produce aggressiveness in others. Aggressive listeners seem to be unusually difficult to persuade; they are likely to reject speakers' proposals uncritically, unless those proposals call for aggressive or punitive action, in which case aggressive listeners may *accept* them uncritically. Furthermore, listeners whose self-esteem or safety are threatened may develop unusually strong desires for affiliation (misery loves company, safety in numbers) or for achievement to restore that lost self-esteem. If the failure, frustration, or threat is too strong, listeners may develop high levels of anxiety or fear which will interfere with their abilities to critically evaluate messages and to make decisions.

All these are personality characteristics that people have at all times and in which they differ: self-esteem, security, need for affiliation, need for achievement, aggressiveness, and anxiety. But they are also temporary psychological states that can develop as a result of events we encounter, states that may affect the extent to which our speaking is responsible and our listening critical. Certainly, they are characteristics and states of which participants in public deliberation should be aware.

REFERENCE PERSONS AND REFERENCE GROUPS

Speakers and listeners are haunted by the ghosts of people they have encountered in the past, people who, for one reason or another, have influenced their opinions in the past and may continue to influence their opinions now and in the future. One of the things speakers need to know about their listeners is who those influential people are, the functions they serve for the listeners, and what opinions they tend to support as well as new opinions they might tend to oppose. Listeners, on the other hand, devoted to making critical decisions ought to give some thought to their own reference persons and groups so that they can decide the extent to which those reference persons and groups might prevent or facilitate such critical decisions. They might also give some thought to the reference persons and groups that may influence speakers to take the positions they do. Reference persons are not necessarily those who are well regarded. Reference persons may be influential because they are well liked and considered to be experts. But they may be influential in the negative sense in that they are disliked and considered to be very inexpert so that individuals will react against their influence. Consequently, I will refer to negative and positive reference persons and reference groups.

Reference Persons and Credibility

Positive reference persons are those whose opinions listeners are likely to accept, and negative reference persons are those whose opinions they are likely to reject. Speakers who expect to change their listeners' opinions are likely to be more successful to the extent that they know where those opinions come from—that is, to the extent that they know who their listeners consider to be authorities, who they pattern their opinions after and who they consider to be consistently wrong so that they are likely to adopt opinions opposite to those expressed by such persons. Since public deliberation is usually involved with policy decisions, frequently in the areas of politics and product purchasing, it is especially likely to be concerned with the *credibility of sources*.

Public deliberation operates in areas in which listeners have little opportunity for first-hand experience. They probably have not met the people they vote for; they are unlikely to have had first-hand experience with ballot propositions and issues of public concern; and although they may have had first-hand experience with some product, given the wide range of different types of products manufactured today, it is obviously impossible for them to have sampled all products. Consequently, listeners have probably formed their opinions in the areas in which public deliberation deals as a result of second-hand information. The question we are dealing with here is what kind of people does that second-hand information come from?

There has been a great deal of research in the area of credibility in the past few years, and a number of studies have concluded that, in general, there may be three major dimensions on which the credibility of other persons is judged. Such research seems to have concluded that sources of information are judged to be credible if they are believed to be competent, trustworthy, and dynamic.[4] Individuals may serve as credible sources of information if they are competent in that they appear to know what they are talking about, if they are trustworthy in that they appear to be willing to testify truthfully and to have the best interests of the listeners at heart, and if they are dynamic in that they are capable of capturing the attention of listeners in some way.

This third dimension is somewhat suspect and confusing because although sources of information are generally judged as more or less dynamic, it is not quite clear that more dynamic speakers are always more credible. Consequently, we will reserve judgment on that third dimension until we clarify just what its relationship is to credibility. But it does appear that credible speakers are expected to be competent and trustworthy.

A fourth dimension that has been identified more recently is that of similarity to the listener. It now appears that listeners are more likely to believe those who are similar to them in a variety of ways, in terms of opinions, of course, but also in terms of demographic variables and personality characteristics that we have already discussed.

Source Functions

There are some problems with this approach, however, because what constitutes competence and what constitutes trustworthiness seems to change depending upon the situation and depending upon the topic.

I am inclined to take a functional approach to the analysis of source credibility. A very specific source performs many different functions at different times. For example, sometimes newscaster Walter Cronkite provides information; sometimes he teaches; sometimes he verifies or reflects one's own perception; sometimes he contributes stability to chaotic crisis situations; sometimes he consoles. In each of those roles different dimensions of his image are relevant. If that is true of a single individual whose functions are rather restricted by the fact that he is trapped in a television tube, think what a variety of functions different sources perform, and what a variety of dimensions of credibility are relevant to each of those sources at different times. That is why it is important to be able to decide what makes the source credible or not credible in a specific topic situation. To decide that, one must have some idea of the kinds of functions sources can perform with respect to their listeners.

Sources probably function in capacities of *information gathering, cooperation facilitation, and self-actualization* just as does public deliberation in general. In the next chapter I will describe some of the functions of opinions and policies. Sources perform some of those functions: maintaining consistency, maximizing social reward, and assisting the individual in ego maintenance. Another person can be a source of information or consistency maintenance, a source of social reward or punishment designed to facilitate cooperation, or a source of social transaction by which one develops, maintains, or regulates his or her own ego or identity. Insofar as another person functions as a source of information, there are certain criteria that seem relevant to his or her credibility. Such a source can be expected to be most reliable if:

1. The source is or was in a position to observe the facts.
2. The source is capable of observing in the sense of (a) being physically capable, (b) being intellectually capable, (c) being psychologically or emotionally capable, (d) being sensitive to the facts in question, and (e) having had experience in making such observations.
3. The source is motivated to perceive and report accurately in that he or she (a) has nothing to gain by deceiving the listener and (b) has goals similar to, or compatible with, those of the listener.

4. The source has reported accurately in the past on this and other topics.
5. The source is responsible in the sense of being in a position to be held accountable for what he or she says.

Thus, although you may respect your professor in this course and although he or she may be in a position to know about communication, he or she may or may not know more about political events than does anyone else. People frequently assume consciously or unconsciously that because another person knows a great deal in one area, that person is an authority about everything.

Similarly, persons capable of making one kind of observation are not necessarily capable of making another, sometimes because they are emotionally disturbed by the second situation, sometimes because they are sensitive to one type of observation but not to another, and sometimes because they lack experience in making the second type of observation. For example, I find I can make fairly respectable cocktail conversation about the races at Laguna Seca, but I don't even pretend to know what to look for at a diving match.

Even when a source is both capable and has had full opportunity to observe the facts, the source may not report accurately if he or she has some stake in the outcome of the decision. Not that such a person will necessarily lie; it is just very difficult to be objective in a case one really cares about. One of the most obvious studies ever reported in the field of social psychology is by Hasdorf and Cantril titled "They Saw a Game."[5] Students from rival schools saw a film of a game between the two schools. Their task was fairly simple. They were to count the rule violations on the part of both teams. Guess which team committed more fouls according to the students from university A. Guess which team committed more fouls according to the students from university B. Right. Talk about empirical confirmation of the obvious.

Now even using a functional approach, the rules only suggest some general criteria for credibility. The actual decision as to who is to be believed still has to come from the specific case. A source functioning to induce or facilitate cooperation can be judged by the same criteria, but there is special emphasis on the third criterion. The crucial question in such situations is which party will benefit by the cooperation? If the source is going to benefit a great deal, the listener should be mighty suspicious. On the other hand, if the source does not appear to have anything to gain but is still trying very hard to persuade, the listener is advised to be even more suspicious. The object of this game is to determine who will gain what by cooperation so a decision can be made in full view of the motives, goals, and benefits of everyone concerned. Refusing to cooperate when it is in the best interest of everyone can be just as irrational as being too gullible.

Finally, consider the situation in which a source functions to develop or maintain a listener's ego or self-identity. Generally, the criteria that apply to sources serving other functions apply here as well. A listener would hardly choose to form a close interpersonal relationship with an ignorant, incompetent, untrustworthy, inexperienced, irresponsible liar if a better alternative were available. But the criteria we have discussed apply a little differently here. Sources can best serve a self-actualizing function for listeners if they have been in a position to observe listeners, are physically, intellectually, psychologically, emotionally, sensitively, and experientially capable of observing the listeners accurately, are motivated to observe and report observations about the listeners accurately and have done so in the past, and are responsible in the sense of having a continuing relationship with the listeners. There must be some basis for mutual trust, usually a mutually reflective relationship in which the speakers and listeners define one another's identities.

Now if you are in the role of speaker, what you need to do is to think about the sources available to your listeners, the extent to which they function in at least these three types of roles and the extent to which they match the criteria for becoming positive reference persons for your listeners. One good way to find out about their reference persons is, of course, to talk to them. You can then determine who their positive reference sources are—that is, the people whose opinions they are likely to accept—as well as who their negative reference persons are, the persons whose opinions they are likely to reject. They may have a great number of positive and negative reference persons, of course, but what you are looking for is a list of their positive and negative reference persons who are relevant to the issue you are going to discuss in your speech. This will give you some idea of the kind of person you ought to quote in your speech to support your own proposition.

In your role as a listener, it is important that you be aware of your own reference persons, both positive and negative, so that you can decide whether you are reacting to a speaker's proposal on the basis of the merits of the proposal or reacting to it on the basis of the credibility of the people the speaker cites as being in favor of his or her proposal.

Reference Groups

Groups may serve much the same function as reference persons; that is, there may be some group that is especially influential in forming an individual's opinions. The individual may be a member of the group or may not. *A group qualifies as a reference group if it influences the opinions of the individual.* The individual does not necessarily have to be a member in order for that influence to occur. You may respect the opinions of the American Medical Association, the American Civil Liberties Union, or the Federal Aviation Administration without being a member of any of those groups. Your opinions may be negatively influenced by other groups, the American Nazi Party or the Ku Klux Klan, for example. If so, these are positive and negative reference groups for you even though you do not maintain membership in them.

What is it about the perception of groupness or relationship vis-à-vis a number of others that causes the group to maintain influence over a period of time? For one thing, *groups provide social support.* Especially when judgments to be made are ambiguous, individuals come to depend upon the perceptions of the others they consider similar to themselves in various ways to provide social reinforcement for opinions. To some extent, this may be due to liking or trusting the members of such a group but not entirely. Being liked by the group seems to be a very important incentive in this case.

Groups may also serve to define social reality. Individuals impose their perceptions on social reality probably to a greater extent than upon physical reality because social reality is more ambiguous. Thus, one builds expectations regarding various groups and is threatened if those expectations are not fulfilled. The left-leaning radical who finds his own opinion on a specific issue supported by the Young Americans for Freedom may begin to feel he is losing his grip on social reality.

If an individual values membership in a group or values some relationship to a group, she may use her opinions to maintain that relationship or membership. Some groups demand greater opinion conformity than do others as the price of continued membership. Some groups demand opinion conformity in only certain areas. The group may not demand anything of the individual. He may not be a member of the group, and it may be that no one in the group has ever heard of the person, yet he may arrange his opinions so as to maintain a self-satisfying relationship to that group. This effect is especially pronounced when an individual occupies a lower power position within or relative to the group and when she expects to continue to be associated with the group in the future.

In your role of speaker, you need to know not only what individuals serve as reference persons for your listeners but also what groups serve as reference groups for them in that they are influential in determining the opinions that they hold. You may find that their reference groups are very similar to yours or that they are very different. In either case you will be much better off as you try to inform or persuade them if you are aware of those similarities and differences.

As a listener, it will be important for you to be aware of your own reference groups in order that you can be certain that you are accepting or rejecting the speaker's proposal on its merits or lack of merit rather than on the basis of its agreement or disagreement with the opinions of one of your reference groups.

SUMMARY

As a speaker analyzing listeners in order to better inform or persuade them and as a listener analyzing a speaker in order to respond more objectively, there are a number of differences to be considered in addition to demographic ones. People differ also in *personality* characteristics: they are more or less authoritarian and dogmatic, and they are more or less "Machiavellian" or manipulative, among other differences. People differ with respect to the *reference groups* they allow to influence them and with respect to the individual *reference persons* they consider to be credible.

ILLUSTRATIVE SPEECH

This speech of Richard Nixon is *not* presented here as a model for speakers to emulate. As a matter of fact it is a widely heralded example of the unscrupulous use of public speaking. What Nixon did here was to take advantage of lines of argument based on some of the "personality" analyses we have considered. He invoked the names of both positive and negative reference persons and groups, and—above all—he related himself to a long list of "typical" American beliefs and values (cultural assumptions). Thus, the speech seems well suited as an object upon which to practice analytic skills of critical listening.

This speech was delivered to a nationwide radio and television audience on September 23, 1952. At that time Nixon was a candidate for vice-president, General Dwight Eisenhower's running mate. The *New York Post* had revealed that a group of Californians had created a fund of $18,000, ostensibly to help Nixon pay his office and travel expenses. Nixon was not accused of accepting an illegal bribe as was his own Vice President, Spiro Agnew, a little over two decades later. Rather, the question concerned the political ethics of accepting such an amount of money from a small group of people who might later expect favors in return, especially since there was no immediately apparent way of determining that Nixon had not converted the money to personal use. The revelation caused a considerable outcry for Eisenhower to remove Nixon from the ticket. This speech, however, produced such favorable public reaction that Eisenhower instead publicly reaffirmed his confidence in Nixon. Critical response was less enthusiastic, of course. The speech is usually labeled the "Checkers" speech, with reference to Nixon's revelation that the family's pet cocker spaniel, Checkers, had also been a gift—and his protestation that, despite what his critics might say, he was going to keep it.

At the beginning of the speech, Nixon presents himself as an honest, forthright person who is going to "tell the truth" rather than "ignore them [the charges] or deny them without giving details." Next, he set up three questions which he said he was going to answer: (a) Did any of the money go to him for his own personal use? (b) Was the fund secretly given or secretly handled? (c) Did any of the contributors get special favors for their contributions?

This introduction indicates that Nixon clearly understood the issues involved, and it indicated to his audience that he was going to deal with those issues in an organized, specific fashion. Does he, in fact, get specific? What "evidence" does Nixon offer? And what problems are there with the evidence?

Nixon's line of argument is interesting, because it gave him the opportunity to present himself as a poor but honest "common man," similar to most of his listeners and in agreement with their beliefs and values. He certainly made the most of that opportunity.

One of the many critics who have analyzed this speech is Henry McGuckin, Jr. [see "A Value Analysis of Richard Nixon's 1952 Campaign-fund Speech," *Southern Speech Journal* 33 (1968), 259-269]. McGuckin listed 39 instances of appeals to 17 different "American values," including thrift, hard work, honesty, service, plain living, propriety, the individual, equality, rejection of authority, quantification, success, sociality, patriotism, modesty, courage, generosity, and practicality. The actual number to be found, of course, depends on whose list of American beliefs and values one uses and how detailed an analysis one conducts. How many can you find?

Notice also he allies himself with a variety of reference persons and groups, who were positively regarded by the listeners he wanted to persuade, and opposes himself to those they disliked. Remember that he had essentially two audiences: staunch Republicans, whose response would largely determine whether he stayed on the ticket, and uncommitted voters, whose response would determine whether he and Ike were elected. The first audience was the more important at the moment, since his first task was to retain his place as the Republican vice-presidential candidate. Can you list some cultural assumptions to which Nixon appeals when he speaks of his wife, Abraham Lincoln, a wife of a Marine, Dwight D. Eisenhower, the Republican Party, and Americans in general?

In appealing to these values and to reference persons and groups, he also uses persuasive techniques related to certain personality characteristics, especially dogmatism. Now when a speaker uses such techniques, it is difficult to know whether he does so because he himself is dogmatic (for example) or because he believes his listeners are. We can only observe the techniques he uses without attempting to infer reasons. What dogmatic techniques does he use in relation to authority, contradiction, peripheral evidence, call for truth, and devotion to a cause?

In going through the speech, it is easy to classify every name he mentions as unambiguously friend or enemy. Finally, it is easy to identify the dogmatic characteristic of devotion to a cause at all costs, especially in the later parts of the speech. His cause at that time was the anti-Communist crusade. It is obvious he indicates strong agreement with the item from the dogmatism scale, "The United States and Russia have just about nothing in common."

Can you find any further instances of dogmatic appeals? Can you find instances of appeals that seem to reflect Nixon's own self-esteem (or lack of it), aggressiveness (or lack of it), Machiavellianism, anomie, or any of the other personality characteristics mentioned? Can you find appeals that seem to be based on the assumption that the listeners have any of these personality characteristics?

The "Checkers" Speech
Richard M. Nixon

My fellow Americans: I come before you tonight as a candidate for the vice presidency and as a man whose honesty and integrity has been questioned. Now, the usual political thing to do when charges are made against you is to either ignore them or to deny them without giving details. I believe we've had enough of that in the United States, particularly with the present Administration in Washington, D.C. To me the office of the vice presidency of the United States is a great office, and I feel that the people have got to have confidence in the integrity of the men who run for that office and who might attain it. I have a theory, too, that the best and only answer to a smear or to an honest misunderstanding of the facts is to tell the truth. And that's why I am here tonight. I want to tell you my side of the case.

I'm sure you have read the charge, and you have heard it, that I, Senator Nixon, took $18,000 from a group of my supporters. Now, was that wrong? And let me say that it was wrong—I am saying, incidentally, that it was wrong [sic, asking, incidentally, if it was wrong], not just illegal, because it isn't a question of whether it was legal or illegal, that isn't enough. The question is, "Was it morally wrong?" I say that it was morally wrong if any of that $18,000 went to Senator Nixon for my personal use. I say that it was morally wrong if it was secretly given and secretly handled. And I say that it was morally wrong if any of the contributors got special favors for the contributions that they made.

And now to answer those questions let me say this: Not one cent of the $18,000 or any other money of that type ever went to me for my personal use. Every penny of it was used to pay for political expenses that I did not think should be charged to the taxpayers of the United States. It was not a secret fund. As a matter of fact, when I was on "Meet the Press"—some of you may have seen it last Sunday—Peter Edson came up to me after the program and he said, "Dick, what about this fund we hear about?" And I said, "Well, there's no secret about it. Go out and see Dana Smith," who was the administrator of the fund. And I gave him his address, and I said, "You will find that the purpose of the fund simply was to defray political expenses that I did not feel should be charged to the Government." And third, let me point out, and I want to make this particularly clear, that no contributor to this fund, no contributor to any of my campaign, has ever received any consideration that he would not have received as an ordinary constituent. I just don't believe in that and I can say that never, while I have been in the Senate of the United States, as far as the people that contributed to this fund are concerned, have I made a telephone call for them to an agency, or have I gone down to an agency in their behalf. And the records will show that, the records which are in the hands of the Administration.

Well, then, some of you will say, and rightly, "Well, what did you use the fund for, Senator? Why did you have to have it?" Let me tell you in just a word how a Senate office operates. First of all, a senator gets $15,000 a year in salary. He gets enough money to pay for one trip a year, a round trip, that is, for himself and his family between his home and Washington, D.C. And then he gets an allowance to handle the people that work in his office, to handle his mail. And the allowance for my state of California is enough to hire thirteen people. And let me say, incidentally, that that allowance is not paid to the senator—it's paid directly to the individuals that the senator puts on his payroll—but all of these people and all of these allowances are for strictly official business. Business, for example, when a constituent writes in and wants you to go down to the Veterans' Administration and get some information about his GI policy. Items of that type, for example.

But there are other expenses which are not covered by the Government. And I think I can best discuss those expenses by asking you some questions. Do you think that when I or any other senator makes a political speech, has it printed, should charge the printing of that speech and the mailing of that speech to the taxpayers? Do you think, for example, when I or any other senator makes a trip to his home state to make a purely political speech that the cost of that trip should be charged to the taxpayers? Do you think when a senator makes political broadcasts or political television broadcasts, radio or television, that the expense of those broadcasts should be charged to the taxpayer? Why, I know what your answer is. It's the same answer the audiences give me whenever I discuss this particular problem. The answer is, "No, the taxpayers shouldn't be required to finance items which are not official business but which are primarily political business."

Well then the question arises: You say, "Well, how do you pay for these and how can you do it legally?" And there are several ways that it can be done, incidentally, and that it is done legally in the United States Senate and in the Congress. The first way is to be a rich man. I don't happen to be a rich man so I couldn't use that way. Another way that is used is to put your wife on the payroll. Let me say, incidentally, that my opponent, my opposite number for the vice presidency on the Democratic ticket, does have his wife on the payroll. And has had it, her on his payroll for the ten years—for the past ten years. Now, just let me say this. That's his business and I'm not critical of him for doing that. You will have to pass judgment on that particular point. But I have never done that for this reason: I have found that there are so many deserving stenographers and secretaries in Washington that needed the work that I just didn't feel it was right to put my wife on the payroll. My wife's sitting over here. She's a wonderful stenographer. She used to teach stenography and she used to teach shorthand in high school. That was when I met her. And I can tell you folks that she's worked many hours at night and many hours on Saturdays and Sundays in my office and she's done a fine job. And I'm proud to say tonight that in the six years I've been in the House and the Senate of the United States, Pat Nixon has never been on the Government payroll. What are other ways that these finances can be taken care of? Some who are lawyers, and I happen to be a lawyer, continue to practice. But I haven't been able to do that. I'm so far away from California and I've been busy with my senatorial work that I have not engaged in any legal practice. And also as far as law practice is concerned, it seemed to me that the relationship between an attorney and the client was so personal that you couldn't possibly represent a man as an attorney and then have an unbiased view when he presented his case to you in the event that he had one before the Government.

And so I felt that the best way to handle these necessary political expenses, of getting my message to the American people, and the speeches I made, the speeches that I had printed, for the most part, concerned this one message—of exposing this Administration, the communism in it, the corruption in it—the only way that I could do that was to accept the aid which people in my home state of California who contributed to my campaign and who continued to make these contributions after I was elected, were glad to make. And let me say I'm proud of the fact that not one of them has ever asked me for a special favor. I'm proud of the fact that not one of them has ever asked me to vote on a bill other than as my own conscience would dictate. And I'm proud of the fact that the taxpayers by subterfuge or otherwise have never paid one dime for expenses which I thought were political and shouldn't be charged to the taxpayers.

Let me say, incidentally, that some of you may say, "Well, that's all right, Senator; that's your explanation, but have you got any proof?" And I'd like to tell you this evening that just an hour ago we received an independent audit of this entire fund. I suggested to Governor Sherman Adams, who is the chief of staff of the Dwight Esienhower campaign, that an independent audit and legal report be obtained. And I have that audit here in my hand. It's an audit made by the Price, Waterhouse and Company firm, and the legal opinion by Gibson, Dunn and Crutcher, lawyers in Los Angeles, the biggest law firm and incidentally one of the best ones in Los Angeles. I'm proud to be able to report to you tonight that this audit and this legal opinion is being forwarded to General Eisenhower. And I'd like to read to you the opinion that was prepared by Gibson, Dunn and Crutcher and based on all the pertinent laws and statutes, together with the audit report prepared by the certified public accounts, quote,

> It is our conclusion that Senator Nixon did not obtain any financial gain from the collection and disbursement of the fund by Dana Smith; that Senator Nixon did not violate any Federal or state law by reason of the operation of the fund, and that neither the portion of the fund paid by Dana Smith directly to third persons nor the portion paid to Senator Nixon to reimburse him for designated office expenses constituted income to the Senator which was either reportable or taxable as income under applicable tax laws. (Signed) Gibson, Dunn and Crutcher by Elmo H. Conway.

Now that, my friends, is not Nixon speaking, but that's an independent audit which was requested because I want the American people to know all the facts and I'm not afraid of having independent people go in and check the facts, and that is exactly what they did.

But then I realize that there are still some who may say, and rightly so—and let me say that I recognize that some will continue to smear regardless of what the truth may be, but that there has been understandably some honest misunderstanding on this matter—and there's some that will say, "Well, maybe you were able, Senator, to fake this thing. How can we believe what you say? After all, is there a possibility that maybe you got some sums in cash? Is there a possibility that you may have feathered your own nest?" And so now what I am going to do—and incidentally this is unprecedented in the history of American politics—I am going at this time to give to this television and radio audit, audience, a complete financial history; everything I've earned; everything I've spent; everything I owe. And I want you to know the facts.

I'll have to start early. I was born in 1913. Our family was one of modest circumstances and most of my early life was spent in a store out in East Whittier. It was a grocery store—one of those family enterprises. The only reason we were able to make it go was because my mother and dad have five boys and we all worked in the store. I worked my way through college and to a great extent through law school. And then, in 1940, probably the best thing that ever happened to me happened. I married Pat—she's sitting over here. We had a rather difficult time after we were married, like so many of the young couples who may be listening to us. I practiced law; she continued to teach school. Then in 1942, I went into the service. Let me say that my service record was not a particularly unusual one. I went to the South Pacific. I guess I'm entitled to a couple of battle stars. I got a couple of letters of commendation, but I was just there when the bombs were falling and then I returned. I returned to the United States and in 1946 I ran for the Congress. When we came out of the war, Pat and I—Pat during the war had worked as a stenographer and in a bank and as an economist for a Government agency—and when we came out, the total of our savings from both my law practice, her teaching, and all the time that I was in the war—the total for that entire period was just a little less than $10,000. Every cent of that, incidentally, was in Government bonds.

Well, that's where we start when I go into politics. Now what have I earned since I went into politics? Well, here it is—I jotted it down—let me read the notes. First of all, I've had my salary as a congressman and as a senator; second, I have received a total in this past six years of $1,600 from estates which were in my law firm at the time that I severed my connection with it. And, incidentally, as I said before, I have not engaged in any legal practice and have not accepted any fees from business that came into the firm after I went into politics. I have made an average of approximately $1,500 a year from nonpolitical speaking engagements and lectures. And then, fortunately, we've inherited a little money. Pat sold her interest in her father's estate for $3,000 and I inherited $1,500 from my grandfather. We lived rather modestly. For four years we lived in an apartment in Park Fairfax in Alexandria, Virginia. The rent was $80 a month. And we saved for the time that we could buy a house.

Now, that was what we took in. What did we do with this money? What do we have today to show for it? This will surprise you, because it is so little, I suppose, as standards generally go, of people in public life. First of all, we've got a house in Washington which cost $41,000 and on which we owe $20,000. We have a house in Whittier, California, which cost $13,000 and on which we owe $3,000. My folks are living there at the present time. I have just $4,000 in life insurance, plus my GI policy which I've never been able to convert and which will run out in two years. I have no life insurance whatever on Pat. I have no life insurance on our two youngsters, Patricia and Julie. I own a 1950 Oldsmobile car. We have our furniture. We have no stocks and bonds of any type. We have no interest of any kind, direct or indirect, in any business.

Now, that's what we have. What do we owe? Well, in addition to the mortgage, the $20,000 mortgage on the house in Washington, the $10,000 one on the house in Whittier, I owe $4,500 to the Riggs Bank in Washington, D. C., with interest at 4½ percent. I owe $3,500 to my parents and the interest on that loan—which I pay regularly, because it's part of the savings they made through the years they were working so hard—I pay regularly 4 per cent interest. And then I have a $500 loan which I have on my life insurance. Well, that's about it. That's what we have and that's what we owe. It isn't very much, but Pat and I have the satisfaction that every dime that we've got is honestly ours. I should say this—that Pat doesn't have a mink coat. But she does have a respectable Republican cloth coat. And I always tell her that she'd look good in anything.

One other thing I probably should tell you because if I don't they'll probably be saying this about me too. We did get something—a gift—after the election [nomination]. A man down in Texas heard Pat on the radio mention the fact that our two youngsters would like to have a dog. And believe it or not, the day before we left on this campaign trip, we got a message from the Union Station in Baltimore saying that they had a package for us. We went down to get it. You know what it was? It was a little cocker spaniel dog, in a crate that he had sent all the way from Texas, black and white, spotted, and our little girl, Tricia, the six-year-old, named it Checkers. And, you know, the kids, like all kids, love the dog, and I just want to say this, right now, that regardless of what they say about it, we're going to keep it.

It isn't easy to come before a nation-wide audience and bare your life, as I have done. But I want to say some things before I conclude, that I think most of you will agree on. Mr. Mitchell, the Chairman of the Democratic National Committee, made the statement that if a man couldn't afford to be in the United States Senate, he shouldn't run for the Senate. And I just want to make my position clear. I don't agree with Mr. Mitchell when he says that only a rich man should serve his

Government in the United States Senate or in the Congress. I don't believe that represents the thinking of the Democratic Party, and I know that it doesn't represent the thinking of the Republican Party. I believe that it's fine that a man like Governor Stevenson, who inherited a fortune from his father, can run for President. But I also feel that it is essential in this country of ours that a man of modest means can also run for President, because, you know—remember Abraham Lincoln—you remember what he said—"God must have loved the common people, he made so many of them."

And now I'm going to suggest some courses of conduct. First of all, you have read in the papers about other funds, now. Mr. Stevenson apparently had a couple. One of them in which a group of business people paid and helped to supplement the salaries of state employees. Here is where the money went directly into their pockets, and I think that what Mr. Stevenson should do should be to come before the American people, as I have, give the names of the people that contributed to that fund, give the names of the people who put this money into their pockets at the same time that they were receiving money from their state government and see what favors, if any, they gave out for that. I don't condemn Mr. Stevenson for what he did, but until the facts are in there is a doubt that will be raised. And as far as Mr. Sparkman is concerned, I would suggest the same thing. He's had his wife on the payroll. I don't condemn him for that, but I think that he should come before the American people and indicate what outside sources of income he has had. I would suggest that under the circumstances both Mr. Sparkman and Mr. Stevenson should come before the American people, as I have, and make a complete financial statement as to their financial history, and if they don't it will be an admission that they have something to hide. And I think you will agree with me—because, folks, remember, a man that's to be President of the United States, a man that's to be Vice President of the United States, must have the confidence of all the people. And that's why I'm doing what I'm doing, and that's why I suggest that Mr. Stevenson and Mr. Sparkman, since they are under attack, should do what they're doing.

Now, let me say this: I know that this is not the last of the smears. In spite of my explanation tonight, other smears will be made. Others have been made in the past. And the purpose of the smears, I know, is this, to silence me, to make me let up. Well, they just don't know who they are dealing with. I'm going to tell you this: I remember in the dark days of the Hiss case, some of the same columnists, some of the same radio commentators who are attacking me now and misrepresenting my position, were violently opposing me at the time I was after Alger Hiss. But I continued to fight, because I knew I was right, and I can say to this great television and radio audience that I have no apologies to the

American people for my part in putting Alger Hiss where he is today. And as far as this is concerned, I intend to continue to fight.

Why do I feel so deeply? Why do I feel that in spite of the smears, the misunderstanding, the necessity for a man to come up here and bare his soul, as I have, why is it necessary for me to continue this fight? And I want to tell you why. Because, you see, I love my country. And I think my country is in danger. And I think the only man that can save America at this time is the man that's running for President on my ticket, Dwight Eisenhower. You say, "Why do I think it's in danger?" and I say, "Look at the record." Seven years of the Truman-Acheson administration and what's happened? Six hundred million people lost to the Communists. And a war in Korea, in which we have lost 117,000 American casualties. And I say to all of you that a policy that results in a loss of six hundred million people to the Communists and a war which costs us 117,000 American casualties isn't good enough for America. And I say that those in the State Department that made the mistakes which caused that war and which resulted in those losses should be kicked out of the State Department just as fast as we get them out of there. And let me say that I know Mr. Stevenson won't do that because he defends the Truman policies. And I know that Dwight Eisenhower will do that and that he will give America the leadership that it needs. Take the problem of corruption. You've read about the mess in Washington. Mr. Stevenson can't clean it up because he was picked by the man, Truman, under whose administration the mess was made. You wouldn't trust the man who made the mess to clean it up—that's Truman—and by the same token, you can't trust the man who was picked by the man that made the mess to clean it up—and that's Stevenson. And so I say, Eisenhower, who owes nothing to Truman, nothing to the big city bosses. He is the man that can clean up the mess in Washington.

Take Communism. I'd say, as far as that subject is concerned, the danger is great to America. In the Hiss case, they got the secrets which enabled them to break the American secret State Department code. They got secrets in the Atomic Bomb case which enabled them to get the secret of the atomic bomb five years before they would have gotten it by their own devices. And I say that any man who calls the Alger Hiss case a red herring, isn't fit to be President of the United States. I say that a man who, like Mr. Stevenson, has pooh-poohed and ridiculed the Communist threat in the United States—he said that they are phantoms among ourselves; he has accused us that have attempted to expose the Communists of looking for Communists in the Bureau of Fisheries and Wild Life—I say that a man who says that isn't qualified to be President of the United States. And I say that the only man who can lead us in this fight to rid the government of both those who are Communists and those who have corrupted this government is Eisenhower because Eisenhower, you can be sure, recognizes the problem and he knows how to deal with it.

And let me say, finally this evening, I want to read to you, just briefly, excerpts from a letter which I received. A letter which after all this is over no one can take away from me. It reads as follows:

Dear Senator Nixon:

Since I am only nineteen years of age I can't vote in this presidential election, but believe me, if I could, you and General Eisenhower would certainly get my vote. My husband is in the Fleet Marines in Korea. He's a Corpsman on the front lines, and we have a two-month-old son he's never seen. And I feel confident that with great Americans like you and General Eisenhower in the White House, lonely Americans like myself will be united with their loved ones now in Korea. I only pray to God that you won't be too late. Enclosed is a small check to help you in your campaign. Living on eighty-five dollars a month, it is all I can afford at present, but let me know what else I can do.

Folks, it's a check for ten dollars, and it's one that I will never cash. And just let me say this; we hear a lot about prosperity these days, but I say, "Why can't we have prosperity built on peace, rather than prosperity built on war? Why can't we have prosperity and an honest government in Washington, D.C., at the same time?" Believe me, we can. And Eisenhower is the man that can lead this crusade to bring us that kind of prosperity.

And now, finally, I know that you wonder whether or not I am going to stay on the Republican ticket or resign. Let me say this: I don't believe that I ought to quit, because I am not a quitter. And, incidentally, Pat's not a quitter. After all, her name was Patricia Ryan, and she was born on St. Patrick's Day, and you know the Irish never quit. But the decision, my friends, is not mine. I would do nothing that would harm the possibilities of Dwight Eisenhower to become President of the United States, and for that reason, I am submitting to the Republican National Committee tonight, through this television broadcast, the decision which it is theirs to make. Let them decide whether my position on the ticket will help or hurt. And I'm going to ask you to help them decide. Wire and write the Republican National Committee whether you think I should stay on or whether I should get off. And whatever their decision is, I will abide by it.

But just let me say this last word. Regardless of what happens, I'm going to continue this fight. I'm going to campaign up and down in

America until we drive the crooks and Communists and those that defend them out of Washington.

And remember, Folks, Eisenhower is a great man. Believe me, he's a great man, [Announcer in background, simultaneously: *This program has been sponsored by the Republican Senatorial Committee and the Republican Congressional Committee.*] and a vote for Eisenhower is a vote for what's good for America.

Chapter Three References

1 T. W. Adorno, et al., *The Authoritarian Personality* (New York: Harper, 1950).

2 Milton Rokeach, *The Open and Closed Mind* (New York: Basic Books, 1960).

3 Richard Christie and Florence Geis, "Some Consequences of Taking Machiavelli Seriously," in *Handbook of Personality Theory and Research*, ed. Edgar F. Borgatta and William W. Lambert (Chicago: Rand-McNally, 1968), pp. 959–973.

4 This research has been reviewed and critiqued most recently in Gary Cronkhite and Jo Liska, "A Critique of Factor-Analytic Approaches to the Study of Credibility," *Communication Monographs* (1976), pp. 91–107.

5 A. Hasdorf and H. Cantril, "They Saw a Game," *Journal of Abnormal and Social Psychology* (1954), pp. 129–134.

CHAPTER FOUR
Opinions and Policies

Interpersonal differences in such matters as age, sex, educational level, socioeconomic status, and for that matter, interpersonal differences having to do with personality characteristics are not important in public deliberation in and of themselves, but rather because people who differ in demographic and personality characteristics may also differ in what they believe, in what they value, and in the plans and policies they adopt for dealing with the world as they confront it. Empathizing with people who differ from us demographically or in personality characteristics really involves coming to understand what those other people believe, value, and plan to do under circumstances as well as understanding the reasons for their beliefs, values, and plans.

Now that we have given some thought to such differences among people, suppose we go more directly to the heart of the matter and consider how people process information cognitively and how they reach decisions. Speakers who have some understanding of such cognitive dynamics will be better able to empathize with and analyze their listeners and consequently will be better able to inform and persuade them. On the other hand, listeners who have such an understanding will be better able to empathize with the speaker and better able to make judgments about the speaker's sincerity and truthfulness.

BELIEVING—VALUING—PLANNING

The model of cognitive processing that I am going to use throughout the remainder of the book I will refer to as the Image: Belief–Value–Plan model. Kenneth Boulding, who is an economist now at the University of Colorado, has described what he calls a person's image of his world.[1] He wrote his description during the year he spent at Stanford University on leave from the University of Michigan. He begins by describing his image of himself in space surrounded by the Stanford campus with the coast range on one side and the Pacific Ocean beyond, with the Hamilton range on the other side, the Central Valley of California beyond that, then the Sierra, other mountain ranges and desert, the Rocky Mountains, the Great Plains, the Mississippi, and the great cities of the East and Midwest, all of which constitute the United States as one part of a planet spinning through space.

He then describes his image of himself in time—how he came to be at Stanford, and what he will do in the immediate future and how all that relates to his life as a whole, how his lifetime is part of the history of the human race, and how the history of the human race is part of the greater history. Boulding then turns to a description of himself in a field of personal relations, his roles, expectations, and obligations as a professor, a husband, a father, a friend, and a member of groups in society. He describes his image of his place in a world of natural relationships in which certain events are followed by others in a fairly stable and predictable sequence and in which he can predict with some confidence that certain acts on his part will produce certain consequences.

Finally, he describes his image of himself in a world of feeling in which he is sometimes elated, sometimes a little depressed, sometimes happy, sometimes sad, sometimes inspired, sometimes open to "subtle intimations of a presence beyond the world of space and time and sense."

I like Boulding's description of the image, and I hope you will have a chance to read it. Now, however, I would like to divide his general description of human thought processes into three parts: beliefs, values, and plans.

Beliefs

Beliefs are feelings about the probable existence of, and relationships among, the objects, people, concepts, events, and ideas that constitute one's image of the world; that is, I can believe *in* a thing, and I can believe *about* a thing. I have a very strong belief in the existence of automobiles, a weaker belief in the existence of black holes in space, and an infinitely weak belief in the existence of unicorns. I not only believe *in* automobiles, I also believe certain things about them—that they have wheels, that they provide transportation, and that they can kill, for example. Thus, I believe that automobiles are related to other concepts—wheels, transportation, and death, among other things.

I believe in different types of relationships among concepts. These types of relationships can be labeled "similarity," "approval," "categorization," and "contingency." Thus, I believe that automobiles are *similar* to trucks in some respects and that Ralph Nader does not *approve* of them. I believe that the concept of "automobile" bears relationships of *categorization* to "wheels" and "Porsche" since both are part of the "automobile" category although in rather different ways, and I believe that there is a *contingency* relationship between automobiles and death; that is, *if* I ride in an automobile, *then* I may be killed.

The strengths of these relationships may vary. I may see automobiles as very similar to trucks but less similar to trains. I may believe Nader strongly disapproves of automobiles or only mildly disapproves. A Porsche necessarily falls in the automobile category because at this time, at least, Porsche does not build trucks, but a Chevrolet may or may not fall in the automobile category. It is less probable that I will be killed if I ride in a train than if I ride in an automobile. Furthermore, the strength of my beliefs in these relationships may vary. I may have a strong belief that Nader disapproves of automobiles; my belief may be quite weak; or I may, in fact, disbelieve. Finally, my beliefs are related to one another. Obviously, it is going to be difficult for me to believe that God created the universe if I do not believe in the existence of God. I say it is difficult instead of impossible because, as I will note later in this chapter, people do maintain logically contradictory beliefs. Nevertheless, they seem to work toward eliminating such contradictions when they become aware of them. Beliefs, then, are feelings that things exist or that they are related to one another. Values are something different.

Values

Values are feelings of liking or disliking for the objects, people, concepts, events, and ideas that constitute one's image of the world. They differ from beliefs in that clearly one must have a belief in the existence of a thing or at least in its possibility before one can begin to have feelings of liking or disliking that thing.

Now, if asked to do so, I can make lists of things I like and dislike. In fact, I can to some extent rank these things in terms of how much I like them. But my value order may change from time to time just as my beliefs may change. As a matter of fact, my values usually change *because* my beliefs change. To understand that, suppose we consider how values relate to beliefs.

Generally speaking, one's values *depend upon* one's beliefs. Imagine yourself as a speaker who owns a sports car. You want to talk to the class about why you own a sports car rather than a station wagon or a four-wheel drive vehicle of some sort. You begin to analyze why it is that you prefer a sports car. You might think first that you value it because you believe it corners well; it has quick acceleration; it has good gas mileage; and it does not require many repairs. You also value cornering; you value quick acceleration; you value gas mileage; but you do not value repairs. If these things were not true, you probably would not own a sports car. Unfortunately, you have some other beliefs that detract from your evaluation of your sports car. You believe, for example, that it has limited interior space, has limited bumper strength, and has limited ground clearance.

The values you place on those concepts depend in turn upon other beliefs. Perhaps, for example, you believe you own a bicycle; you believe that you are going to have to move in a few weeks; and you believe that there are many times when you are going to want to drive your car on secondary or even dirt roads in the Sierra, Rockies, or Appalachians. On the whole, you value your sports car. That could change if you came to believe less strongly in its cornering, its acceleration, and its gas mileage, if you came to value the cornering, acceleration, and gas mileage less, or if you came to place more value on carrying your bicycle, pulling a trailer, or driving on dirt roads. In short, the value one places on something depends on the value he or she placed on other things to which he or she believes it is related.

Sometimes, however, the opposite is true. To a certain extent, one's beliefs depend upon one's values. Perhaps because you value your sports car in general, you may find yourself rationalizing, talking about how much luggage you can cram into it, how it is possible after all to put a bicycle on top of it, how surprisingly well it negotiates back roads or, alternatively, how seldom you need to drive on back roads. As you prepare to convince a group of listeners that they, too, might value sports cars, you are going to have to lead them to believe certain things about sports cars. You are going to have to lead them to believe that certain things they value are related to the owning of a sports car.

One of the first steps in audience analysis is to prepare a list of the probable beliefs that your listeners hold with respect to your topic, the probable values they place on each of the items, and how those beliefs relate to your topic. You can do the same for yourself. You can make a list of your own beliefs and values that are relevant to your topic and then lay the two lists side by side to get some idea of the extent to which they coincide. What you are generally trying to do in a speech is to bring a certain part of your listeners' mental image to match your own mental image, and the way you proceed to do that is by trying to cause their beliefs and values to match your own, at least in the area under consideration.

But beliefs and values are rather abstract and have little consequence in and of themselves. They acquire their importance because they have consequences for what people plan to do.

Plans

Plans are feelings about the sequences in which behaviors must be performed in order to achieve certain outcomes. Miller, Galanter, and Pribram, who also spent a year at Stanford sometime after Boulding was there, found a copy of his book in the library and were inspired to elaborate on his concept of the image by describing how plans form a part of that image.[2] Plans can be thought of as a special type of belief in a contingency relationship. "If I perform this sequence of behaviors, *then* these outcomes will occur." Three important characteristics of plans are: first, they range from very specific to very general; second, they are hierarchically related to one another; and third, the plans one chooses depend upon one's beliefs and values.

You may have a very specific plan for speaking, a plan that obviously was learned a long time ago, a plan for moving your tongue in a particular way, forming your lips in a certain way, aspirating certain sounds and not aspirating others. Obviously, this is a very specific plan, and it is a plan you do not have to think about as you do it. On the other hand, you may have a very general plan of completing a degree at the college or university in which you are now enrolled. The specific plan for speaking is hierarchically related to the general plan for completing your degree because you are going to use the more specific plan of speaking many times in executing the more general one. The plan for completing your degree includes subordinate plans for taking a certain number of courses that are generally required. The plan may be quite formal. It may actually be written and filed somewhere as a plan of study. The plan for passing this course is part of this more general plan. You probably have not written it down, but you have some idea of the sequence of behaviors you are going to perform to accomplish it. That sequence of behaviors may have been given some shape by a syllabus your professor gave you the first day of class or by his or her description of the course requirement.

Among those requirements is undoubtedly the giving of a speech. You may not have given that much thought yet, but when the time comes you are going to put together a plan for that speech. The plan will consist of a number of subordinate plans that you already have stored and should be able to recall when they are needed—plans for talking to your professor about a topic, for finding books in the library, for making an outline, and then finally for actually producing the words in a public speech.

At the bottom of the hierarchy are a number of plans that were learned so long ago and learned so thoroughly that you will not even have to think about them when you have to do them. Among those very specific plans is the one I mentioned earlier—that is, actually moving your tongue, your lips, and aspirating so that your sounds will be intelligible to your listeners. Obviously, you did not have to plan this physical act of speaking when you planned to finish your degree because the speaking plan was stored and ready to become part of a more general plan to which it is hierarchically related. Your choice of the general plan of completing your college degree was made because of certain beliefs and values you had. You believe certain outcomes will occur as a result of executing that plan. On the whole, you apparently value those outcomes more than those of alternative plans, such as getting a full-time job immediately after high school or hiking into the wilderness and living off of the land. Some of the outcomes of the degree plan are undesirable, of course: having to read textbooks, take exams, write papers, give speeches, and live in poverty, among other things. But in light of what you believe will be the outcome and in light of how much you value those outcomes, the degree plan seems to have the advantage at the moment.

Sensation and Perception

A sensation is an item of data that comes to you through one of your senses. A perception occurs when a number of sensations are organized into a pattern and find a place in the image. Sometimes the sensations do not fit into the image very well. In that case, two things can be done. One can see, hear, or feel the sensations in such a way that they *do* fit, or one can change the image so that it will absorb sensations more easily.

In the discussion of plans I described plans as if they were blueprints for actual, observable physical behavior for dealing with the real world. Frequently they are, but there are other kinds of plans, which I will call perceptual plans, that are blueprints for fitting incoming information or sensation into one's cognitive image. Suppose I have a good friend whom I have known for several years and whose friendship I really value. Chances are that I believe that my friend is honest and fair and has a good many other virtues. I am unlikely to listen sympathetically to other people who tell me that my friend is dishonest, unfair, insincere, and the like. I am very likely to perceive such reports from others as being motivated by their jealousy or insincerity or a desire to gain something at my friend's expense. This is essentially a plan for perceiving information regarding my friend. That perceptual plan may change, of course, if I hear enough bad things about this friend or if I begin to encounter incidents that I myself can observe and that suggest my friend may be dishonest or insincere. The point is, however, so long as I maintain the perceptual plan of believing my friend to be honest and sincere, I will be likely to perceive incoming information in a way that allows me to maintain those beliefs about my friend.

The Perception of Messages

The communication message one receives is initially a sensation that must be integrated into the image. Messages have to conform to certain rules or expectations that are part of the image. Otherwise, they may be judged as unintelligible or meaningless. For example, messages presumed to be spoken in English have to conform to certain rules for English sound combinations, or they are likely to be perceived as gibberish; and they have to conform to certain rules for English sentence structure, or they are likely to be perceived as nonsensical. They have to conform to certain rules of English meaning, or they will be perceived as meaningless;

and they have to conform to rules for appropriate use, or they will be perceived as tactless, crude, or inappropriate. Those rules are going to be discussed at greater length in the chapters dealing with language. What we want to focus on right now is the fact that people can misperceive messages in a variety of ways if those messages do not fit the images they have already formed.

If I hear a message about the friend I used in the preceding example, I have at least four kinds of misperceptions that I can use to avoid changing my opinion of that friend. First, I can simply misunderstand the sounds that I have heard. If I am listening to a delivery of a talk of which a part is a discussion of my friend, it is possible for me to misperceive the sounds of that friend's name so that I believe they are talking about somebody else, or I can hear the word *dishonest* and misperceive it as honest. That is possible, of course, if the delivery is only barely audible and if there is other noise occurring in the audience. If the words are plain enough that I cannot possibly misunderstand them, then I might go to some higher level of misperception. For example, I might misperceive the sentence structure in a way that reflects well on my friend, or I might misperceive some of the semantic rules or rules of meaning. I might

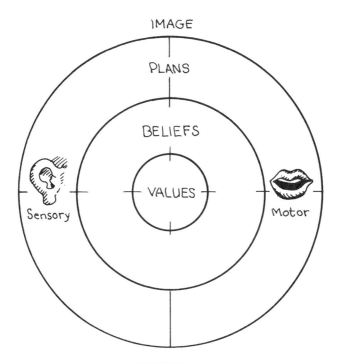

FIGURE 4-1
The Image: Belief—Value—Plan

perceive the speaker who is making a derogatory statement about my friend to be speaking ironically, so that when he says "Joe is really a bad dude," I am much more likely to perceive that in its complimentary sense than in its derogatory sense. Finally, I can perceive the message as failing to conform to certain rules for appropriate use, in which case I can dismiss the speaker as a tactless or crude individual and thus avoid having his statements in any way reflect upon my friend.

Figure 4-1 shows a diagram of the Image:Belief–Value–Plan model. The outside ring labeled Plans is the only one that has any contact with the external world. But there are two types of plans represented here: perceptual and behavioral. The ring labeled Beliefs has contact with both plans and values, but its only contact with the external world is through plans. Beliefs are affected by incoming stimuli after those stimuli are filtered through sensory or perceptual plans. Beliefs, in turn, affect the plans that the individual chooses. The inside circle labeled Values is affected by the individual's beliefs and can, in turn, affect those beliefs. The values have no direct contact with either plans or the external world.

Policies

It seems convenient to add one more word to our list. I have defined a plan as a feeling about the sequence in which a number of acts are to be performed in order to achieve certain outcomes. In fact, people seem to have collections of such plans organized in such a way that if such and such occurs, then they will perform this sequence, but if something else occurs, they will perform a different sequence.

I would like to use the term policy *to cover a collection of plans for dealing with particular aspects of reality.* We are quite accustomed to talking about organizations having policies. For example, we talk about banks having loan policies, by which we mean that banks will loan certain amounts of money to certain types of people with certain credit references, past credit experience, and certain amounts of collateral. The complex organization of plans that the United States maintains with respect to other nations we label "foreign policy" under which are a number of different plans for dealing with specific contingencies in various parts of the world. We also talk about organizations having hiring policies, by which we similarly refer to a set of more specific plans for determining who will be hired and who will not when the job positions are open. I am simply suggesting that we use the word *policy* to apply to collections of plans that individuals use in dealing with a certain segment of their world. For example, I have a policy with respect to picking up hitchhikers. I make the decision about whether to stop for a hitchhiker on the basis of a number of criteria, some having to do with who is riding in the car with me at the time, how much money I am carrying, whether it is day or night, whether the road is well traveled, what the location is, and, of course, what the hitchhiker looks like. Using the present terminology, I would call this my policy for picking up hitchhikers. As a teacher, I also have a grading policy that includes a collection of plans for dealing with specific contingencies, assigning grades on the basis of certain criteria. We all have many such policies, some of which are fairly rigidly maintained and fairly stable and others of which are constructed on a more or less ad hoc basis as the need arises.

Unfortunately, when I use the terms *plans* and *policies*, they may suggest that I believe there is more premeditation and stability to human behavior than is the case. In fact, plans and policies are not always conscious; they are not always premeditated; and they are only more or less stable in that they do change from day to day at the very least. Some of that change, of course, can be incorporated into a policy. For instance, I adopt different policies for picking up hitchhikers depending on how I am feeling on a given day. If I feel that I want to be alone for one reason or another, I simply will not pick up hitchhikers at all. On other days, I will pick up a considerable variety of people. We can think of it as the same policy operating from day to day simply including the specification of what my mood may be and how my moods may change from day to day.

Be that as it may, policies are important in public deliberation because frequently speakers attempt to change listeners' policies rather than attempting to change their specific plans. Any change that a speaker is able to produce in the listener's policy is probably going to be more far-reaching than change he or she produces in some specific plan, since a change in policy represents change in a number of subsidiary plans.

OBJECTIVITY AND SUBJECTIVITY

It is important for everyone involved in public deliberation to be able to evaluate critically the rationality of speakers' proposals. Therefore, in Chapter 7 I will be talking about tests of reasoning and evidence, of criteria by which reasoning and evidence can be judged as satisfactory or unsatisfactory from both rational and empirical points of view. However, it is important to realize that, although rationality is an ideal toward which we ought to work, human thought processes are frequently something less than purely rational.

It is important to a speaker to realize this because speakers frequently build towering edifices of logical reasoning and hard objective evidence before which they expect their listeners to bow in abject submission.

Listeners are not always so cooperative. On the other hand, it is important to listeners to understand the sources of irrationality in their own thinking so that they can prevent unethical speakers from taking advantage of such irrationality, so that they can better evaluate the product of their own thinking and make more critical decisions in response to speeches they may encounter.

I am a little uncomfortable using the term *rational* because what is rational to one individual may not be rational to another. Consequently, I have chosen to use the terms *objective* and *subjective*, which are capable of being specified a little more clearly. When I talk about an objective decision, I refer to a decision that is based primarily upon the external data—that is, data external to the individual. An objective decision, in other words, is one that is object-oriented. It is oriented toward the objective judgment. The subjective decision, on the other hand, is one that depends primarily on the internal characteristics or mental dynamics of the individual making the decision. It depends more heavily upon the characteristics of the subject of the decision, the characteristics of the individual making the decision.

To the extent that an individual makes objective judgments, those judgments will be verified by other individuals under the same circumstances; that is, an objective decision produces reliability between individuals or intersubjective reliability. On the other hand, decisions that are subjective will not produce a great reliability between individuals since those judgments will depend upon different characteristics of the individuals making the decisions and will, of course, involve the kind of interpersonal differences that we have been discussing in this and the preceding chapter.

Decisions that have clear reference in reality can be tested for their objectivity. If I ask you to judge how long a line is and you tell me it is five inches long, I can determine fairly quickly just how objective your decision is in that I can place a ruler next to the line and measure it to see how close your guess is to the actual length of the line. On the other hand, if I ask you to judge whether a given action is good or bad, it is almost impossible, and probably *is* impossible, to determine whether your judgment is objective or not. In fact, it may be impossible to give an objective response to such a question since it involves something that is very subjective, namely, certain values that relate to the action and that differ from one individual to another.

Suppose we consider some of the characteristics of the human thought processes that make decisions somewhat subjective. People tend to use their beliefs, values, plans, and policies to serve certain functions. One of those functions, of course, is the preservation of their lives, their continued health, well-being, and comfort. But they also use those opinions and policies to serve at least three other functions including the maintenance of social reward and the avoidance of social punishment; maintenance of consistency among the beliefs, values, plans, and policies themselves; and maintenance of a satisfactory self-image. Suppose we consider each of those in order.

Social Learning

It is important for you as a speaker to think about how your listeners have learned their opinions and policies and especially what kinds of social reward and punishment have reinforced that learning. As a listener it is equally important that you know how that speaker learned his or her opinion and policies and know about the rewards and punishments that are responsible for them. Finally, as either speaker or listener trying to make critical decisions, it is important for you to know how social learning has shaped your own opinions and policies.

People use their own opinions and policies to increase the social rewards they receive from others and to reduce or avoid social punishment. They learn to express those opinions and pursue those policies that will be socially rewarding.

Suppose we put this in terms of a public deliberation situation. Imagine a situation in which a speaker wants to argue that United States law enforcement agencies should never negotiate with terrorists who threaten to kill hostages unless their demands are met. His major argument is that giving into terrorists' demands simply encourages other terrorists to try the same tactics, and there is no telling where all that may end. Although he deplores the fact that some lives of hostages may be lost initially, he believes that in the long run more lives will be saved than lost because terrorists will have to abandon those tactics when they see they are no longer effective and when they see that their violence is turning public opinion against them. Here is where the empathy must begin.

In order to empathize with his listeners he is going to have to ask himself where their present opinions and policies regarding terrorism have come from. Listeners may be thinking of the terrorists who hijacked the plane containing a number of Israeli nationalists, flew it to Entebbe, and then demanded that Israel release certain prisoners they held, or they may be thinking of the incident at the 1972 summer Olympics in which hostages were kidnapped, demands were made, Israel refused to negotiate, and then the resulting shootout in which both the hostages and the terrorists were killed. It is a fair guess that listeners' values for terrorist kidnapping are strongly negative. It is also a fair bet that their value for human lives is strongly favorable. They have learned those values by a process of social reinforcement. Much of that social reinforcement has probably occurred as a result of watching the television reports of these incidents. The speaker wants the listeners to come to believe that his policy of refusing to negotiate with terrorists will lead to defeat of terrorism and to the pereservation of human life. In a straightforward conditioning experiment one would teach a pigeon that pressing or pecking a lever will result in food pellets dropping into the cage and a reduction of hunger.

The situations are somewhat analogous. What the speaker is trying to do is to some extent analogous to conditioning, but the problem is that he cannot put the listeners into the situation and have them actually reinforced. Instead, he has to describe the situations to them and give them verbal reinforcement. Thus, a speech becomes a sort of conditioning device analogous to conditioning. But which of the incidents should he use for his description? Should he use the example of the Munich Olympics in which the law enforcement agencies as well as the Israeli government refused to negotiate with the terrorists and not only the terrorists but all the hostages were killed, or should he use the incident at the Entebbe airport in which the Israelis refused to negotiate with the terrorists (although they gave them some false hope that they might negotiate) but instead carried out a daring raid and freed all but a few hostages? Obviously, the incident at Entebbe in which refusal to negotiate coupled with decisive action saved almost all the hostages will most clearly reinforce the kind of policy that he is proposing. But he would be foolish to ignore the kidnapping at the Munich Olympics in which refusal to negotiate turned out to be very unsuccessful because his listeners almost certainly have heard of that incident or others like it. Real empathy with the listeners, a real understanding of how they have learned their beliefs, values, plans, and policies with respect to terrorists and terrorism, will require that the speaker not only present examples that clearly illustrate his position but also that he deal with doubts they may have that result from negative examples.

Listeners, too, can use the concepts of conditioning to empathize with the speaker. They can try to understand why he may have come to the conclusion he has reached. He may have learned the general policy very early in life; that is, he may have learned very early that being tough, although it may bring pain in the short term, may result in less pain in the long run.

If public deliberation is to proceed to a satisfactory conclusion in this case or in any other case, both the speaker and the listener must be aware insofar as possible of the extent to which their beliefs, values, plans, and policies may be the result of something similar to conditioning.

Consistency

People also act as if they not only have to acquire knowledge about their environments and to maintain and maximize social reward but also as if they have to see and maintain consistency in their knowledge. I have already mentioned gathering of information as a major function in public deliberation. What has not been discussed yet is the apparently overwhelming need for *consistent* information.

Consistency has a great reputation. To some extent, the reputation is deserved. Consistency is the basis for logical reasoning. People who are consistent are to be depended upon; to the extent that we find consistent, dependable relationships in a world, we can make plans to deal with the world. That, after all, is what the image is all about. One's image as described earlier is a set of consistencies one perceives in the world upon which one bases his or her expectations. But in his essay on self-reliance Ralph Waldo Emerson was so brash as to say:

> A foolish consistency is the hobgoblin of little minds, adored by little statesmen, and philosophers and divines. Speak what you think today in words as hard as cannonballs and tomorrow speak what tomorrow thinks in hard words again though it contradict everything you think today.

What on earth was he thinking? Since Einstein we are accustomed to hearing about how parallel lines do eventually meet, about space-time warps and the like. We have learned to live without knowing whether the universe is expanding or contracting. We have all heard the story of physicists who must one day treat light as if it were composed of particles and the next day as if it were composed of waves. And we have managed some semblance of sanity, probably because it does not really matter if the sidewalk is a whirling mass of electrons so long as one can walk on it. But Emerson was not talking about that sort of inconsistency, which is largely irrelevant to our daily lives. He was arguing that relying too heavily on consistency in everyday reasoning can be irrational. How can consistency ever be irrational? Well, a variety of types of consistency that have been identified are certainly potentially irrational. Let's consider a few examples.

Source-concept-message consistency   One of the most pervasive types of consistency and one of the types of consistency that is most damaging to rational thinking is the consistency people try to maintain between their opinions of other people and their opinions of what other people say. Roger and Darrell have been good friends for months. The question of legalization of marijuana has simply never been discussed.

However, Darrell favors its legalization and, in fact, smokes it on occasion. Roger strongly opposes legalization of marijuana because a favorite cousin of his who smoked marijuana became hooked on heroin. One day in class, Darrell gives a speech arguing for the legalization of marijuana. Roger listens in amazement and horror. After class Roger and Darrell have a long discussion about their opinions of marijuana, a discussion that becomes more and more heated until it brings their friendship to an end.

The general rule for this type of inconsistency seems to be that it is inconsistent to disagree with a friend's opinion or to agree with the opinion of an enemy. If one discovers that a friend has an opinion with which one disagrees, one then rejects the friend or accepts the opinion. A number of theorists and researchers have explored this phenomenon. One of the earliest was Heider,[5] whose basic formulation was expanded by Osgood and Tannebaum.[6] Without delving into the complexities of the various theories, suppose we deal with the basic question: Is this type of consistency rational or irrational?

Even the most likeable people are wrong sometimes. When one is trying to reach a reliable decision, the opinions of those one strongly dislikes or likes can interfere because of the temptation to agree with friends and disagree with enemies. Friends are not always right, and enemies are not always wrong. Consequently, their opinions must be evaluated objectively with special attention to the reasons they are offering the advice or holding the opinions. Trying too hard to maintain consistency between one's opinions of a source and one's opinions of what that source says can destroy that objectivity. Further, one need not come to like another person less just because he or she is wrong occasionally. Everyone is. People who are always right are not necessarily the most enjoyable people to be around. Public speakers frequently try to make use of their likeableness in order to get listeners to do things that they otherwise would not do. This is a frequently used technique in advertising as well, where we see famous sports figures or famous stage or screen personalities endorsing products that they probably do not use, not testifying on the basis of expertise, but simply using their likeableness or fame to get the listeners or viewers to buy the product without giving a valid reason why it would be advantageous. There is a fine line here between likeableness and expertise of the speaker. There is nothing irrational about agreeing with the speaker if that speaker has some expert knowledge that the listener does not have. But to agree with the speaker simply because the speaker is likeable is the stuff of which irrational decisions are made.

Choice-outcome consistency   Leon Festinger has advanced a theory that suggests that after an individual has made a choice, there is greater dissonance created to the extent that the choice is important, and the dissonance is maximum when the alternatives are nearly equal in desirability and so similar as to make compromise impossible. The individual must perceive that he or she alone was responsible for making the choice, and she or he must perceive that the choice is irrevocable.[7]

For example, suppose a person had just chosen between a Datsun 280Z and a Porsche 924. Such a choice is important in that it represents a considerable cash outlay. It is irrevocable, at least for some time, since most people cannot switch cars whenever they change their minds. The alternatives are probably perceived as nearly equal in desirability, and the individual probably perceives that he or she alone has made a choice. Consequently, the dissonance created by such a choice would be considerable. What would prevent it from being maximal is that the two cars have very similar advantages and disadvantages. Making a choice between a sports car and a pickup truck with a camper would create even greater dissonance because of the dissimilarity of the two vehicles. Speakers attempting to analyze audiences will try to determine whether the listeners have made choices of this sort that might freeze the opinions they are trying to change. People under the influence of choice-produced dissonance will try to reduce the dissonance by perceiving the choice to be less important, the alternatives to be more similar, the choice less voluntary and irrevocable, by seeking information or social support for the decision, and most importantly, by becoming more favorable toward the chosen and less favorable toward the unchosen alternative. If the speaker's arguments are bucking any of those attempts to reduce dissonance, he or she will have to provide the listener with an alternative means of dissonance reduction or see the proposal rejected.

On the other hand, listeners should be aware that they are especially susceptible to irrational attempts to justify a choice when these conditions are satisfied, and they should be alert to the possibility that they may be misled into making additional unfortunate decisions in order to justify the original. Let's take an example. Suppose you give a speech explaining why you decided to major in engineering. During your speech you give a very dismal report of how majors in liberal arts and humanities are begging on the streets while certain types of engineers are in great demand. After your speech you are astonished at the vehemence with which many of your listeners attack what you have said. Why? After all, you were merely explaining why you decided to major in engineering. Then it begins to dawn on you that most of the people in the class are majors in the liberal arts and humanities. They have invested a great deal of time and energy in classes required for their majors, and they know if they were to change majors now, they would have to stay in college a year or two longer. But they also know that they are soon going to be out looking for jobs. You have increased their postdecision dissonance tremendously. To bring that dissonance back down, they are attacking your credibility, they are attacking your statistics, and they are attacking the field of engineering, not because they hate you or believe you would lie to them, not because they hate engineers, but because they have made an important, almost irrevocable decision that they have to justify.

The best way for speakers to avoid problems of that sort is, of course, to talk to some of their listeners before they speak. If an engineering major giving a speech of this sort had talked to a group of people in the class, including some majors in liberal arts and humanities, she or he would probably have avoided these problems. On the other hand, listeners ought to be aware of the things that their own dissonance may do to them. The listeners in this case, for instance, are responding in an irrational way, in that they are rejecting the speaker's explanations and probably rejecting the speaker to a greater extent than was called for because they are being affected by the psychological discomfort of dissonance and are doing everything in their power to reduce it.

One of the irrevocable choices some of your listeners may have made is to commit themselves to certain opinions in the presence of people they respect. That is going to make it difficult to change those opinions unless you provide them with some face-saving way of doing it. Apparently changing one's mind is not something to be done in public. It is difficult enough to do in private. Further, opinion change seems to be retarded even more when one has chosen to perform numerous irrevocable acts that are consistent with that opinion. In essence, commitment by means such as these imposes psychological limitations on opinion change, making an individual more rigid, less adaptable, less free, and thus less capable of objectively evaluating new information.

Understanding the general role of commitment in the communication process is important to anyone involved in that process. The speaker trying to influence another wants to prevent that other person from becoming committed to a position other than his or her own or wants to reduce the effect of any commitment that has occurred. After the speaker has successfully changed the opinion of the other, he or she generally tries to get commitment to the new position so that opinion change will endure. A listener trying to make rational decisions, however, wants to avoid commitments that might limit freedom to change opinions in the future if he or she should encounter new information. Thus, communicators, regardless of the role they play in public deliberation, can only benefit in knowing the commitments that all the participants have made which might affect the outcome of that public deliberation.

One of the fraternities at the school where I teach had been requiring its pledges to memorize a rather vulgar song about a Mexican prostitute named "Lupe." One of the Chicano organizations on the campus found out about it and protested to the university administration and the national office of the fraternity. They and other Chicano organizations also marched from the fraternity house to the Quad where they held a noon rally that featured several speakers. Then they marched to the administration building where they demanded some sort of action. The protests and the fraternity's apology received a great deal of coverage in the student newspaper and other local media, and the whole thing was the topic of conversation for several weeks, as is fairly predictable with controversial issues. It also became a topic of discussion in speech classes.

Now suppose you decided to give a speech condemning the use of the song, but you knew that about half of the class were members of fraternities or sororities. You could be fairly certain that some commitment was operating for these people, commitment to the Greek system, at least. How would you handle that commitment? You probably would not have much luck persuading them to renounce their commitments to fraternities or sororities. You would have to find some face-saving way that would allow them to maintain their commitment and still join with you in condemning the use of the song. One thing you would reasonably avoid, because it probably would not work and because it would be manifestly unfair, is to blame the incident on the Greek system in general. A good approach would be to point out that the whole thing had unfairly reflected on fraternities and sororities in general so that Greeks ought to be among the first to condemn them. It would probably also be more effective and again more fair to point out that many of the people who sang the song probably never reflected on its racist nature. That could easily lead into a discussion of the unconscious racism that affects so many of us, not because we are evil people, but because we do not consciously examine our hidden assumptions until someone suddenly confronts us with them. Such a discussion would probably be much more valuable than self-righteous condemnation of a small group of people who certainly received their share of condemnation during those few days, and it is a point that the Greeks in the class could accept without renouncing their commitment.

Belief–belief consistency and wishful thinking   People also seem to maintain certain types of consistency among their beliefs. But the consistency between their beliefs is sometimes destroyed by a second type of consistency they try to maintain, consistency between what they *think* will be true and what they *hope* will be true.

Belief–belief consistency, or what McGuire[8] calls "logical thinking," can probably be best illustrated by the example of trying to estimate the chances of successfully drawing a good hand in poker. Suppose you already have the ace, king, queen, and ten of hearts and a queen of clubs. If you can exchange the queen of clubs for the jack of hearts, you will have a royal flush and you will undoubtedly win the pot. On the other hand, if you stand with what you have, you have only a pair of queens. Would you discard the queen of clubs and draw to a royal flush, or would you stand? Thinking about it in terms of logical belief–belief consistency, you know that there is only one card in the deck that could bring in your royal flush, and since there are only 47 cards that you do not have, you have one chance in 47 of successfully drawing to your royal flush. You have four chances in 47 of making at least a straight since there are four jacks out, and you have nine chances in 47 of completing a flush since there are nine hearts out. If you make your decision strictly on the basis of those probabilities, you are engaging in strict belief–belief consistency, or what McGuire calls logical thinking. But the temptation and the traditional gambler's nemesis is to overestimate the odds in your favor, which is wishful thinking. But wishful thinking is not just the gambler's nemesis, it is also the nemesis of speakers and listeners involved in public deliberation.

In persuading listeners to take some action, a speaker usually has to convince listeners that there is something wrong with the action they have been taking, that some undesirable consequences are going to ensue if they continue to do what they are doing. That puts such a speaker in the position of operating against the listeners' wishful thinking. The listeners are, of course, motivated to overestimate the probability that things will come out all right. On the other hand, wishful thinking puts listeners in a bind, too, since they are more likely to attend to speakers who tell them what they want to hear. In either case, it is clear that wishful thinking militates against the making of objective decisions.

Ego Maintenance

When I refer to the ego I am not using the term in the almost mystical, highly speculative sense in which Freud and his followers have used it. Actually the terms *self-concept* and *identity* will serve equally well, and I will use them frequently and interchangeably. In terms of the Image: Belief–Value–Plan model I am really referring to a person's image of self and place in the world. For most people, this self-image seems to be the center of the image in general. When Boulding described his own image, he described it by beginning with himself and moving outward. I suspect most other people would do the same. Thus, the image is egocentric. I do not mean egocentric in a bad sense, even though in popular use the term usually has negative connotations. I only mean that a person's perceptions of the world are necessarily from his or her own point of view. After all, that is the only vantage point one has. Even the person who succeeds in empathizing with another does so by imagining how he or she would feel in the other person's position. It should not be surprising that maintenance of one's self-image is important, since one has to spend so much time there.

Value expression   Katz has written with special clarity about the function of value expression.[9] He says that *opinions and policies serving the value expressive function are developed for the purpose of maintaining self-identity, enhancing favorable self-imge, self-expression, and self-determination.* They are aroused by cues associated with the individual's values, by appeals to the individual to reassert the self-image, or when the individual faces ambiguities that threaten his or her self-concept. They are likely to change when the individual changes this self-concept or discovers new opinions consistent with the existing self-concept. Thus, the individual who perceives himself or herself to be politically liberal subscribes to those magazines, buys those books, and watches those television programs that describe the opinions and policies political liberals are supposed to maintain. A man who wants to be a sophisticated, urbane playboy is likely to buy *Playboy* or *Penthouse* if he believes those magazines will tell him what sophisticated playboys are supposed to believe and how they are supposed to act. The woman who has just become conscious of her potential as a liberated woman may consult *Ms.* or *Cosmopolitan* or *Playgirl*, depending on what kind of liberated woman she wants to be.

Now you may have noticed that I seem to be writing about two self-images here, and, in fact, I am. There is the image one perceives as *actually* representing oneself at a given time, and there is the *ideal* self-image one would like to become. For some people, the perceived self-image may coincide with the ideal self-image, and for others, the two may be very different. Of course, persons whose self-images coincide can publicly advertise the fact, in which case they are likely to be seen as very smug and egotistical, or they may simply go about their business confidently and unobtrusively. Similarly, persons whose self-images differ drastically may respond by working hard to make them coincide, or they may become discouraged and apathetic. Communication enters the picture because one's perceived self-image can become quite unrealistic if never tested against someone else's perceptions.

It is important to know how others perceive us. It would be absurd, of course, to revise one's perceived self-image whenever it fails to conform to one or two others' perceptions. But if it does not match the consensus of others, and especially of others who might be expected to know one well, there may be cause for concern. It may be that one is misperceiving himself or herself or is communicating a false image. In either case, there may be a problem. Similarly, communication with others can help one maintain a realistic ideal self-image. Without knowing how others perceive one's abilities, it is easy to set one's aspirations too low or too high. Self-actualization requires one to adopt an ideal self-image that is attainable but not too easily attainable, and then work toward that self-image. This process of self-actualization depends heavily upon socially meaningful communication. We have all known people who seem to have no clear anchors for their self-images, who go from day to day trying on new personalities as they might try on new costumes. We all go through phases when we are dissatisfied with ourselves but are not quite sure just what we want to be. That is perfectly natural if it does not last too long. At such times it is important to have friends capable of understanding us, friends with whom it is possible to communicate on a fairly intimate level. Such understanding and capacity for intimate communication is not likely to be developed at a moment's notice. It has to be developed and practiced before it is needed.

It is very important to speakers' self-confidence that they have stable and realistic self-concepts and that their speech reflect internal stability and realism. Stable self-concepts are equally important to critical listeners since their decisions about how to respond to a speech will be based on what they conceive themselves to be and how they believe they should respond in such a situation.

There is always someone around to tell us what we ought to be and how to achieve it at a very superficial level, which is frequently to their advantage rather than ours. The best examples of the use of self-images in public deliberation for unethical purposes come from advertising. Remember the advertising campaign used by the makers of Camel cigarettes that pictured several people in some situation and the reader was challenged to find the Camel Filter smoker in the picture? Strangely, everyone except the Camel Filter smoker had some sort of unattractive gimmick that really amounted to a superficial, unattractive, and obviously fake image he or she was trying to project. That image invariably involved smoking some sort of weird cigarette. The Camel smoker, of course, was obviously natural, sincere, and self-confident. Guess whose image the Camel manufacturers were trying to get the reader to imitate?

What has loosely been labeled sex advertising seems to rely on a similar approach. Of course, sex is frequently used in ads simply to get attention. Usually, however, there is more to it than that. At first, it may appear that the sexy nude or semi-nude woman in the ad is offering herself to any man who buys whatever product is being sold. Some men are gullible, but I do not know many who are *that* gullible, and most of those I do know are locked up. Instead, what such ads are usually portraying the woman as saying seems to be something like this: "The kind of man who can have me is the kind of man who uses Satyr deodorant, wears Body-Form clothes, drives a Studmobile (your product name here). If you want to be the kind of man who can make it with women like me, then you ought to use Satyr deodorant or wear Body-Form clothes or drive a Studmobile." Such ads talk directly to the self-image and, I might add, bypass the brain. Similar ads in women's magazines say, in essence, "If you want to be the kind of woman who can compete with me, you had better use Mink perfume, wear Next-to-Nothing swimwear, etc." Self-images have to be carefully tailored, and they cost more than money. Buy one off the rack, and you will find when you get it home that you look ridiculous in it.

Speakers have to be concerned not only with their own self-images but with those of their listeners. A part of audience analysis or empathy with the audience is trying to decide what images the listeners have of themselves and recommending one's proposals in terms that do not violate the components of their self-images. This is an area in which an ethical speaker must tread very carefully, since the use of appeals to listeners' self-images is a powerful weapon and one that is altogether too easy to use unethically.

Listeners, on the other hand, should be aware of the ways in which speakers may attempt to tell them what their self-images ought to be and then attach their proposals to those recommended self-images. If public deliberation is to take its place in the general evolution of ideas, moving toward the ideal of critical decision-making, both speakers and listeners will have to proceed on the basis of self-images of which they are consciously aware.

Ego defense   Opinions and policies serving the function of ego defense develop to protect against *internal conflict* and *external threats* to the ego. Threat and frustration, appeals to hatred and repressed impulses, and authoritarian suggestion lead to arousal of these attitudes. Change occurs when the threat is removed, after successful aggression or catharsis, or after recognition and acknowledgement of the defense mechanisms. It is important to remember that *ego defense mechanisms are those of which the individual is not consciously aware, by definition.* The mechanisms, in fact, serve to eliminate threat and fear from conscious awareness, but general anxiety level remains high without being related to any specific threat the individual can verbalize. Obviously, these threats are not those we encounter every day. They are threats that tend to produce fear so strong that the individual will not or cannot deal with it. One cannot very well ask another if certain opinions and policies are ego defensive, since the other person does not know. If he or she knew, by definition, they would not be ego defensive. These mechanisms have to be inferred from behavior which is frequently designed (although not consciously) to be misleading.

Katz, McClintock, and Sarnoff reduced racial prejudice by instructing prejudiced people in the dynamics of ego defense. Actually, racial prejudice is very frequently the result of a person being insecure and using a particular racial group as a means of reducing his or her insecurity. Thus, one may feel threatened by blacks or guilty about their treatment but may deny it, repress it, profess to like them ("some of my best friends are black"), or model his or her own behavior and appearance after them. He or she may feel socially unacceptable motives such as high sexual desire and may project that sexual motive, attributing sexual promiscuity to blacks or other racial or cultural groups.[10]

People who are especially concerned that they may be homosexual are the most likely to refer to others as "fairies," "queers," "gay," "butch," and the like. People may feel guilty about their own affluence when there is so much poverty and may accuse welfare recipients of being lazy, or they may feel threatened by high taxes and inflation and blame "lazy niggers," "lazy hippies," unwed mothers on Aid to Dependent Children, or any other available scapegoat. People may feel highly anxious, incapable of coping with the world, and guilty about their failures so that one convenient escape is to blame it all on a conspiracy of Communism, the devil, rednecks, Catholics, or the Establishment. They may feel frustrated by their bosses, frustrated by the success of competitors, or frustrated by rivals for girlfriends or boyfriends, but they may not be willing to take the consequences of aggression against those bosses, competitors or rivals, so they take it out on someone similar to the frustrating person, a person or group safer to attack. They may feel so guilty about something they have done that they feel the need to be punished, but the act may be so unacceptable that they are unwilling to admit it and accept the punishment. Instead, they act in self-destructive ways that are at least socially acceptable but will bring the punishment they feel they deserve. Such analyses explain a great deal of behavior, both in oneself and in others, which otherwise seems unexplainable.

Such knowledge is useful to speakers in that listener resistance to the speakers' ideas may be due to their uses of some of these ego defense mechanisms, and if that is true, then speakers may be able to devise ways of getting their listeners to abandon these ego defenses and at the same time advance their own proposals.

Suppose we first take an example of a short speech a speaker might give that appeals directly to many of these ego defense mechanisms. The speaker is a member of an all-male department at a university. The department is considering hiring a woman for a faculty position. The occasion is a department meeting devoted to making a hiring decision.

Some people have argued that women don't belong in the academic world and that if we allow them to compete for jobs, it's going to increase the supply in a market that is already glutted with qualified men. Now, I don't believe that and I'm sure you don't either. I, for one, like women. My wife has accused me of liking them too much. I certainly wouldn't mind having a woman in this department. As much as I like you people, a woman would certainly improve the scenery. But I am worried about why Mrs. Rogers, excuse me, *Dr.* Rogers, wants this job. After all, she has a pretty good life now. Her husband is a well-known attorney, and he must be making $30,000 or $40,000 a year. I wonder if she is just out to prove something to herself or to her husband or to us or to the rest of the world. I'm not sure we want to introduce that kind of competitive spirit into this department. We get along pretty well together, and I wouldn't like to see that change. I wonder, too, if it would be in our best interests to put her in a position of competing with her husband. That could play hell with her marriage. And if her marriage is a little shaky, it isn't going to help to have her spending all day with seventeen men. But what I am most bothered by is the fact that she is a friend of Mary Jane, the woman who heads that affirmative action group. It is just possible that Mary put her up to applying for this job and that affirmative action bunch has made it almost impossible for the university to hire an Anglo male no matter how qualified. Take Jack Douglass, for example, who has applied for this job. He has had his Ph.D. for two years and has two publications, and he hasn't been able to get a steady teaching job anywhere because everyone is hiring women. And he has a family to support.

The speaker starts out with what may be an example of denial, and he goes next into what may be reaction formation. But before long he seems to be using the device of projecting motives that he himself probably feels onto the female applicant for the job. Then he begins to use arguments that seem to be based on displacement, paranoid reactions, and scapegoating. The speech is rather transparent because I deliberately made it so to provide some obvious examples of how ego defense mechanisms can operate in public speaking. The examples you will encounter in real life may be far more subtle, and the motives may be far more difficult to recognize. It is much more difficult to provide examples of speeches that reduce the listeners' use of ego defense mechanisms.

The best way is to provide extreme examples of the use of defense mechanisms so that the listeners can laugh at the examples but at the same time recognize some of those ego defense mechanisms in their own behavior. In that way, they do not have to openly admit that they have been using the mechanisms. They do not have to confront the use of the mechanisms so directly, and it does not constitute such a threat to their own self-concepts. Yet, at a low level of awareness, they may recognize what they have been doing and begin to take steps to correct it. I think that is what the television program "All In The Family" was designed to do. It probably has had some success, although various analyses of that program have noted that Archie's tremendous popularity may have had the opposite effect for some people. Nevertheless, it is much easier to see the operation of these defense mechanisms in other people or in a television character than it is to see the operation of the mechanisms in oneself when one is openly accused of them.

If you perceive that your listeners are also using ego defense mechanisms, this sort of indirect approach is probably going to be much more effective than to openly accuse them of using those mechanisms, which will only invite hostile reactions.

Ego involvement   To say one is ego-involved in an opinion or policy generally suggests that the opinion or policy is closely related to one's own self-image and necessary to the maintenance of a satisfactory self-image. Defined that broadly, value expression and ego-defense can be considered subfunctions of ego involvement. I want to use the term more narrowly to apply to opinions and policies that are used not merely to express one's self-image or to defend it, but rather are so closely related to the self-image as to actually *define* it. These are opinions and policies so closely related to one's self-imge that, without them, one would be essentially a different person.

For example, Rokeach talks about an overriding general policy that guides one's behavior through a large number of areas.[11] These especially important kinds of policies are those regarding what kinds of authorities one will choose to consider credible, and how one goes about deriving one's beliefs from statements of authorities. Such policies are very important in ego maintenance since they essentially define the ego or self-image. They are policies that rest upon what the person considers ultimately good or bad, right or wrong, worth attaining or not worth attaining. The individual makes decisions about how he or she is going to act, what to do and not do on the basis of these general principles. When one talks about choice situations, he or she is usually talking about the situations in which two or more of these central policies are brought into conflict so that the individual must decide which of the conflicting values are more essential to his or her own self-image. That is no mere expression of perceived or ideal self-image, nor is it a defense of that self-image against some sort of threat. Rather, it is a decision as to what the individual considers to be his or her essential self-image, without which he or she would not be the same person.

Rokeach does not apply the term *ego involvement* to his own theory. That is my doing. Another theorist, Muzafer Sherif, uses the term *ego involvement* to describe his theory.[12] In fact, the key term in Sherif's theory is *ego involvement*. But that term as used by Sherif does not mean exactly what it means in common usage, nor is it used in quite the same sense as intended by other theorists. Taking note of his own research and that of others, Sherif concludes that there is a *latitude of acceptance* around an individual's own opinion. This latitude of acceptance is a range of opinion such that any opinions of others falling within the range will be not only accepted but perceived as lying closer to the individual's own opinion than they really are. It is the width of this range of acceptable opinon that Sherif uses to define ego involvement. The narrower the range, the greater the involvement.

On either side of the latitude of acceptance lies a latitude of noncommitment in which opinions are perceived relatively objectively and are neither consistently accepted nor consistently rejected. Still farther out on either side lies the latitude of rejection, within which opinions are not only rejected but also perceived as being more divergent from the individual's own opinion than they really are. Beyond the identification of these latitudes, Sherif's most important contribution seems to be the conclusion that the latitude of acceptance is smaller and the latitude of rejection is greater when the individual's own opinion is near the extremes on either end of the scale.

Thus, although ego involvement is defined as the narrowness of the latitude of acceptance, it is also presumed (with considerable research support) that ego involvement is greater if an individual's own opinion is extreme. I see this conclusion as indicating that people are very discriminating about opinions that are ego involving. They make fine distinctions among opinions close to their own, but they are very intolerant of opinions that are very different from their own. I am discussing this theory in relation to Rokeach's because I suspect that extreme opinions that have narrow latitudes of acceptance and wide latitudes of rejection are either the central policies Rokeach refers to or they are closely related to those central policies. This is only a suspicion; I do not have any conclusive evidence for it. But if it is true, it certainly has implications for communication, especially for critical listening.

Notice that the thing Sherif says people do with opinions in which they are highly ego-involved are very similar to the things Rokeach says closed-minded people do most of the time. In other words, *everyone is closed-minded or dogmatic about opinions in which he is ego-involved.* We can see that happening constantly. Extreme left-wing groups make fine distinctions among left-wing opinions, but anyone to the right of Castro is a "capitalist insect" or a "facist pig." The John Birch Society member can make fine distinctions among right-wing groups such as the American Nazi Party, the Ku Klux Klan, the Minutemen, and the White Citizens Council, but anyone to the left of Barry Goldwater or Ronald Reagan is either a Communist or a dupe of the Communist Party. Are you exempt from that sort of thinking? I am sure I am not, on opinions that are really ego involving, that serve to define the essence of my self-image. Yet, that kind of thinking would be hard to defend as rational and objective. The disturbing point about this analysis is that it suggests we are *least rational and objective* about those opinions and policies that are *most important* to us.

The implications for a speaker in a public speaking situation seem to be clear. If you are dealing with opinions that are central to your listeners' self-concepts or opinions upon which they feel very strongly, then you will have little success in changing them by expressing opinions widely at variance with their own. In fact, you may cause them to move in the opposite direction. The best thing to do in such a case is to try to move them a little bit at a time.

By moving the listener step by step on opinions that are very ego involving for them, a speaker will avoid the possibility of having proposals being rejected altogether. On the other hand, listeners ought to be aware that they are most likely to be closed-minded and rejecting on those opinions that are most ego-involving and on which they feel most strongly.

SUMMARY

All these differences among people—demographic, personality, and reference—are important in public deliberation largely because they produce or accompany differences in beliefs, values, plans, and policies. Public deliberation is critically concerned with these opinions and policies. A speaker whose purpose is to inform is trying to *add new beliefs and plans to listeners' repertoires*; a speaker whose purpose is to persuade is trying to *change listeners' beliefs, values, plans, or policies*. Whether informing or persuading, a speaker is faced with the fact that listeners' opinions and policies may cause them to misperceive his or her explanations or arguments.

Thus, in order for public deliberation to proceed effectively and objectively, it is important for both speaker and listener to understand that opinions and policies serve the functions of maximizing social reward and minimizing social punishment, maintaining internal consistency, and maintaining one's ego or self-image. We maintain internal consistency between our opinions of sources and our opinions of what sources say, between the choices we have made and what we perceive to be the outcomes of those choices, between our beliefs, and between our expectations and what we wish to be true. We try to maintain our self-images by *expressing* them in opinions and policies, by *defending* them using opinions and policies, and by *becoming so involved* in certain opinions and policies that, in fact, they constitute our self-images.

ILLUSTRATIVE SPEECHES

Any speech that successfully changes beliefs will necessarily change listener values as well, since the two are integrally related and since changes in one's values change one's policies. Any speech designed to change listener values will do so by changing beliefs, and if value change occurs, it will have implications for future policies. And if a speech is *designed* to change policies, it must do so by changing beliefs and values.

Given this, however, it is still possible to look at speeches that *overtly advocate* propositions regarding beliefs, values, and policies. (Other writers generally refer to these as propositions of *fact*, value, and policy.)

We have already encountered speeches that overtly advocated propositions regarding beliefs and values. Look back at the speeches used to illustrate concepts in Chapter One. I used the speech by Carolyn Kay Geiman, "Are They Really Unteachable?" (p. 27), to illustrate good techniques of explanation. But Ms. Geiman went beyond pure explanation; she also tried to *persuade* her listeners to *accept new beliefs*. She listed those beliefs in the conclusion: "[Underprivileged children] can be encouraged to communicate and [their] apathy and antagonism can be conquered." Thus, her purpose was to persuade her listeners to believe, in the language of the title, that underprivileged children are *not* unteachable.

Looking over her speech, one can see that her evidence was chosen specifically to support those beliefs. Her first hypothetical description of the home life of a typical underprivileged child was designed to instill the belief that it is the child's early training (or lack of it) that makes him or her appear unteachable. Her example of the successful educational program conducted by Dr. Deutch was designed to demonstrate that the effects of such a home life can be overcome. Her paraphrase of Frank Reissman was designed to encourage the belief that "Children and parents in slum areas . . . are apathetic, and even antagonistic, not toward education, but rather toward the school system which writes them off as hopeless."

Thus, the thesis and supporting evidence of this speech related directly to *beliefs*; consequently, it is an example of a speech specifically designed to change beliefs. But that does not mean it has no consequences for *values* and *policies*. A listener who adopted these new beliefs would certainly be expected to *value* underprivileged children more and to support policies that include allocation of more money for educational programs such as the one she described. Ms. Geiman asked *explicitly* for belief change, but change in values and policies was certainly implied.

On the other hand, Martin Luther King's speech, "I Have a Dream" (p. 23), seems to call most explicitly for change in *values*: greater devotion to *justice, freedom, equality,* and *faith* in a better future. Those words and their derivatives were used constantly throughout the speech, and *freedom* and *faith* were used repetitively to achieve a peak of emotional impact in the conclusion. *Of course,* the speech dealt with beliefs as well (see if you can identify them), and *of course,* the speech has implications for future policies. (What policies do you think King would recommend?) But the *explicit* call in the speech was for greater devotion to specific values.

With this experience in critical analysis behind you, look ahead to the speech presented in connection with Chapter Nine: Dean's "Anti-Westernism: Cause and Cure" (p. 242). This speech *explicitly* advocated certain *policies.* The policies are easy to find because they were described clearly and specifically, which was not the case with the Geiman and King speeches. But in advocating her policies, Dean certainly dealt with listener beliefs and values. There is no other rational way; critical listeners adopt policies because they *believe* those policies will produce consequences they *value.* See if you can find how Dean tried to cause listeners to believe the proposed policies are related to consequences they value.

In a sense, persuasive speakers *always* advocate policies: sometimes policies of adopting new beliefs, sometimes policies of adopting new values, and sometimes policies of adopting new overt behaviors. I hope that is not too confusing. The point is that persuasive speakers always try to get their listeners to *do* something, although sometimes (as in the Geiman and King speeches) what the speakers want the listeners to "do" most immediately is to change their beliefs and/or values.

Chapter Four References

1 Kenneth Boulding, *The Image* (Ann Arbor: University of Michigan Press, Ann Arbor Paperbacks, 1956).

2 George Miller, Eugene Galanter, and Karl Pribram, *Plans and the Structure of Behavior* (New York: Holt, Rinehart, and Winston, 1960).

3 Leonard Doob, "The Behavior of Attitudes," *Psychological Review* (1947), 135–156.

4 Charles Osgood, "On Understanding and Creating Sentences" (Presidential address to the American Psychological Association in 1962), printed in *Readings in the Psychology of Language,* ed. Leon Jakobovitz and Murray S. Miron (Englewood Cliffs, N.J.: Prentice-Hall, 1967).

5 Fritz Heider, "Attitudes and Cognitive Organization," *Journal of Psychology* (1946), 107–112.

6 Charles Osgood and Percy Tannenbaum, "The Principle of Congruity in the Prediction of Attitude Change," *Psychological Review* (1955), 42–55.

7 Leon Festinger, *A Theory of Cognitive Dissonance* (Stanford, Calif.: Stanford University Press, 1957).

8 William J. McGuire, "A Syllogistic Analysis of Cognitive Relationships," in M. J. Rosenberg, et al., eds., *Attitude Organization and Change* (New Haven, Connecticut: Yale University Press, 1960), pp. 65–111.

9 Daniel Katz, "The Functional Approach to the Study of Attitudes," *Public Opinion Quarterly* (1960), pp. 163–204.

10 Daniel Katz, Charles McClintock, and Irving Sarnoff, "The Measurement of Ego-Defense as Related to Attitude Change," *Journal of Personality* (1957), pp. 465–474.

11 Milton Rokeach, *Beliefs, Attitudes, and Values* (San Francisco: Jossey-Bass, 1968), and *The Nature of Human Values* (New York: Collier-Macmillan, The Free Press, 1973).

12 Muzafer Sherif, Carolyn Sherif, and Roger Nebergall, *Attitude and Attitude Change* (Philadelphia: W. B. Saunders, 1965).

PART ONE
QUESTIONS FOR SELF-EVALUATION

Speaking Objectives

Audience analysis

1. Have you considered what motives your listeners have that are relevant to your topic in this situation?
2. Have you considered what interests your listeners have and the ways those interests will make them attentive or inattentive to your speech?
3. Have you considered how the opinions and policies of your listeners relate to your speech?
4. Have you considered how the reference groups of your listeners will shape their responses to your speech?
5. Have you considered what people or organizations your listeners are most likely to believe on this topic?
6. Have you considered what images your listeners might be trying to maintain?
7. Have you thought about what beliefs, values, and plans your listeners hold?
8. Have you thought about external (objective) data and internal (subjective) characteristics that your audience is sensitive to?
9. Have you considered what social rewards or punishments your listeners are sensitive to?
10. Have you thought about consistency in your arguments and presentation of data?
11. Have you thought about the role of your ego and that of your listeners in overcoming barriers to good communication?

12. Are you sincerely and respectfully attempting to empathize with your listeners and their demographic, personality, and belief differences and similarities?
13. Have you considered which model best fits your needs—Johari window, Stewart, MYLAR, Image: Belief-Value-Plan?

Listening Objectives

Analysis of self and speaker

1. Are you actively trying to empathize with the speaker to determine what motivates him or her to present this speech?
2. Are you earnestly working to minimize or at least recognize the effects of any differences between yourself and the speaker?
3. Do you have any demographic characteristics, personality characteristics, reference persons, reference groups, beliefs, values, plans, or policies that might hinder your attention or comprehension or cause you to *reject* uncritically this speaker or the speech?
4. Do you have any such characteristics (as in item 3) that might cause you to *accept* uncritically this speaker or the speech?
5. Have you considered the age, sex, race, socioeconomic status, education of the speaker and how similar or different they are from your own background?
6. Have you thought about the cultural assumptions that are being made by the speaker and by yourself?
7. Is the speaker dogmatic or open-minded? Which are you?
8. Is the speaker high in self-esteem, need to influence, trusting, and other personality characteristics? How similar are you in these areas?
9. What authorities is the speaker citing and do they meet the reliability tests:
   a) in a position to observe the facts?
   b) capable of observing the facts?
   c) objective or subjective?
   d) reliable in the past?
   e) accountable?
10. What beliefs, plans, or policies is the speaker asking you to understand or change?
11. What rewards are possible from this speaker? Is he or she delivering them?
12. Is the speaker appealing to any consistencies or inconsistencies in your image? What about the speaker's image?
13. Is the speaker ego-defensive or ego-involved? How defensive are you and how ego-involved?

PART TWO

Message Content and Structure

It is impossible to discuss message content intelligently without considering speakers' and listeners' purposes. I have already said that speakers and listeners may have many purposes for participating in public deliberation: to impress one another or some third party, to entertain or be entertained, to pay respect to those who have done something commendable, to earn money or academic credits and grades . . . the list is endless. I have chosen to focus on two major purposes: the transfer of information *and deliberation regarding whether to* cooperate with (accept) *a speaker's proposals.*

INFORMATION AND PERSUASION

I have also pointed out that transfer of information *is an underlying purpose of any speech, since without the transfer of information, the other purposes could not be accomplished. Thus, all speeches are "informative" in the sense that the speaker wishes to inform or the listener wishes to be informed. (Note, however, that labeling a speech as "informative" in this sense does not mean the speech actually* does *a good job of informing, only that the speaker and/or listeners* wish *it to.)*

A second purpose may be imposed over the first: that of persuading *(a speaker's purpose) or* deciding whether to be persuaded *(a listener's purpose). To the extent that this second purpose is superimposed on the first, we generally label a speech "persuasive." (Again, labeling a speech as "persuasive" in this sense does not mean that the speech* succeeds *in getting listeners to accept what the speaker says, only that some listeners feel they must* decide *whether to accept it, and/or the speaker is* trying *to get them to.) Thus, a speech is labeled "persuasive" in this sense to the extent that there is any question of listener* acceptance.

Another way to approach this problem of definition might be to refer to persuasive situations *as those that involve any question of listener acceptance. (This may be somewhat similar to Bitzer's definition of a rhetorical situation.)[1] Then we could define a persuasive* speech *as one delivered in a persuasive* situation—*one in which listener acceptance is in question.*

Incidentally, some experts believe all *speeches are persuasive as well as informative. I have no problem with that, and it is perfectly compatible with my definition. It simply means such experts believe listener acceptance is* always *in question to some extent, and that may well be true.*

INFORMATION, PERSUASION, AND CONTENT

Now the point of all this is that the content of messages is different; the procedures for constructing messages are different; and the specific criteria for evaluating message content are different to the extent that a speech is persuasive as well as informative.

To understand why, it may be helpful to think in terms of McGuire's analysis of the process of persuasion.[2] *McGuire points out that in order for listeners to be persuaded, they must: (a)* receive a message, *(b)* attend *to it, (c)* comprehend *it, (d)* yield *to it, (e)* retain *it, (f)* act *on it.*

*I am sure you can see very quickly that in order for listeners to be in-*formed, *at least four of those items must be accomplished: that is, in order to be informed, listeners must* receive a message, attend *to it,* comprehend *it, and* retain *it. If there is no question that the listeners will also* yield *to the message and* act *on it, then the speech is only informative, but if the speaker must take additional steps to get them to* yield *and* act *(or be willing to act), the speech is also said to be persuasive.*

These can be viewed as the subordinate goals or purposes of a speaker, which when accomplished individually, constitute accomplishment of the primary purposes of informing or persuading.

Now is applying these component purposes of informative and persuasive speaking to message content, we can drop the first—receiving—because it is affected by a speaker's delivery rather than the content. The content of an informative speech, then, must be designed in such a way as to promote listener attention, comprehension, *and* retention. *The content of a successful persuasive speech ("successful" from the speaker's point of view) will be designed to promote* yielding *and* action *as well.*

Now suppose we proceed to consider how content can be made to serve these purposes. In Chapter Five I will deal with the use of explanation and amplification for the purpose of informing and in Chapter Six with the basic dynamics of persuasive appeals. Chapters Seven and Eight present tests of reasoning and evidence and explain how to find and prepare information. Both chapters will be useful whether the speech is strictly informative or also persuasive. Chapter Nine explains how to plan the structure of informative and persuasive speeches and deals with some additional considerations involving the effects on one another of messages occurring in a sequence.

Part Two Introduction References

1 Lloyd Bitzer, "The Rhetorical Situation," *Philosophy and Rhetoric*, 1 (1968), pp. 1–14.

2 William J. McGuire, "Persuasion," in *Communication, Language, and Meaning*, ed. George A. Miller (New York: Basic Books, 1973), pp. 242–255.

CHAPTER FIVE
Explanation and Amplification

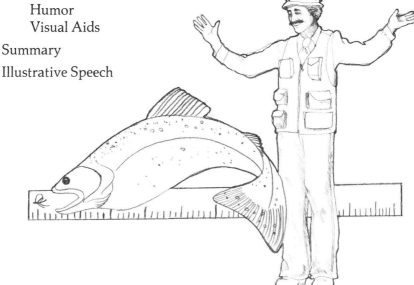

In this book I have frequently used the terms *information* and *persuasion* as if they referred to two different types of speeches or two different types of speech purposes. That is not exactly how I intend to use them. All public speaking is informative, or at least it had better be, to the extent that listeners do not initially accept what the speaker has to say. However, information is also necessary for persuasion to take place. What I will be talking about in this chapter relates especially to informative speaking and its major purposes of clarity and interest. However, since informative speaking underlies even the most clearly persuasive speech, explanation and amplification are important in persuasive speaking as well. What I will not be discussing in this chapter are the means of gaining acceptance once one has made an explanation clear.

TYPES OF INFORMATIVE SPEAKING

There are certain types of speeches in which the purpose of transmitting information seems to predominate and in which the question of listener acceptance seems to be minimal. Let's consider each of those types of speeches briefly before proceeding to discuss methods of explanation and amplification.

Spatial Description

You may be interested in describing specific objects or areas to an audience. You do that frequently in interpersonal conversation when you give directions on how to get someplace. A travelogue would qualify as this type of speech. Similarly, a description of how some city is laid out, a description of how the boroughs in New York City are related to one another geographically, a description of how Chicago curves against the tip of Lake Michigan, or a description of how San Francisco occupies the peninsula on which it is located are examples. Someday you may give a speech describing a building, particularly if you are an architect or archeologist or a historian interested in the structures erected by past civilizations. You may describe an object that is of particular interest for one reason or another. I recall one particularly interesting student speech describing the structure of a space satellite and others describing such things as genetic structures, atomic and subatomic structures, automobiles, sewing machines, and the like. Sometimes when objects that have moving parts are described, the descriptions might equally well be descriptions of processes. An assembly line is probably the best example. An assembly line could be described as an object or as a process, and, in fact, the two types of descriptions might not differ a great deal.

Process Description

Thus, when you are interested in describing not only how an object is constructed, but how it works, your description must begin to deal with the concept of process. The operation of an automobile engine follows a particular chronological sequence, even though it is a repetitive sequence that you can really enter at any point. Two volumes entitled simply "How Things Work," which you can probably find at your local book store, offer excellent examples and endless ideas for this type of speech.

Another type of process description is the how-to-do-it kind of speech. If you are an expert at skiing, surfing, sewing, automobile mechanics or if you are a pilot, you may want to explain to the other students in your class how to perform a particular operation, which is, in reality, a description of a process.

A third type of process speech is the description of an event that for some reason has significance to you and your listeners. You may describe some event from the distant past if you can make it interesting to a contemporary audience, some event currently in the news, or even some fictitious, hypothetical future event such as a nuclear power plant disaster or the discovery of life on a distant planet. Occasionally, events that have occurred to you or your acquaintances may be of interest to your listeners, although this can, unfortunately, disintegrate into the "How-I-Spent-My-Summer" kind of speech. You should probably be especially cautious about describing events of a personal nature because they may be of considerably more interest to you and your friends than they are to a general audience.

Two kinds of speeches that are, in fact, descriptions of events, but that are not usually considered under that category are research reports and investigative reports. If you have conducted an interesting experiment in one of your classes in the physical, biological, or social sciences, it might be of interest to your listeners and would probably be best described as a process. Similarly, an investigative report of the sort you might conduct as a reporter for a newspaper might very well become a report of an event or a series of events.

Critical Analysis

A review of a film, a gallery exhibit, or even a book you have read might be viewed as a description of an event, but it will probably be more interesting to your listeners if you go beyond mere description and provide some critical commentary. If you have encountered some art work or exhibit of particular interest and if you feel that you can make the work or exhibit interesting to your listeners, especially if you have some particular artistic expertise that is applicable, that could make an interesting topic for an informative speech as could a critical analysis of poetry, a movie, a musical performance, or some literary work.

Exposition of Issues

One final type of explanatory speech that I would like to mention approaches, but stops just short of being, persuasion. Perhaps there is some controversial issue or controversial person that occupies your listeners' attention or could be made to occupy their attention. For example, there may be a ballot proposition in their state dealing with legalization of marijuana, banning nuclear reactors, regulating abortion, establishing rights for homosexuals, or legalizing capital punishment. Such topics would make good material for persuasion if you wanted to take a position on one side or the other. But they also make good material for explanation if you want to analyze the issues involved in such controversial questions and present a balanced treatment of pro and con arguments. The issues involved in such controversial questions are usually ones of definition, fact, value, and policy. For example, you might compare and contrast the various definitions of life—human life, in particular—that are adopted by advocates on different sides of the abortion question. You might try to clarify the facts to which advocates and opponents of nuclear power reactors appeal. You might discuss the values accepted and alluded to by those who favor and oppose capital punishment. You might describe various alternative policies that have been proposed for dealing with such problems as inflation, crime, or the conflict between the environment and progress. This brief survey is certainly not intended to exhaust the possible types of explanation but rather to suggest some possibilities for speeches and some of the ways in which explanatory speeches may differ.

METHODS OF EXPLANATION AND AMPLIFICATION

In the remainder of this chapter, I will be dealing with a large number of methods and techniques that you can use to clarify your explanation and make it interesting to your audience. Before I do that, however, I would like to pause briefly to discuss some criteria that can, and probably should, be applied to such methods and techniques. I believe we can identify three general criteria and then discuss how those criteria can be applied to specific methods. I am not presenting these criteria in order of importance because I feel all three are of equal importance, but they must, of course, be presented in some order.

Criteria for Using Methods

The first important question you need to ask of any method of amplification is this: *Is it relevant to the point you are trying to make?* You can ask whether it is relevant to the point of the entire speech, and you can also ask whether it is relevant to the specific subject with which you are dealing at a given moment. The criterion may seem like an easy one to meet. After all, why would you use a particular technique if it were not relevant to the point you are trying to make? The problem is that it is very tempting to include material that is dramatic, attention-getting, and perhaps ego-enhancing, even when it is not particularly helpful and clarifying to what you are trying to say. Speakers sometimes become so fascinated by their own material that it is difficult for them to judge its relevance. Testing your material on a group of acquaintances before you actually deliver your speech will help you to overcome that problem.

The second criterion to be applied is the question: *Is the material logical, reasonable, and fair?* Now that may sound like a criterion to be applied in persuasion rather than in explanation. Certainly, it is a criterion that is likely to be more critical in persuasion, but it applies to explanatory material as well because the material may be so desirable from some other standpoint that it becomes really difficult to exclude it because it does not meet the criteria for sound reasoning and reliable evidence I describe in the next chapter. For example, a description of the issues involved in a controversy may present the issues so clearly that it seems a tragedy to discard it simply because it is an obvious oversimplification. A scathing indictment of the mayor of your city may be so forceful and/or humorous that it seems to cry out for inclusion, even though it is an exaggeration. Remember, however, that you have a considerable advantage in an explanatory speech in that as long as that speech remains predominantly explanatory, listeners are not likely to question what you have to say. If you begin to present material that they consider illogical, unreasonable, and unfair, you may lose your credibility and find yourself embroiled in an argument when your original purpose was to present an unbiased explanation.

The third criterion I want to mention is this: *Does the material make your speech more interesting?* Does it engage your listeners' attention?

That criterion seems to be self-explanatory. Obviously, you want to present interesting material so your listeners do not fall asleep, leave, begin to talk among themselves, or interrupt you. But you can avoid all those unpleasant reactions and still fall short of what you are trying to accomplish, which is, after all, causing your listeners to understand and remember what you have to say. You will not accomplish that purpose if their attention begins to wander, and the material you use in explanation and amplification ought to capture and securely hold their attention at a high level thoughout the speech in order to facilitate that purpose.

Given these criteria, suppose we turn to a consideration of some of the specific methods of explanation and amplification that you can use for the purpose of maintaining clarity. Obviously, the basic techniques, the underlying fabric of expository speech, are explanation and description. But there are a variety of ways to weave, stitch, embellish, and adorn that basic fabric.

Fact and "Factoid"

Facts are probably the most basic threads of which this fabric of explanation is woven. Of course, the problem is that we could probably discuss endlessly what constitutes a fact. We have heard it said more often than we care to remember that one man's fact is another man's fantasy. Practically speaking, I mean to suggest that there are certain items of information that you will want to present to your listeners as part of your explanation. Those items of information may come from your own experience; that is, they may be reports of sensory experiences you yourself have had, in which case it is your own credibility that attests to their truth. The best I can say is that you should believe them to be accurate and, since we are dealing here with explanation rather than persuasion, the matter of personal bias is less likely to arise.

Another kind of fact is the kind that you have obtained from some authoritative source. In that case, of course, you probably will want to tell your listeners what that source is, although, again, extensive qualification of your sources is not nearly as important in explanation as it is in persuasion, and you will probably want to avoid littering your speech with very extensive citations. What is of the greatest importance here is to avoid presenting as fact something that is inference—either on your part or the part of your source. Events that you have personally experienced should be identified as such, and inferences that you have made from those experiences should be equally clearly identified.

Quotation and Testimony

Testimony is a quotation used in support of some proposition. It is used to gain acceptance and, consequently, it is essentially a quotation used in persuasion. However, quotations are also used simply to clarify explanations. You may be quite a competent mechanic, and your listeners may be willing to accept what you tell them about the internal workings of an automobile engine so you do not really need the testimony of an authority to convince or persuade them. However, you may find a particularly concise explanation that you would like to quote in your speech simply because its language is clearer than that in your own explanation. It is perfectly acceptable to do so, so long as you give credit to the person or institution that produced the explanation. In this case, you will cite your source—not for the purpose of causing your listeners to accept what is said, but rather to avoid presenting the explanation as your own when, in fact, it was produced by someone else.

Quotations can be very useful in explanation, and you should not hesitate to use them. In fact, much of the research you conduct in preparation for your speech will probably be devoted to finding quotations that will help clarify your explanation at crucial points. Here is an example to clarify the distinction between testimony and explanatory quotation: I would consider the statement from an automotive engineer, "The rotary engine is superior in efficiency to the piston engine," to be testimony, whereas the statement from the same automotive engineer, "The piston engine operates by means of pistons moving in a straight line, whereas the rotary engine operates by means of a modified triangular rotor rotating within a cylinder," to be simply an explanatory quotation.

Specific Instances

Specific instances are another type of amplification that you will use frequently. I discuss these in Chapter Seven as forms of support rather than as forms of clarification. A specific instance is a means of making an abstract generalization concrete and capable of being visualized by your listeners. Specific instances may be ones that you yourself have experienced, but it is even better if they have been experienced by your listeners as well. If you cannot find enough specific instances that you and your listeners have experienced, you may want to resort to specific instances that have been described by others.

Specific instances are especially useful when you are trying to define a term or make a distinction clear to your audience. I used that device a few lines ago when I provided what I considered to be specific instances of testimony as opposed to explanatory quotations.

Extended Examples and Illustrations

Extended examples and illustrations differ from specific instances in that they are described in more detail. One of my students recently tried to explain what he meant by a "prime-time soap opera." He mentioned the names of several television programs that he considered to be specific instances of prime-time soap operas, but he also chose two programs that he described in considerable detail and that he used to exemplify the criteria by which he defined such television shows. You will frequently find extended examples and illustrations very useful in clarifying your own explanations.

What my student used were real examples—that is, examples drawn from his own experience and from the experience of his listeners. As I have mentioned, real examples can also be drawn from the experiences of others, but examples and illustrations, if used for the purpose of explanation rather than proof, need not be real. Instead, they can be hypothetical. Obviously, the hypothetical nature of your example ought to be clearly indicated to the audience. Suppose, for example, you want to explain how U.S. air defenses would react to the intrusion of an enemy missile into U.S. air space. Since there has been no *real* instance of an enemy missile intruding into our air space (at least as far as I know), it would be rather difficult for you to provide one. Instead, you would be perfectly justified in describing a hypothetical example of such an intrusion and the response of our air defense system as long as you made it clear that your example was hypothetical. The specific detail you could provide by describing the point of intrusion, the system that detected the intrusion, and the weapons deployed to destroy the missile would allow your listeners to visualize our air defense system in much more concrete fashion than would a more abstract description. Please note, incidentally, that I have just used a hypothetical example of a hypothetical example which I hope does not prove too confusing.

Statistics

Statistics are not always used to support controversial propositions in persuasion. They can also be used as a means of informing your audience. The first means of amplification that I mentioned in this section was the use of facts. Statistics are really summaries of facts and summaries of specific instances, whereas the individual facts and the specific instances, and for that matter, the extended examples allow your listeners to visualize conditions you are describing. In addition to facts and specific instances, statistical summaries will be useful in giving your audience some indication of the extent of those conditions. Of course, they should conform to the tests mentioned in Chapter Seven so that they do not mislead your audience.

If the statistics are based on a sample of cases, it is especially important that the sample be chosen in such a way as to represent the entire population of cases. This really emphasizes the criterion that the methods and techniques of explanation and amplification ought to be *fair*. That criterion applies especially well to the use of statistics. It also applies to the use of specific instances, extended examples, and illustrations since—whether real or hypothetical—they ought to be chosen so that they are, in fact, typical and representative of all the instances that might be encountered.

Comparison and/or Contrast

It is very useful in explanation to take advantage of things your listeners already know about in order to clarify for them the things they do not know about. The way to do that is to take something known to them and compare and/or contrast it with the unknown that is the object of your explanation.

If your are trying to explain to your listeners how to operate a motorcycle, for instance, it will be a great help if they are familiar with riding a bicycle. Then you can tell them the ways in which operating a motorcycle is similar and move on to the ways in which it is different. If you are reviewing a musical performance by an unknown singer, it will help if you can tell them she sounds like Judy Collins in terms of her vocal quality, but maintains a much more definite rhythm.

Literal and Figurative Analogies

Analogies are more extensive comparisons. They are discussed in Chapter Seven in terms of their value as proof rather than in terms of their value as explanation. In that chapter I state that analogies are rather suspect in terms of their proof value. Certainly they are much less suspect in terms of their value as explanatory devices.

An analogy involves an extended comparison between the known and the unknown. What is probably most important here is the distinction between literal and figurative analogies. A literal analogy is an extended comparison between the known and the unknown in which the similarities are, in fact, quite extensive.

Suppose you are trying to describe the dynamics of ocean currents, waves, and tides, and you find that you have a great deal of difficulty finding anything with which your audience is familiar that bears a literal similarity to the dynamics of an ocean. It might then be useful to compare the various periodic movements of the ocean to the periodic movements of a clock, pointing out that the clock has rapid periodic movements superimposed upon much slower movements. You might point out that waves are, in a sense, related to tides as the movement of the second hand of the clock is related to the movement of the hour hand. With a little creativity you could probably come up with a much better analogy, but I hope the example at least gives you a picture of the way in which figurative analogies can be used to clarify explanations.

Figurative analogies can also be used as, or considered as, devices of language style and will be taken up in some more detail in Chapter Ten, "Language Style."

Laws and Principles

Sometimes you will give speeches explaining scientific laws and principles, but scientific laws and principles can also be used to explain the operations of mechanisms and specific occurrences difficult to understand in any other way. For example, what keeps an airplane in the air? The most satisfactory explanation requires reference to something called Bernoulli's Principle. This principle specifies that liquids and gases in rapid motion generate less pressure than do liquids and gases at rest or in slow motion. An airplane wing is shaped in such a way that the molecules of air passing over the top of the wing must travel further than the molecules of air passing underneath the wing; they must also travel faster if they are to reach the trailing edge at the same time as the molecules passing under the wing. Because the air passing over the top of the wing is traveling faster, it generates less air pressure and this reduced air pressure on the top of the wing causes the wing—and the airplane to which it is attached—to become airborne. Such an explanation is not so much an explanation of Bernoulli's Principle as it is a use of Bernoulli's Principle to explain the phenomenon of flight of heavier-than-air aircraft.

Causes and Effects

In a similar vein, it is sometimes useful to specify the cause/effect relationships involved in a particular phenomenon as a means of amplification. Sometimes this takes the form of detailing the causes of a particular effect, which a speaker might do if he or she were trying to clarify the development of heart disease within the larger explanation of how one can avoid succumbing to such a disease. On the other hand, it may sometimes take the form of detailing the effects of a given cause. To use a similar example, a speaker might explain the various physical effects attributed to excessive smoking, one of which might be heart disease.

Logical Definition and Synonym

Definition sometimes proceeds by means of examples representative of the term. Logical definition, however, proceeds in somewhat the opposite fashion in that an unknown term is defined as being part of a larger category with which the listeners are familiar. Following this initial assignment of the unkown term to a larger class, the term is then differentiated from the other members of the class until its specific characteristics become clear.

Let's take a simple example. Suppose I am speaking to a group of listeners who have never encountered a platypus, and I want to define the term for them. Actually, I suspect that it would be rather difficult to find a group of listeners who *had* encountered a platypus, so the situation should not be too difficult to imagine except that it might be difficult to imagine why anyone would want to define such an animal. Be that as it may, the first part of such a definition would undoubtedly consist of a statement such as, "The platypus is a mammal that . . ." The definition would then go on the specify the characteristics by which a platypus differs from other mammals. The use of synonyms is somewhat different and probably requires very little explanation. I mention it primarily to remind you that it is a technique useful in explanatory speaking. Sometimes it is helpful when trying to explain an unknown term to provide synonyms, or near-synonyms, with which the listeners are familiar so that they can begin to distill from that list the characteristics covered by the unknown term. Antonyms may be useful for much the same purpose in that the speaker can provide a list of words approximately opposite in meaning to the unknown term so that we have essentially the process of comparison and contrast described earlier applied specifically to the problem of familiarizing an audience with the meaning of a word.

Restatement

Restatement is a legitimate and very useful technique of amplification as long as it is clearly distinguished from mere repetition. Restatement consists of saying the same thing in different words. It not only provides listeners with more time to grasp the idea, it essentially provides them with an alternative explanation in case some of the explanations are not adequately clear. It is not far removed from the technique of providing synonyms. Restatement is an easy technique to use badly but a difficult one to use well. Too frequently speakers restate an idea not to assist their listeners but to provide themselves time to think of what they are going to say next. This use of the technique can become very boring very quickly if the listeners grasped the idea after its first explanation. Too many speakers begin with a clear statement or explanation and then provide successively more difficult and confusing explanations, which, in fact, appear to contradict the earlier ones until the listeners lose their grip on what was once perfectly clear to them.

Your restatements should approach the explanation from different points of view but always to add clarity rather than confusion and to provide time for listeners to comprehend rather than to buy time for the speaker to compose his or her thoughts.

Restatement is probably most useful at the major transition points in a speech and most useful when applied to crucial ideas that the listeners must grasp in order to be able to understand what is to follow. Thus, it is particularly appropriate in introductions and conclusions, at the beginning and end of major divisions of the body of the speech, and following the statements of major points in the speech.

Humor

I cannot begin to emphasize how important humor can be in gaining rapport with an audience and in keeping their attention. Conversely, I cannot begin to emphasize how quickly the clumsy use of humor can destroy the speaker's rapport with the audience and lose their attention. Humor, per se, is probably not particularly important in clarifying a speaker's explanation although I have encountered instances in which it did contribute to clarity. But it will not contribute even to audience rapport and attention, let alone clarity, if it does not conform to the criteria I mentioned at the beginning of this section. Dropping humorous anecdotes into a speech at random may produce laughter, but if they are unrelated to the explanation, they may also very effectively distract the listeners. If that distraction continues very long, the listeners will begin to recognize it for what it is and you will lose whatever rapport you may have gained.

Humor that operates at the expense of another person or group—especially if it characterizes the other unfairly—is very likely to backfire to the detriment of the speaker. The third criterion mentioned earlier has to be modified a little bit in the case of humor because humor—if it is humor—is almost bound to be interesting. But is it fresh and original? The telling of stale jokes will not only bore your listeners, it is bound to reflect on your own intelligence and creativity. The use of verbal humor—that is, humor that springs from the *way* something is said, from the language that is used—is discussed in considerable detail in

Chapter Ten. The kind of humor that qualifies as amplification is predominantly the use of humorous examples or anecdotes, whether real or fictitious. Once again, I think it is very important to try such anecdotes on some of your acquaintances so that any mistakes you may make in this area will be made in relative privacy.

Another particularly important consideration with respect to humor is that it ought to be appropriate to the listeners and to the occasion. Not only are sexual and scatological references inappropriate in some contexts before some audiences, but, in fact, any humor at all is inappropriate in certain contexts with certain topics, and there is a wide variety of specific types of humor that can offend specific listeners. The placement of humor within the speech is also important. Humor can be distracting if it is not relevant. But it can even be distracting when it is relevant. If it occurs in the middle of a difficult explanation, it should occur at points when the audience either needs some relief from tension or some rest from difficult mental activity. Unfortunately, I do not even pretend to be capable of telling you how to be funny, so I have had to settle for cautioning you about how to avoid some common pitfalls.

Visual Aids

Because I regard the preparation of visual aids as being quite similar to the finding of information, they are discussed in much more detail in Chapter Eight. At this point, all I want to do is to remind you of the wide variety of visual aids available to you and to emphasize the overwhelming importance of visual aids in explanation. You can prepare diagrams and sketches; you can bring to class the actual objects you want to explain if they are of appropriate size; or you can construct or acquire models of the objects if the objects themselves are too small or too large. You can prepare and acquire charts and graphs to illustrate processes and organizational complexities. You can use cutaway diagrams and pictographs, line graphs, profile graphs, and bar graphs to summarize and more dramatically illustrate your statistics. You can use photographs, audio tapes, video tapes, film, slides, and maps for other specific purposes. Sometimes these are difficult to acquire or prepare, but they are frequently much more accessible than you might think.

In addition to helping your audience visualize parts of your explanation that would otherwise depend upon their imagination and in addition to providing a sometimes welcome diversion from the repetitive visual image of a single person standing before them, visual aids can also be a welcome distraction for you—a distraction from the tension and anxiety you may feel in a speaking situation.

SUMMARY

Informative speeches are those designed to produce listener attention, comprehension, and retention in cases when acceptance and action can be assumed. Such speeches sometimes provide spatial descriptions of objects or areas, or they may describe processes: how things work, how to do something, how a particular event occurred, or how some research or investigation was conducted. Other informative speeches may provide critical analyses of literary, musical, or artistic works or performances, or they may consist of explanations of aspects of controversial issues on which the speaker does not want to take a position.

Informative speeches use a variety of methods of explanation and amplification, including: generally accepted facts, quotations and testimony, specific instances, extended examples and illustrations (real or hypothetical), statistics, comparison and/or contrast, literal and figurative analogies, laws and principles, causes and effects, logical definitions and synonyms, restatement, humor, and visual aids.

It seems self-evident that speakers must know these types of informative speeches and methods of explanation and amplification. Listeners, however, should also be familiar with them for two reasons. First, listeners will be better able to comprehend if they understand the function a particular method serves in a particular type of speech. Second, speakers sometimes smuggle persuasion in the guise of mere information—sometimes without even being aware of it. Listeners who know what constitutes informative speaking will be better able to detect such ploys.

ILLUSTRATIVE SPEECH

I have already asked you to notice the methods of explanation and amplification used by Carolyn Kay Geiman in her speech "Are They Really Unteachable?" which was used as an example following the first chapter. What you did not have at that time was a list and descriptions of the various methods available. Now that such a list and such descriptions have been presented in this chapter, I would like to propose that you go back to her speech and see if you can not only notice but also *identify* the methods or techniques she used.

Another speech that seems useful for the same purpose is the one that follows by Karl Menninger, titled "Healthier Than Healthy," delivered to a general (nonspecialist) audience at the Chautauqua Amphitheater in Chautauqua, New York, on April 5, 1958. His topic lay in his own technical specialty, but the speech was addressed to a general audience;

therefore, it is especially interesting to note and identify the techniques of explanation and amplification he used for the sake of clarity.

Healthier Than Healthy*
Karl Menninger

I want to report four observations to you. I would call these "facts," except that I have an aversion for the expression, "Let's get the facts." One of the most untruthful things possible, you know, is a collection of facts, because they can be made to appear so many different ways. I was somewhat interested in sleight of hand when I was younger, and what always intrigued me was that the obvious facts could be so untruthful. It was a fact that here something was and a minute later it was there. It was a fact but it wasn't the truth, because what was over there wasn't what was here. There was something phoney about it.

Here are four observations I want you to consider. The first observation is that mental illness is something that may occur in the lives of any of us. It always develops rather unexpectedly. Nobody plans to get mentally ill, you know, and nobody expects to get mentally ill. We all expect we may get pneumonia or we may get a bad cold next winter. We expect physical illnesses of certain kinds, but no one expects a mental illness.

Nevertheless, mental illness does come; it strikes down friends and acquaintances, the prominent and the lowly, rich victims and poor ones. It is no respecter of persons. It may come to any one of us.

I do not want you to be alarmed by this statement. But I do want to break through the barrier of misapprehensions that divide the world into "those people"—meaning this time those impossible, outlandish, afflicted "crazy" people—and "us"—us sane, sensible people. That is the perfectly understandable, aristocratic view, but it is a mistaken one.

Mental illness used to be thought of only in the extreme forms or stages which render its victims incapacitated by reason of such symptoms as overwhelming depressions, paralyzing fear, delusional misapprehensions, or uncontrolled impulses toward unprofitable or undesirable behavior. Such individuals have to be taken in hand and cared for, even over their protests. True.

But surely many of us have experienced *some* degree of depression, some inhibition from irrational fear, some loss of self-control in social behavior. And, while it is true that one swallow does not make a summer, these *are* symptoms of mental illness, and mental illness can be mild in degree, or severe, and it can be "in between."

*From *A Psychiatrist's World: The Selected Papers of Karl Menninger, M.D.* Copyright 1959 by Karl Menninger. Reprinted by permission of the Viking Press.

This, of course, is not quite like the notion of some physical diseases. One can have many degrees of arthritis. But one either *has* malaria or does not have it. The same is true with many other diseases. But in the case of mental illness, it seems that any of us can—indeed, all of us *do*—have some degree of it, at some times.

That is my first observation. Now for a second observation.

The general notion has long prevailed that, once mental illness has appeared, the victim is doomed. The illness progresses, the disability increases, the spector of dementia looms inevitably ahead. "Once insane, always insane," they said. Mental illness is incurable. Kindly and well-meaning doctors in state hospitals sometimes used to counsel relatives to go home and try to forget their poor father or sister or whoever it was; "He can never recover and you should remake your life as if he were dead."

This all seems incredible to us today, because we have quite the opposite view. Most attacks of mental illness subside; most of the patients recover. The trend of mental illness is *usually* back toward health, not toward permanent disability and incurability, and we believe that we know some ways to encourage that return to health, one of which is the sustained and sustaining love of friends and relatives. This is something *they* can do, while the doctors (and nurses and therapists) do what *they* can; all contribute to the patient's recovery from mental illness.

The third observation I am going to make is that some mental illnesses seem to recover for a while and then stop and other mental illnesses recover slowly and others may recover more rapidly but may recur. They come back again. People often ask me, "You say that eighty-five to ninety per cent of all the patients in the state hospitals that you know about are out within a year. How many of them come back?" They always say this with a knowing look in their eye. "Ah, we've got you there." They haven't got me at all. I admit that something like a fifth of them come back, perhaps even as many as a fourth. "Well," they say, "in other words, they weren't cured." "Well, I do not agree with that. I have had pneumonia three or four times and I don't consider that I wasn't cured of it." Well, I guess I am likely to have another attack. I expect to get over it if I do. Similarly, I think people with a mental illness can have another attack. It is something they will recover from, in all probability. But now you see this is a different attitude. This attitude of "He is probably a little crazy underneath and just waiting for it to appear," is the old medieval, suspicious, devil-possession attitude toward mental illness which we psychiatrists and those interested in mental health wish so much that the public could learn to renounce. They will learn to renounce it when they have had more experience. That is why we wish everybody could have more exposure, more contact, and more communication with the mentally ill. It is a pity that every one of you can't visit some of our patients and make life a little more enjoyable for them. Go and read to them if you like; go and talk with them; go and chat with them about things; they would enjoy it. They would like to have you. You do have to be screened by the hospital authorities, but they will be glad to do it. Most state hospitals now have hundreds of volunteers.

The fourth observation I wanted to make is that some patients may have a mental illness and then get well, and then may even get "weller"! I mean they get better than they ever were. They get even better than they were before. This is an extraordinary and little-realized truth—and it constitutes the main point of my talk today. Take an instance familir to all of you. Abraham Lincoln was undoubtedly a far more productive, a far bigger man, and a far broader and wiser man after his attack of mental illness than he was before. Prior to it he had seemed to fail at everything—in his profession, in politics, in love. After his terrible year of depression, he rose to the great heights of vision and accomplishment for which we all know him. And Lincoln is not the only one; there are many others, but he is a conspicuous one. Now I ask you, does this occur in physical illness?

It was noticed in England by a very observing doctor, Dr. Jenner, that some of the milkmaids caught a disease called "cowpox." They subsequently seemed to be a little healthier in some respects than did the other people. Particularly when smallpox came, which was one of the great plagues of the world, as you know, it was noticed that these milkmaids didn't get it. From that it was gradually discovered through a process of some numerous steps that if you get cowpox, you are in some way or other protected against getting smallpox. Now this idea of inoculation, giving you one disease to prevent your getting another, is a kind of a way of making you "weller" than you were before, in that you are protected against something that you previously haven't been protected against. Cowpox being less serious than smallpox, most of us are glad to have it. Of course most of us have had it now. Cowpox got to be one of the great popular diseases of the world and everybody tried to get it, just as we try to have our little girls and boys get the German measles to protect them against serious trouble later.

Now for another illustration. People who have arthritis noticed long ago that if they have a fever of some kind from another cause, their arthritis gets much better. So the treatment was tried of giving them a fever artificaly in various ways. We tried giving them an abscess. Now an abscess is pretty painful, but not necessarily as painful as the arthritis, and so a severe abscess will sometimes seem to improve the arthritis. We have better ways of producing fever now with fever machines which don't cause infections. I am just giving you the principle. . . .

This idea that illness can be replaced or changed is one that I am asking you to concentrate on because I want to go back now to mental illnesses. We have thought for a long time that various drugs could cure illnesses in various ways by neutralizing the infection, or by stimulating certain responses in the body to combat them. Now I want to invite your thinking for a few minutes on what the word "recovery" means. . . .

Suppose you think of somebody who is ill—not yourself, somebody else; there one can be more objective. He is ill, but somebody says he has recovered. Now who says he has recovered? Let's say that *he* says he is recovered. What does he mean? I suppose he means that he doesn't have any pain any more; or perhaps he means that he doesn't have the disability he had had . . . he doesn't limp so much, or he can move his arm more freely; or perhaps he merely means that he doesn't feel so hopeless and the world looks bright again; or maybe he means that he is not so aware of a rapid degeneration and disintegration of his corporal frame and in that sense feels that death is somewhat postponed. . . .

Now look at it from the standpoint of the oberver. The observer cannot see the pain, and he cannot feel the pain. He can only be told about it. If the patient says "I have pain," you have to believe it; or if he says, "I don't have pain," you accept that. But the observer, who might be a physician, has other ways of examining. *You* may say you feel perfectly well and think you have recovered, but *I* don't think so. The doctor may say, "I think you have recovered," and the patient says, "I don't think I have, as I still feel awful." Or it may be the other way. The physician may say, "I have evidence from tests and from X-ray that you haven't recovered. You'll have to stay in bed a few more days." But the patient says, "But doctor, I feel fine, I want to get up." Now you have two judges. You could have another judge, couldn't you? What do the neighbors say? They may say, "Well, *he* may think he has recovered and the doctor may think so, but *I* don't think so. And I'll tell you why." And they tell you. Well, the neighbors have a point of view about this and it is one that we shouldn't neglect. Maybe the neighbors are the best judge of all; they may say, "He has never done a constructive thing for this community. He doesn't act like there was anybody but him on this earth. I don't call that recovery."

Suppose the neighbors say, "Oh, he looks fine; he has recovered." Let's suppose that the doctor says, "I have X-rayed you, I've made some blood tests, I have made some urine tests, I have observed you, I have taken your temperature, etc., and I think you have recovered." Suppose the patient himself says, "I am glad I have. The doctor says I have recovered, the neighbors say I have recovered, my wife says I have recovered; I guess I have recovered." Now suppose we give psychological tests to such an individual. A psychologist might conceivably say, "He is able to fool people pretty well, even himself, but he just thinks he has recovered. He hasn't recovered." In what way hasn't he recovered? He still continues to think loosely. He continues to misjudge people slightly. He still tends to project the blame to others. The question of whether and to what degree a person has recovered is all relative and is capable of being judged differently by different people.

This abstract case I am giving you, you may find a little dull. Let me give you a more dramatic one and you will see immediately what it means. Suppose I ask you if a certain person in your community, who has done a violent crime, has recovered. First you will say "Recovered from what?" I'll ask you, "Did you think he was sick?" "Well," you say right away, "I don't think a healthy-minded person would do what he did." Well, then you assume that he must have been sick. "Do you think he has recovered?" "No, I don't. I think he is dangerous." Very well, let's all agree with you for the moment. Let's say, here is a person whose illness took a form worse than cancer, worse than penumonia, worse than hemorrhoids, worse than diabetes, worse than any of these things. It took the form that made him hurt one of his fellow men. He has become dangerous. Certainly, then, somebody has to deny him liberty for a while. Let's leave vengeance and punishment and smug righteousness out of it. Let's just treat him objectively and say, "This is a dangerous person and he mustn't be in the position to hurt other people as he has a tendency to do. So let's watch him. We will watch him all year, and we will watch him next year, and the next, and the next." So we do, and this man develops a good many talents and becomes useful and decorous. Has he recovered? Let's ask the doctor to examine him. The doctor examines him and says, "I find no sickness. I find no evidence of sickness." Let's ask the people who have been in his vicinity— his neighbors. They say, "Well, he doesn't offend us. He is not a difficult person for us to adjust ourselves to. We find nothing that can be called a sickness. If he had one, so far as we are concerned, he is recovered." Then let's ask the person himself. He will say, "I think I am perfectly safe to be trusted. I don't think I would hurt anybody. I think I am recovered." Then let's ask the psychologist.

Now suppose they all agree. There will still be other people in the general public who will say, "We don't think he has recovered. We don't think he has ceased to be dangerous. We don't want him near us." You ask them on what basis they say that and they reply, "We just don't think he has. We don't want to believe that this could be possible." Now this isn't just a theoretical matter; it is one of the most puzzling problems for the federal government and the state government at the present time.

We don't want to be responsible for releasing people who are going to be dangerous, but we are just as alarmed today about retaining people in custody at your expense—and a very considerable expense—who are not only not dangerous but who are capable of doing splendid things, doing useful things and being community assets....

Nevertheless it is hard to say, when an individual has been detained in public custody for a while, that he is well enough to go. Everybody in the country has been angered, at times, by reading that such-and-such a terrible crime had been committed by a man who was recently discharged from such-and-such a prison. You know why? Many times the prison officials would like very much to keep the man; they know he is dangerous, but the judge didn't sentence him to stay until he was cured, or until he was recovered. The judge sentenced him to five years according to the statutes of the state law, or whatever it is. Therefore he served five years and then he is out. Penological people are very much distressed by this because the men that ought to be released they can't release and men they ought not to release they have to release, and this is because of the present rigid structure of the penal system.

I want to talk about the fact that people improve and we don't know how to handle people who have improved. If you have pneumonia, or if you have bronchitis or a bad cold, you don't feel as well as before you had it. You wait until it has run its course and then you say, "I am well again. I am just as well as ever. I am my old self." Of course you are not your old self. You are a different self because time has moved on. You have learned something. Maybe the cold did you some good. You theoretically could be better. Now in the case of mental illness it is very definitely and obviously true that frequently you are better....

Sometimes some people have a mental illness and grow beyond that. They begin suddenly to see they want to have fun in the broad sense of the word. They want to grow. They want to enjoy the gratitude of people. "I want to enjoy trees, I want to enjoy music, I want to enjoy the world." This represents a kind of growth that we frequently see in our patients who have been mentally ill and some who don't know that they have been mentally ill, and even some who haven't been ill at all. I think, in short, that this is my notion of the gradual and progressive growth that we all make in the direction of mental health. This is what I think mental hygiene is. Now, as I have been speaking perhaps you have been thinking, "Well that is what is done at Chautauqua." That is the whole spirit of Chautauqua and that is what I meant you to think. That is what I think mental health is.

CHAPTER SIX
Persuasion and Appeals to Motives

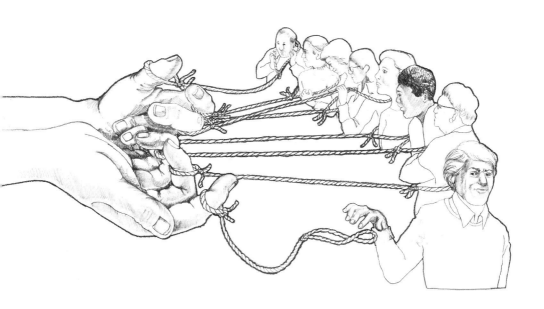

Imagine a mob gathered outside a jail in an old western town. One of the townspeople is holding a shirt drenched with blood. He says that Dr. Farley, a popular and well-respected citizen of the town, has been murdered. He is arguing that Jake, a local tramp, should be lynched for the murder of Dr. Farley. The shirt is a horrible sight, and it is strongly motivating to some sort of action, but what sort of action? Does that shirt actually belong to Dr. Farley? Is that his blood? Does the blood on the shirt mean Farley has actually been murdered? Did Jake do it? If so, should Jake be lynched or turned over to the sheriff? These are all questions that have to be answered by mutual reasoning between the speaker and the listeners. We can talk about that reasoning very conveniently in terms of the Image: Belief–Value–Plan model.

THE ESSENCE OF PERSUASION

Reasoning in a public speech is speakers' attempts to change some beliefs of groups of listeners. Speakers may try to establish new beliefs or try to strengthen, weaken, or eradicate old ones. They usually try to do all of those. The new beliefs the speaker in the example will probably try to establish are that Dr. Farley has been murdered and that Jake has committed the murder. If his listeners accept those new beliefs, they have two apparent alternative courses of action—or plans, in my terminology. They could turn Jake over to the sheriff for trial, or they could lynch him. For listeners who already believe that the sheriff and the local court system are effective, the speaker's job, if he is to persuade them to lynch Jake, is to eradicate that belief, or at least to weaken it to the point that they will consider his alternative plan. Some of his listeners, however, probably already believe that the sheriff and the local courts are ineffective. In that case the speaker will work to strengthen their old belief. Of course, when beliefs are changed, so are values. The value in which the speaker is primarily interested here is the value the listeners attach to his plan of lynching Jake. He wants them to come to value that plan more, and to value less the alternative plan of turning Jake over to the sheriff. To produce that change in value, he is going to try to relate his plan to other strong values that the listeners already hold. He may argue that the plan of lynching Jake is positively related to a positive value such as "safety in our homes and streets," so he may say, "If we don't hang this murdering tramp, no one of us will be safe from any other no-good drifter who wants our money, our horses, or our women." Or he may argue that the plan is negatively related to a negative value, the negative value of allowing criminals to go unpunished. So he might say, "Is there anyone here who's going to stand up and say that murder should go unpunished?" Of course, since every positive value has an equal and opposite negative value, any argument can be thought of in either way. Thus, when beliefs and values are changed, so are specific plans, and the collection of plans I have called policies. The specific plan is that of lynching Jake. Indirectly, however, the speaker is arguing for a more general policy—lynching in dealing with violent crimes.

Relating Values to Plans

The speaker does two things in deciding how to argue. First, he chooses those values he thinks are most important to the listeners, and second, he tries to make the listeners believe that those values are related to the proposed plan. In deciding how to respond, listeners must answer two parallel questions: "Are these the values on which I want to make this decision?" and "Are these the values that are actually most related to this plan?" These two questions imply some others. There may be other values the speaker does not mention that may be quite relevant. Since lynching is illegal, this particular plan is related to the value of *abiding by law*, which the speaker is not likely to mention. There may also be alternative plans—in this case turning Jake over to the sheriff—that have most of the advantages of lynching and few of its disadvantages. Sometimes an abstract value such as safety requires more complete elaboration before it is strong enough to be really motivating. A speaker frequently elaborates an abstract value by associating it with more concrete values toward which listeners have even stronger feelings. So he might argue:

> If we ain't safe from murder, we ain't safe from nothing. What about the money from the cattle sale that ya have in the strongbox? Ya think it's safe for one day if word gets around that we set a murderer free in this town? What are ya gonna do about it? How're ya gonna pay the mortgage? Your cattle ain't gonna be safe on the range. You'll be wiped out. Yer children are gonna be beggin' for food on the streets. Yer wife and daughters are gonna be sellin' themselves to the miners in Central City and Cripple Creek to keep body and soul together. All because you was too spineless to stand up and protect them against outlaws here in Rock Ridge.

Some of the relationships among these beliefs, plans, and values are diagrammed in Figure 6-1. Thus, in a persuasive speech, the speaker tries to get his or her listeners to adopt new plans or policies. The new plans may be ones for overt behavior—in this case lynching Jake. They may be perceptual plans for seeing things differently in the future: the listeners in our example may come to see any future inaction or hesitation on the part of the sheriff as evidence of the inefficiency or ineffectiveness of local law enforcement. Or they may be new cognitive plans for thinking

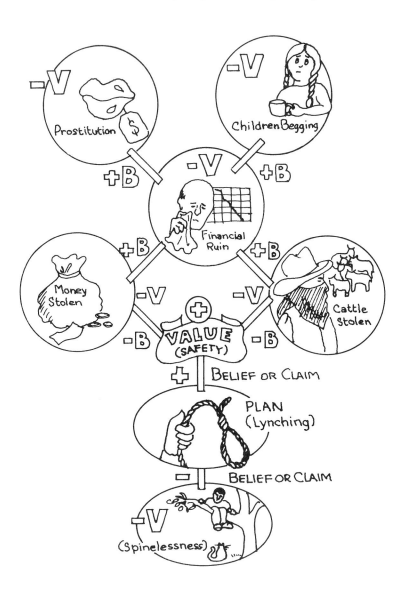

FIGURE 6-1
Relationships among beliefs, plans, and values expressed by speaker urging Jake's lynching.

about things differently, so that in the future the listeners may come to see any violation of the law as being a direct threat to their personal safety. Frequently, a persuasive speech involves all three kinds of plans—behavioral, perceptual, and cognitive. Remember the speaker is always dealing directly with beliefs. Values and plans change as a result of belief change. That is why I defined reasoning earlier as the speaker's attempt to change some beliefs of a group of listeners.

Persuasion and Information

Now, we usually talk about using reasoning in speeches intended to persuade, but it is used in informative speeches as well. If speeches of persuasion and information are to be distinguished, the distinction must be made on the basis of whether acceptance is in question. If a situation calls for persuasion, it does so because there is some question of whether the listeners will accept what the speaker has to say. In the example there is obviously some question about acceptance. The listeners have to be persuaded that Dr. Farley has been murdered; they have to be persuaded that Jake committed the murder; and they have to be persuaded that lynching is the best way to deal with the situation.

Sometimes listeners know so little about the speech topic or they perceive the speaker as so much of an expert that his or her statements will be accepted with little reservation. In such cases the speech situation is primarily informative. For example, if I were to attend a lecture on nuclear physics by a famous nuclear physicist, I would be very likely to accept what the lecturer had to say without ever raising the question of acceptance. I know so little about nuclear physics and the speaker would be such an expert in the field of nuclear physics that I would be attending the speech primarily to gather information rather than to decide whether I should accept or reject what he or she has to say. However, even in informative situations reasoning is important, because it is always possible for a speaker to bungle reasoning so badly that he himself raises the question of acceptance. Usually informative situations do not involve strong values, either. If strong values are involved, acceptance is almost always in question. If the speaker is arguing that nuclear power plants are the only way to solve our energy problem, he or she is going to automatically involve some strong values of mine. And although I may be provided with information, the speaker has to persuade me, too.

Supporting Claims Relating Values to Plans

So far, all of the statements I have used as examples have been unsupported claims. Now suppose we turn to a description of how claims can be supported.

Toulmin[1] has provided a model that can be plugged into the one diagrammed in Figure 6-1. I will use only three parts of the Toulmin model: data, warrant, and claim. A claim is the speaker's statement that the plan is related to a value—in our example, that lynching Jake is necessary to safety. Data are statements supporting that claim. For example, "Second Mesa has had three murders since the town let that gunslinger go last spring." The warrant is a statement connecting the datum to the claim: "Rock Ridge ain't no different from Second Mesa." Any argument consists of an assertion of fact or something assumed to be a fact and an assertion that the fact is related to the claim. Either one may be omitted if the speaker assumes that the listeners will supply it themselves. "Look what happened in Second Mesa!" might be enough to make that whole argument, if the listeners knew what had happened and believed that Second Mesa was enough like Rock Ridge.

On the other hand, someone may question either the datum or the warrant. Up steps Luke who says, "Whaddya mean three murders? I recollect some fair gunfights over there, but they weren't no murders." The speaker must supply a new item of data. "Now, Luke, we all know Fast Eddie drawed first, and shot that sixteen-year-old kid 'fore he even cleared leather. And in the second fight . . ." Then he has to provide a warrant to relate that datum to the first one. "When Fast Eddie drops a kid with no gun in his hand I call it murder." But Josh is not so sure about the first warrant. "Now Second Mesa ain't nothin' like Rock Ridge. They always had a wild bunch and lots of roustin' about over there. We always had a nice clean town here." Then the speaker has to supply data to support the warrant. "Why, I remember, and you do, too, Josh, when nobody in Second Mesa ever shot nothin' but coyotes. It was ever' bit as quiet as Rock Ridge is now. Then they got that easy-goin' constable over there, and now look what they got." And then comes the new warrant to relate that datum to the first warrant. "I say that can happen right here in Rock Ridge. Ain't no different. It's just a matter of time." (See Figure 6-2.)

A speaker may supply several items of data to support the same claim. If the Second Mesa example is not enough, he might have other examples, or he might resort to another kind of data. "You know what Marshall Dillon said how you go about cleanin' up a town, 'Be tough,' that's how." And then the warrant: "Marshall Dillon knows what he's talkin' about. He shore cleaned up Dodge City. And he had a twenty-year run on T.V., too."

I have talked so far as if the only kind of claim speakers use is that in which the plan will lead to favorable consequences or avoid unfavorable ones. Actually, speakers use several other types of claims. Those discussed so far are causal claims in which the speaker claims that adopting his plan will cause safe streets. One may also claim that a given effect must have resulted from some cause. The bloody shirt must have resulted from the murder of Dr. Farley. Claims of sign relationships are closely related to causal claims, but they are not the same. All four

FIGURE 6-2
Relationships among data, warrants, and claims expressed by
speaker urging Jake's lynching.

murders in Second Mesa could be a sign of an unruly town but not necessarily caused by it or by a lazy sheriff. Perhaps Second Mesa is close to a convenient outlaw hideout so that outlaw gangs naturally choose it, causing the disruptions, the murders, and the conveniently easy-going sheriff, who might be dead if he were more conscientious.

Claims of similarity are those in which two things are claimed to be similar, so that if listeners like the one, they will like the other. Dissimilar claims, of course, are the opposite. If listeners dislike the one, they will like the other. Thus, the speaker may argue that the proposed plan is similar to another the listeners like. In our example, the speaker might have compared lynching Jake to defending one's home against an Indian attack.

Claims of categorization are those in which the speaker argues that the proposed plan is part of a larger plan the listeners like. Thus, lynching Jake may be just part of a larger plan to maintain law and order.

Claims of approval are those in which the speaker argues that a well-liked person or agency approves of a plan, so the listeners' feelings about the person will transfer to the plan. This was not the way Marshall Dillon was used in the example. There, he was used to support the relationship between lynching and safety, and his effectiveness depended on his believability. He might also have an approval effect if he were well-liked, since he himself would become a value.

The last type of relationship—coincidental association—can hardly be dignified with the label of claim. Such relationships are seldom openly claimed by a speaker, although they are frequently used. Relationships of coincidental association are those in which the proposed plan becomes associated with certain values, because they appear in the same context. Thus, although there is no very obvious relationship between smoking Salem cigarettes and fresh spring air, years of advertising that has pictured people smoking Salems in pastoral, fresh, green settings have produced that association. In our example, the negative relationship between the word *spineless* and the plan to lynch Jake was coincidental association for the most part. Coincidental association is a type that has really come into its own with the advent of television and film. In a public speech it is difficult to coincidentally associate the plan with anything other than certain words or phrases in the speech. In television, however, it is possible to cut from one scene to another very quickly and thus associate the two scenes. It is also possible to arrange a scene in such a way that the proposed plan is enacted in favorable surroundings, with favorable consequences, or to actually superimpose things viewers value on a background enactment of a plan.

If the speaker in our example had television available to him, he could do some much more persuasive things. He could show a scene of violent murder being committed and then cut quickly to a shot of the town sheriff giving a speech in which he says, "Now, things are perfectly peaceful in the town of Rock Rodge." Without advancing any verbal argument, he could leave the impression that the sherrif was blind to violent crimes occurring in the town. He could show a scene of a violent murder, cut quickly to concerned citizens marching the perpetrator of the crime off to a lynching, and then cut quickly to a scene of a peaceful main street in which all the citizens are going about their business with no fear. Another possibility would be to have two citizens in a peaceful setting discuss the advantages of taking strong action against violent crimes. The speaker could picture a man coming home one night, looking under his bed, discovering his strongbox broken open, then superimpose on this image in a way to suggest the man's picturing in his head images of his wife soliciting on the streets of a mining town. These forms of argument, if they can be dignified with that label, are examples of pure association without support. But they are constantly used in advertising and political campaigns on television, and their very proliferation testifies to their success. Fortunately, it is impossible to use this kind of association so extensively and effectively in a public speech.

In general, if you do not have good evidence that adopting a given plan will cause, or at least contribute to, desirable consequences, why adopt it? The other types of claims are really kinds of verbal conditioning, and although they are certainly capable of changing the value one attaches to a given plan, they do not constitute good reasons for adopting it. As claims in their own right, these forms of association are just not adequate. But they may be used as forms of reasoning to support claims of cause, as I will discuss later. For now, remember the only adequate justification for adopting a plan seems to be the belief that the plan will somehow produce results you value.

Suppose we consider another example, just in case you can't really empathize with Jake or the lynch mob. Imagine that Flora Carpenter is a candidate for mayor of the town in which you live. One of her supporters gives a speech in her behalf. The proposed *plan* is to elect Carpenter. The speaker may make several *claims:* If you elect Carpenter, she will work to (a) reduce property taxes, (b) improve city services, and (c) restrain commercial development. These claims are based on the assumption that the voters *value* (a) reduced property taxes, (b) improved city services, and (c) restraint of commercial development. If those are not consequences the listeners value, the speaker is in trouble already. Assuming they are valued consequences, the speaker must still bring the listeners to *believe* that electing Carpenter will produce those consequences.

The speaker does this by presenting *data:* (a) Carpenter has voted against property taxes as a member of the City council; (b) she improved the water system as director of the water board; and (c) she has spoken against unrestrained commercial development. The *warrant* in all three cases, although probably not stated, seems to be: "What Carpenter has done in the past, she will do in the future."

But those statements that constitute the data may themselves require support, so the speaker may (a) cite the specific times the City Council minutes show Carpenter voted against property taxes, (b) list the improvements to the water system that were instituted while Carpenter was director of the Water Board, and (c) quote from public statements Carpenter has made regarding commercial developments. These supportive data require additional warrants, whether expressed or implied: (a) the City Council minutes are accurate; (b) the list of improvements is accurate, especially as to dates; and (c) the quotes are accurate.

But remember the warrant for the initial data: What Carpenter has done in the past, she will do in the future. That assumption, which serves as a warrant relating each of the original data to the claim, could be questioned in all three cases. For example, Carpenter may have spoken against unbridled commercial development as a member of the City Council, but she may not continue to do so if she is elected and is pressured by housing and shopping center developers. The speaker may have to provide more data to demonstrate that Carpenter has been exposed to and resisted similar pressures in the past. Of course, one can never prove *absolutely* that any part of the future will resemble the past, but one can provide *support* for such a proposition in a variety of ways.

You can begin to see from these examples the general structure of a persuasive speech. Basically, such a speech is an attempt to make listeners believe that the speaker's plan will produce consequences that listeners value positively and avoid consequences they value negatively. The speaker attempts to produce such beliefs by offering the listeners units of proof to support the claims. Each such unit of proof consists of a datum and a warrant, and each datum and warrant may have to be supported by further units of proof, each of which consists of a datum and warrant, and so on until the listeners are satisfied.

In preparing for a persuasive speech, a speaker must (a) decide what consequences of the plan the listeners will consider most valuable and (b) devise chains of reasoning consisting of units of proof that will cause the listeners to believe that the plan will produce those consequences. In devising those chains of reasoning, the speaker must decide which data and warrants will have to be supported by further units of proof and which the listeners will accept without further support.

Let's consider the speaker's first task: choosing the consequences that listeners value because the consequences satisfy certain of their motives.

TYPES OF MOTIVES

Chapters Two, Three, and Four were largely devoted to discussing people's motives. Chapter Four, in particular, described how people use their opinions and policies to serve certain functions. Those functions are, in fact, general categories of motives.

Early textbooks in communication and persuasion sometimes make extensive lists of the biological drives to which a speaker might appeal. I am sure you know that people generally do their best to stay alive and comfortable, that they are motivated by needs to eat, sleep, breathe, have sexual relations, avoid pain, and the like. I would like to deal with some of the more subtle needs people try to satisfy—needs to which speakers are likely to appeal because they *are* subtle. Let's examine three categories of these more subtle motives: social motives, consistency, and ego maintenance.

Social Motives

In Chapter Four I discussed how social reward and punishment shape one's opinions and policies and dealt with the role of social motives in communication. Furthermore, some of the personality characteristics in Chapter Three are very relevant to social motives. At this point I want to pull all of that together into an explanation of ways in which speakers sometimes use social motives to change listeners' opinions and policies.

Recall that some people are unusually likely to conform to the opinions of others in general or to opinions of others they consider to be authorities, whereas other speakers are pushovers for proposed plans to manipulate others. If you have such tendencies, people who know you well may use those characteristic social motives to persuade you.

Remember from Chapter Four that social reward and punishment can be used to change one's opinions and policies in very subtle ways, sometimes so subtly that "social reality" is substituted for one's own sense experiences. Skillful persuaders know that social threats and promises are sometimes even more effective than physical threats and promises, and they are usually easier to make.

Furthermore, recall that once you have committed yourself to an opinion or policy before people or groups who are important to you, it is much more difficult to reevaluate your position in the light of new evidence. Speakers may use your previous commitments to get you to accept plans that do not make good sense. You can avoid this by remaining uncommitted until you are fairly certain all the evidence is in. Speakers may also use your desire for consensus with others you respect to keep you from critically and independently evaluating new proposals. Finally, they may use their own general credibility or the general credibility of others to persuade you on topics to which that credibility is irrelevant, about which they know no more than you do. The opinions of experts can be very useful—even necessary—in specific areas in which you lack adequate expertise of your own, but generalized, uncritical credibility can be a sort of mental Spanish fly to seduce you into accepting opinions and policies which would look foolish in any other light.

So what are you to do with social motives when you are in the role of speaker? My suggestion would be that you first make a list of the *physical* motives your plan will satisfy for your listeners and then add to that list the probable *social* consequences if the listeners were to adopt your plan. Social consequences are frequently more important than are physical consequences. Whether that is good or bad might be an interesting question for class discussion. For my part, I am more concerned that speakers make listeners *aware* of both the physical and social consequences of their plans so the listeners can decide for themselves which are most important.

Consistency

In Chapter Four, we reviewed various ways people attempt to maintain consistency among their beliefs, plans, and values. It is important to remind you that speakers frequently appeal to their listeners to be "consistent" in ways that do not seem very rational: to adopt a plan just because someone they like approves of it; to adopt a policy or an opinion just because it seems to justify a past decision, even though the past decision may have been a bad one; to believe something just because they would like it to be true.

The research in social psychology does provide some illustrations of "consistency" in action. For example, some studies have demonstrated that most people will administer high levels of supposed electrical shock to others who "fail" an experimental task if they are told to do so in the interests of science by a prestigious experimenter. Many subjects continued to administer what they thought were high voltage shocks even after the other person had feigned collapse, even after they had been told that the other person had a weak heart, as long as the experimenter continued to order them to do so.

It has also been repeatedly demonstrated that subjects who believe another person is being painfully shocked for failing to perform an experimental task will reject and dislike the other person, even though they are told the failure was not that person's fault. The dislike and rejection was even greater when the subjects were told they would see the other person suffer more later and when they could do nothing to help. Fate is just and *consistent*, right? And if it is not, we make sure it is. *Life in a maze of irrational "consistency" can be a life in prism, where input from the outside world is distorted beyond objective recognition.*

Again, when you are in the role of speaker, you will have to decide how to use consistency motives. I adopt the straightforward rule that I will appeal to listeners' desires to be *logically* consistent but not to their tendencies toward other types of consistency.

Ego Maintenance

In Chapter Four I also discussed how people use their opinions and policies to serve the function of ego maintenance. Persuaders frequently take advantage of this fact, consciously or unconsciously. When you hear a speaker say something like, "Now I know a sophisticated college student like you isn't going to ... ," you know where he's coming from and you'd best watch where he's going. Statements such as, "We (your group here) have to stick together" are warning flags to alert you that the persuader is trying to use your self-image in order to use *you*. Follow the Pride Piper and he will lead you on a veritable Gullible's Travels, littering generalities all the way.

Persuaders also know and use the ego-defense mechanisms. A persuader may say something like this: "Now some people have accused us of hating college administrators. I don't think that's true. I've known many administrators I've really liked. But this administration is to blame for a lot of our problems around here. Sometimes I think they are deliberately shafting the students so they'll look good with the board of regents." The speaker may be advocating something perfectly reasonable, but up to that point he has not offered one iota of proof. What he has done is to appeal to the ego-defense mechanisms of denial, reaction formation, scapegoating, and paranoid reactions, at least. Nothing he has said up to that point should have any effect on the opinions of a critical listener, who is going to be waiting for the evidence. Instead, these should be warning signs that the speaker is trying to appeal to motives of which the listener may not be totally aware.

Ego involvement is another type of psychological motive in the sense that people want to agree with those who express support for their most central opinions and try to push *all* the opinions of those who disagree with those central opinions as far away from their own as possible. I know an individual whose most central values seem to be "personal" morality, including, especially, sexual monogamy and strong family ties. I watched as that person excused all the excesses of the Nixon Adminis-tration, even after Nixon's resignation. The crucial fact in this judgment was that Nixon and his cohorts all seemed to be sexually faithful to their wives and appeared generally to be "good clean family men," whereas some of his detractors were not. Now I do not know whether Richard Nixon was more "moral" in these respects than was Edward Kennedy, but it is hard to see what "personal" morality defined this way has to do with the public, political morality that was at issue. But *all* the opinions and policies of both men were judged on the basis of these few highly central values. On the other hand, I have known people with different central values for whom Nixon could do no right and Kennedy could do no wrong. Either position seems mistaken and seems to result from contaminating all of one's judgments by relying too heavily on central opinions in which one is too highly ego-involved. When the twin devices of perceptive selection and selective perception are allowed to roam about, murdering offensive facts at will, they can turn one's image of reality into a "wonderland benight."

On the other hand, as a speaker you would be foolish not to try to become aware of the self-images your listeners may be trying to maintain, the ego-defense mechanisms they may be using, and the central beliefs, values, plans, and policies that define their self-images. Being aware of such matters, however, does not mean you will exploit them to your listeners' disadvantage.

ETHICAL USE OF MOTIVES

I began this book with the assumption that speakers operate ethically insofar as they keep their listeners aware of the bases on which they make decisions in response to the speech. Speakers who wish to deal ethically with their listeners will do their best to emphasize what favorably valued consequences will result from adopting the proposed plan or what unfavorably valued consequences will be avoided by adopting that plan; that is, speakers will do their best to make clear which of the listeners' *motives* will be satisfied if the listeners adopt the plan.

Certainly, speakers are justified in warning listeners of undesirable physical consequences a plan may avoid and in describing desirable physical consequences it may achieve. I believe speakers are equally justified in alerting listeners to the *social* consequences of accepting a plan. But when are speakers justified in advertising the *perceptual* and *cognitive* consequences of adopting a plan? That question is a much more difficult one.

The answer may be: *When you feel comfortable making the claim openly*, but not when you are tempted to conceal it. I would not feel comfortable asking listeners to accept a plan to *justify a previous mistaken decision* (dissonance reduction), *because they would like it to work* (wishful thinking), *to agree with someone they like or disagree with someone they dislike*, or *because it would help them avoid facing unpleasant facts about themselves* (ego defense). My feeling is that if I would not use such arguments openly in an atmosphere of mutual awareness, then I ought not use them covertly and subtly as techniques of suggestion. To do so would violate my assumption that mutual awareness is the key to objective decision-making.

On the other hand, I might feel comfortable asking listeners to accept my plan because it would be logically consistent to do so and they want to be logically consistent, because it would express the kind of people they want to be (value expression), or because it would be consistent with certain of their central policies (ego involvement).

These are only examples. I do not mean to say that appeals to value expression, logical consistency, and ego involvement are *always* and *necessarily* ethical. You will have to decide when they are and when they are not. If you cannot make the appeal openly without feeling guilty or embarrassed about it, it is probably an unethical appeal; that is, *if you can't say it straight, it is probably crooked.*

SUMMARY

The essence of persuasion is to cause listeners to *believe* that a proposed *plan* or *policy* will result in consequences they *value*—that is, that it will satisfy certain of their motives. This presupposes reasoning from cause to effect: *If* you adopt this plan or policy, *then* these valued consequences will result. The proposed plans or policies may be for overt, observable behavior change or for change in cognitions and perceptions. A speech is persuasive insofar as it is designed to produce *acceptance* and *action* as well as attention, comprehension, and retention.

Speakers *claim* cause-to-effect relationships between their proposals and valued consequences. Such a claim requires support in the form of at least one *datum* and one *warrant*. The datum is a "fact" or accepted belief, and the warrant is a statement of the relationship between that "fact" and the claim—a statement explaining how the datum supports the claim. If they are not immediately accepted by the listeners, data and warrants themselves become claims, and must be supported by further datum–warrant pairs.

In addition to cause-to-effect relationships, claims can express other relationships of *contingency* (effect-to-cause and sign), relationships of *similarity*, *categorization* (deduction), *approval*, and *coincidental association*. None of these are logically acceptable substitutes for the central cause-to-effect claim that the speaker's proposal will result in valued consequences, although speakers sometimes try to use them that way. With the exception of coincidental association, they can all serve as logically acceptable data and warrants, however. Although *physical* consequences or motives are certainly important in public deliberation, it is important for both speaker and listener to remember that *social* motives and internal motives such as *consistency* and ego maintenance are sometimes equally important in determining what plans and policies listeners will accept.

ILLUSTRATIVE SPEECH

Persuasion is accomplished by causing listeners to believe certain valued consequences will result and/or undesirable consequences will be avoided if they adopt the policy the speaker is advocating. (One type of *policy*, as that word is used here, would include adopting and maintaining a given set of beliefs and values.)

The matter that I believe needs illustration concerns the distinctions among *types of consequences* a speaker can promise or threaten. I have listed three general types of consequences: *physical*, *social*, and *internal* (including perceptual and cognitive). The sermon that follows—Jonathan Edwards' "Sinners in the Hands of an Angry God"—is a clear example of a speaker describing undesirable *physical* consequences to be avoided by adopting the proposed policy. That policy is not described here, but the congregations to whom this sermon was delivered understood perfectly well what the policy was: to go to the altar at the conclusion of the sermon, confess and renounce their sins, and profess their faith in Jesus Christ as their Savior.

Jonathan Edwards was an early colonial minister who conducted "revivals" intended to convert sinners and renew the faith of the faithful, in the manner of Billy Graham. Thus, this sermon was no doubt delivered on numerous occasions. Although it may seem overdone to many, it is unusual only in the force of its imagery. Those of you familiar with conservative, "fundamental" religious traditions, which include belief in Heaven and Hell as actual places, may have encountered similar sermons in "revivals," "camp meetings," "tent meetings," and even in Sunday morning services.

At other times revival preachers choose instead to describe (and promise) *valued* physical consequences of salvation and posthumous residence in Heaven rather than dwelling on the unpleasant consequences to be avoided. In either case the relationship is clearly cause-to-effect and the evidence drawn directly from authority or testimony: the Holy Bible.

Sinners in the Hands of an Angry God*
Jonathan Edwards

Their foot shall slide in due time. Deut. xxxii, 35.

The expression I have chosen for my text, *Their foot shall slide in due time*, seems to imply the following things relating to the punishment and destruction that these wicked Israelites were exposed to.

1. That they were always exposed to *destruction*; as one that stands or walks in slippery places is always exposed to fall. . . .

2. It implies, that they were always exposed to *sudden* unexpected destruction; as he that walks in slippery places is every moment liable to fall, he cannot foresee one moment whether he shall stand or fall the next; and when he does fall, he falls at once, without warning. . . .

3. Another thing implied is, that they are liable to fall *of themselves*, without being thrown down by the hand of another; as he that stands or walks on slippery ground needs nothing but his own weight to throw him down.

4. That the reason why they are not fallen already, and don't fall now, is only that God's appointed time is not come. . . .

The observation from the words that I would now insist upon is this. —"There is nothing that keeps wicked men at any one moment out of hell, but the mere pleasure of God. . . ."

1. There is no want of *power* in God to cast wicked men into hell at any moment. . . . We find it easy to tread on and crush a worm that we see crawling on the earth; so it is easy for us to cut or singe a *slender thread* that any thing hangs by; thus easy it is for God, when he pleases, to cast his enemies down to hell. What are we, that we should think to stand before him, at which rebuke the earth trembles, and before whom the rocks are thrown down?

2. They *deserve* to be cast into hell; so that divine justice never stands in the way, it makes no objection against God's using his power at any moment to destroy them. Yea, on the contrary, justice calls aloud for an infinite punishment of their sins. . . .

3. They are *already* under a sentence of condemnation to hell. They don't only justly deserve to be cast down thither, but the sentence of the law of God, that eternal and immutable rule of righteousness that God has fixed between him and mankind, is gone out against them, and stands against them; so that they are bound over already to hell. . . .

4. They are now the objects of that very *same* anger and wrath of God, that is expressed in the torments of hell; and the reason why they

*The text of this revival address is from *Selected Sermons of Jonathan Edwards*, II. Norman Gardiner (ed.), New York: The Macmillan Company, 1904, pp. 78–97.

don't go down to hell at each moment, is not because God, in whose power they are, is not then very angry with them; as angry as he is with many of those miserable creatures that he is now tormenting in hell, and do there feel and bear the fierceness of his wrath. Yea, God is a great deal more angry with great numbers that are now on earth, yea, doubtless, with many that are now in this congregation, that it may be, are at ease and quiet, then he is with many of those that are now in the flames of hell.

So that it is not because God is unmindful of their wickedness, and don't resent it, that he don't let loose his hand and cut them off. God is not altogether such a one as themselves, though they may imagine him to be so. The wrath of God burns against them; their damnation don't slumber; the pit is prepared; the fire is made ready; the furnace is now hot, ready to receive them; the flames do now rage and glow. The glittering sword is whet, and held over them, and the pit hath opened her mouth under them.

5. The *devil* stands ready to fall upon them, and seize them as his own, at what moment God shall permit him. They belong to him; he has their souls in his possession, and under his dominion. The Scripture represents them as his goods, Luke xi, 21. The devils watch them; they are ever by them, at their right hand; they stand waiting for them, like greedy hungry lions that see their prey, and expect to have it, but are for the present kept back; if God should withdraw his hand, by which they are restrained, they would in one moment fly upon their poor souls. The old serpent is gaping for them; hell opens its mouth wide to receive them; and if God should permit it, they would be hastily swallowed up and lost.

6. There are in the souls of wicked men those hellish *principles* reigning, that would presently kindle and flame out into hell-fire, if it were not for God's restraints. . . .

7. It is no security to wicked men for one moment, that there are no *visible means of death* at hand. It is no security to a natural man, that he is now in health, and that he don't see which way he should now immediately go out of the world by any accident, and that there is no visible danger in any respect in his circumstances. The manifold and continual experience of the world in all ages shows that this is no evidence that a man is not on the very brink of eternity, and that the next step will not be into another world. The unseen, unthought of ways and means of persons' going suddenly out of the world are innumerable and inconceivable. Unconverted men *walk over the pit of hell* on a rotten covering, and there are innumerable places in this covering so weak that they won't bear their weight, and these places are not seen. The arrows of death fly unseen at noonday; the sharpest sight can't discern them. God has so many different, unsearchable ways of taking wicked men out

of the world and sending them to hell, that there is nothing to make it appear that God had need to be at the expense of a miracle, or go out of the ordinary course of his providence, to destroy any wicked man, at any moment. All the means that there are of sinners' going out of the world are so in God's hands, and so absolutely subject to his power and determination, that it don't depend at all less on the mere will of God, whether sinners shall at any moment go to hell, than if means were never made use of, or at all concerned in the case.

8. Natural men's *prudence* and *care* to preserve their own *lives*, or the care of others to preserve them, don't secure them a moment. . . .

9. All wicked men's *pains* and *contrivance* they use to escape *hell*, while they continue to reject Christ, and so remain wicked men, do not secure them from hell one moment. . . .

10. God has laid himself under *no obligation*, by any promise, to keep any natural man out of hell one moment. God certainly has made no promises either of eternal life, or of any deliverance or preservation from eternal death, but what are contained in the covenant of grace, the promises that are given in Christ, in whom all the promises are yea and amen. . . .

So that thus it is, that natural men are held in the hand of God over the pit of hell; they have deserved the fiery pit, and are already sentenced to it; and God is dreadfully provoked, his anger is as great towards them as to those that are actually suffering the executions of the fierceness of his wrath in hell, and they have done nothing in the least to appease or abate that anger, neither is God in the least bound by any promise to hold them up one moment; the devil is waiting for them, hell is gaping for them, the flames gather and flash about them, and would fain lay hold on them and swallow them up; the fire pent up in their own hearts is struggling to break out; and they have no interest in any Mediator, there are no means within reach that can be any security to them. In short they have no refuge, nothing to take hold of; all that preserves them every moment is the mere arbitrary will, and uncovenanted, unobliged forbearance of an incensed God.

The use may be of *awakening* to unconverted persons in this congregation. This that you have heard is the case of every one of you that are out of Christ. That world of misery, that lake of burning brimstone, is extended abroad under you. *There* is the dreadful pit of the glowing flames of the wrath of God; there is hell's wide gaping mouth open; and you have nothing to stand upon, nor any thing to take hold of. There is nothing between you and hell but the air; 'tis only the power and mere pleasure of God that holds you up. . . .

The God that holds you over the pit of hell, much as one holds a spider or some loathsome insect over the fire, abhors you, and is dreadfully provoked; his wrath towards you burns like fire; he looks upon you as worthy of nothing else, but to be cast into the fire; he is of purer eyes than to bear to have you in his sight; you are ten thousand times so abominable in his eyes, as the most hateful and venomous serpent is in ours. You have offended him infinitely more than ever a stubborn rebel did his prince; and yet it is nothing but his hand that holds you from falling into the fire every moment. 'Tis ascribed to nothing else, that you did not go to hell the last night; that you was suffered to awake again in this world after you closed your eyes to sleep; and there is no other reason to be given why you have not dropped into hell since you arose in the morning, but that God's hand has held you up. There is no other reason to be given why you han't gone to hell since you have sat here in the house of God, provoking his pure eyes by your sinful wicked manner of attending his solemn worship. Yea, there is nothing else that is to be given as a reason why you don't this very moment drop down into hell.

O sinner! Consider the fearful danger you are in. 'Tis a great furnace of wrath, a wide and bottomless pit, full of the fire of wrath, that you are held over in the hand of that God whose wrath is provoked and incensed as much against you as against many of the damned in hell. You hang by a slender thread, with the flames of divine wrath flashing about it, and ready every moment to singe it and burn it asunder; and you have no interest in any Mediator, and nothing to lay hold of to save yourself, nothing to keep off the flames of wrath, nothing of your own, nothing that you ever have done, nothing that you can do, to induce God to spare you one moment. . . . can you rest for one moment in such a condition? Are not your souls as precious as the souls of the people at Suffield,* where they are flocking from day to day to Christ?

Are there not many here that have lived long in the world that are not to this day born again, and so are aliens from the commonwealth of Israel and have done nothing ever since they have lived but treasure up wrath against the day of wrath? Oh, sirs, your case in an especial manner is extremely dangerous; your guilt and hardness of heart is extremely great. Don't you see how generally persons of your years are passed over and left in the present remarkable and wonderful dispensation of God's mercy? You had need to consider yourselves and wake thoroughly out of sleep; you cannot bear the fierceness and the wrath of the infinite God.

And you that are young men and young women, will you neglect this precious season that you now enjoy, when so many others of your age are renouncing all youthful vanities and flocking to Christ? You especially have now an extraordinary opportunity; but if you neglect it, it will soon be with you as it is with those persons that spent away all the

*The next neighbor town.

precious days of youth in sin and are now come to such a dreadful pass in blindness and hardness.

And you children that are unconverted, don't you know that you are going down to hell to bear the dreadful wrath of that God that is now angry with you every day and every night? Will you be content to be the children of the devil, when so many other children in the land are converted and are become the holy and happy children of the King of kings?

And let every one that is yet out of Christ and hanging over the pit of hell, whether they be old men and women or middle-aged or young people or little children, now hearken to the loud calls of God's word and providence. This acceptable year of the Lord that is a day of such great favor to some will doubtless be a day of as remarkable vengeance to others. Men's hearts harden and their guilt increases apace at such a day as this, if they neglect their souls. And never was there so great danger of such persons being given up to hardness of heart and blindness of mind. God seems now to be hastily gathering in his elect in all parts of the land; and probably the bigger part of adult persons that ever shall be saved will be brought in now in a little time, and that it will be as it was on that great outpouring of the Spirit upon the Jews in the Apostles' days, the election will obtain and the rest will be blinded. If this should be the case with you, you will eternally curse this day, and will curse the day that ever you was born to see such a season of the pouring out of God's Spirit, and will wish that you had died and gone to hell before you had seen it. Now undoubtedly it is as it was in the days of John the Baptist, the axe is in an extraordinary manner laid at the root of the trees, that every tree that bringeth not forth good fruit may be hewn down and cast into the fire.

Therefore let every one that is out of Christ now awake and fly from the wrath to come. The wrath of Almighty God now undoubtedly hanging over great part of this congregation. Let every one fly out of Sodom. *"Haste and escape for your lives, look not behind you, escape to the mountain, lest ye be consumed."*

Chapter Six Reference

1 Stephen Toulmin, *The Uses of Argument* (Cambridge: Cambridge University Press, 1959).

CHAPTER SEVEN
Reasoning and Evidence

I have assumed throughout this book that public speaking causes listeners to *do* something. However, what they do may not be immediately observable; they may only "change their minds"; that is, they may adopt new perceptual plans or policies, so that they *perceive* and do things differently in the future. They may change their plans or policies regarding future behavior so that, although there is no immediate change in their observable behavior, they *do* things differently in the future. They may change beliefs and values in ways that will eventually change their plans and policies, which will, in turn, have consequences for their future behavior.

This idea that public speaking always causes listeners to do something is important to the way I am going to talk about reasoning in speeches. It means that *a speaker is always implying, even though he may not be aware of it, that the listeners ought to adopt a plan.* Furthermore, listeners are always evaluating the message to decide whether or not they are going to adopt the proposed plan, even though they may not fully realize that a plan is being proposed or that they are evaluating it.

That means *there is one form of reasoning that is always crucial in a speech: reasoning from cause to effect.* The form of the argument is: "If you adopt my plan, it will result in certain desirable consequences." Speakers do not always say it explicitly, but they always imply it. A message as subtle as a raised eyebrow, for example, taken in context, may imply, "If you explain your position further, you may get me to agree; if you don't I'm going to remain skeptical." Thus, the speaker is always trying to get listeners to perceive a relationship between the speaker's proposed plan and the listeners' motives.

Let's look at the statement more closely. Reasoning in response to a speech takes this form: "If I adopt Plan A (the speaker's proposal), then outcomes 1, 2, 3, 4, and 5 will probably occur. If I adopt Plan B (an alternative to the speaker's proposal), then outcomes 3, 5, 7, and 9 will probably occur. If I adopt Plan C, then outcomes 2, 5, 8, 9, and 10 will probably occur. I prefer the combination of outcomes 3, 5, 7, and 9. Therefore, I think I'll choose Plan B."

Let's take a concrete example: the lynching of poor Jake. Here is Amos listening to the speaker telling him he ought to help hang old Jake from a limb of the big cottonwood down by the river. That is Plan A. One alternative, Plan B, is to try to persuade the others to turn Jake over to the sheriff. Another alternative, Plan C, is to sneak home and forget the whole thing. Amos' brain is racing like a computer, calculating the probabilities of all the possible outcomes, weighing the probability of each outcome by the value of that outcome, and trying to figure the total value of each plan to decide which one he wants to adopt. His brain isn't doing all that in terms of numbers, of course; it has to work too fast to fool around with numbers:

Let's see, if I help lynch Jake, the sheriff may call in the federal marshals and arrest us all. We might all be thrown in jail, or we might even be hanged ourselves. But it's a long way to Denver, they prob'ly don't have a jail big enough for all of us, and they surely wouldn't hang us all. Prob'ly what they'll do is get the leaders, 'specially the guy who's talkin' so loud, so chances are I'll get off.

But my wife will raise hell with me, I know, and I wonder what the kids will think. I won't be able to go to Sunday meetin' for months, else for sure the preacher will tell me to my face right there in front of ever'body what *he* thought of it.

Besides, it's murder, and I don't like that. I'd have to live with that the rest of my life, thinkin' I'd *killed* a man. What if it turns out Jake didn't kill old Doc Farley? Then I'd have killed an *innocent* man.

But dammit, the fella's right, we got to protect our homes. Can't have outlaws ridin' through Rock Ridge shootin' up the town and takin' what they want. I'd kill myself if Jody ended up in a saloon in Cripple Creek.

But suppose we turned Jake over to the sherrif? Reckon he'd do anything? Reckon the law would take care of him? The law shore hanged old Mace and his bunch over in Mace's Hole, cleaned up that place 'til it's nice and peaceful, they're callin' it Beulah Valley now.

But these fellers here ain't gonna turn Jake over to no sheriff without somebody stands up and says they should, and that some-body's prob'ly gotta be me. But I don't wanta make no fool of myself. They sure gonna call me a yaller dog, and they might just hang me alongside Jake. They're purty het up 'bout this.

But s'pose I was to just mosey on home, like I had chores to do? Then I ain't gonna kill nobody and I ain't gonna be called yaller neither. Reckon I'll jest meander that way, kinda casual like, and hope nobody sees me.

The plan selected, Plan C, is not ideal, because if Jake were lynched, Amos would still have to live with the fact that he had not spoken up. But he would probably warp his perceptions enough to conclude that the mob was too "het up" for him to have stopped them, that Jake was guilty anyway, that even if he were not guilty, he "shore weren't worth much," and that now there would not be any real outlaws riding through town. Amos would probably change the value he placed on killing, raising it a few notches. But he would almost certainly alter his general plan for dealing with crisis situations in the future: Stay out of mobs!

The point of this example is that decisions in response to speeches are made in terms of *outcomes*: physical outcomes, social outcomes, perceptual outcomes, and cognitive outcomes. Outcomes are the *effects* of which plans are the *causes*. So we will now examine types of reasoning people use as they try to decide what plans will produce what outcomes.

Now I have said the basic claims that a speaker's plan will produce valued consequences are cause-to-effect claims that have the underlying form: "*If* you adopt my plan, *then* (a valued consequence) will result." The units of proof used to support such claims, however, take several forms.

Speakers may try to establish their claims by *comparison and generalization*. They may argue that the problems their plans are designed to remedy are widespread, which is usually a generalization based on specific instances. Then they may argue that other similar plans have solved similar problems in the past. This is usually termed a "need-plan" approach. They may argue directly that similar plans have produced valued consequences, in which case they will not dwell on a list of present problems. This is an "advantages" approach. If they compare the probable advantages of their own plan to those of other alternative plans, they are using a "comparative advantages" approach.

One major type of generalization speakers try to establish are *contingency* generalizations, which include *sign* generalizations and *causal* generalizations. When using the need-plan approach, it is not adequate merely to argue that there are problems in the present system. It is also necessary to try to establish the *causes* of such problems in order to show that the proposed plan will remove the causes. When arguing the advantages of a plan, it is necessary to show that plans similar to the proposed plan have actually *caused* certain favorable conditions rather than merely accompanying those conditions. No one would deny that the development of atomic weapons has *accompanied* prosperity, but showing that development of atomic weapons has *caused* prosperity would be quite another matter. Sign generalizations may be important, too. For example, a speaker may be arguing that one of the problems his or her plan will remedy is the presently unhealthy economy. Of course, the speaker must establish that the economy *is* unhealthy, in which case he or she will try to identify the *signs* of an unhealthy economy. Such *signs* may or may not be *causes*.

Although all claims are "hypotheses" in one sense, the specific form of reasoning termed *hypothesis* is not always used to support them. Frequently it is, however. A prosecuting attorney may try to establish a version of a crime by describing a hypothesis and then showing how specific details of evidence support that hypothesis. In the first of Patty Hearst's trials, the prosecutor advanced the hypothesis that Patty was attracted to her captors, and became a willing participant in their crimes. The discovery that at the time of her arrest she was still wearing an amulet one of the S.L.A. members had given her provided strong support for that hypothesis.

Testimony is frequently used to establish facts listeners could not observe for themselves and to lend support to inferences when those inferences require specialized knowledge and abilities the listeners do not have. Despite its problems, it is a widely used and useful form of support. Because of its problems, it is especially important to know the criteria by which it may be evaluated.

Finally, *categorization* (or deduction) is frequently used to apply a generalization to the specific case under consideration. It provides no "new" information, but it is the means of reasoning used to draw conclusions out of information already available.

COMPARISON AND GENERALIZATION

Probably the most basic method of reasoning—actually the second most basic operation of the brain—is the ability to learn from one experience, so that the first experience affects the way we act in a second, similar situation. Some of the higher animals are capable of learning by observing the experiences of others; humans, in particular, are even capable of learning from experiences that have only been described to them. We learn by example, and speakers try to persuade listeners by offering them examples.

Single Examples

The use of single examples or a limited number of examples is good in that it allows listeners to visualize each specific instance vividly and to decide if it seems representative. The difficulty is that it is usually impossible to enumerate or describe enough examples to constitute an adequate sample.

Usually the question at hand is how similar an example is to the present instance. I went through that question to some extent discussing the similarities and differences between Rock Ridge and Second Mesa. Certainly the two instances should be similar in as many respects as possible, and any differences should be irrelevant or unimportant to the conclusion.

Extended Examples

Sometimes speakers describe the similarities between two instances in great detail; the speaker in our example might have made an extended comparison between Rock Ridge and Second Mesa. Such extended comparisons are sometimes called "analogies." Analogies do not have a very good reputation among logicians, because they do not seem to have the force of evidence some other types of reasoning do. However, if a speaker is going to use an example, it is probably better to carefully enumerate the similarities and differences between the sample and the present case.

Beardsley,[1] for one, rejects analogy as a valid form of induction except as a type of generalization. His argument is that enumerating 13 characteristics that two situations have in common produces no rational grounds for inferring any additional similarities *unless* one of the observed similarities puts both situations into some general class about which we have additional knowledge.

Suppose, for example, the argument is that coffee drinking, like cigarette smoking, is hazardous to one's health. One could construct an extensive analogy between the two: coffee drinkers drink more the longer they have been drinking; they become irritable when deprived. In fact, they show many withdrawal symptoms when they try to break the habit. Both caffeine and nicotine are "artificial" drugs, and on and on. None of these constitute rational grounds for concluding that the two are also similar in being hazardous to one's health. But when we note that coffee and cigarette "addicts" both have chronically fast heart beats, we seem to be on to something important. And we are because we know that chronically fast heart rates are associated with (probably "cause," but are at least symptomatic of) certain types of heart disease. We now have some evidence for the conclusion, but not by force of the *analogy*. Rather, our new evidence comes from the application of a *generalization*.

One good approach may be to describe and enumerate a number of examples and then use statistical means to summarize data based on a larger sample or even based on the entire population. Imagine a speaker arguing that the federal government should consider a family of four with income less than $7000 to be within the official definition of "poverty." He or she might first describe the living conditions of a few typical families at about that income level, allowing listeners to visualize the conditions. Then to demonstrate that the conditions described are in fact typical, the speaker could cite statistical data from some source such as *Statistical Abstracts of the United States* regarding the average number of bedrooms in the living quarters of such families, percentages who own various types of appliances, indebtedness, savings, insurance, number who attend college, and other matters with which his examples may have dealt. The examples without the statistics would be difficult to evaluate for representativeness; the statistics without the examples would be difficult to visualize. The two together can constitute a reliable and vivid argument.

Collections of Examples: Generalizations

Speakers use examples not just to speculate about their present case, but to make generalizations. Reasoning by generalization attributes some *characteristic* to a *class*. To be certain the generalization is sound, one may ask a number of questions:

1. Is the class clearly defined? If not, it is difficult to evaluate the adequacy of any sample from that class.

2. Is the characteristic clearly defined? Any conclusion is going to be at least as ambiguous as the definition of the characteristics. If the definitions of the class and/or the characteristic depend upon measurement, the measurement procedures should be clearly understood and evaluated for adequacy. Remember also that measurement procedures can themselves bias a sample even though the sample may have been unbiased initially. Questions used in an opinion survey, for example, can antagonize respondents or suggest "correct" responses consistent with the bias of the investigator.

3. Is the scope of the generalization clearly specified; that is, does it contain vague terms such as *most* or *many*?

4. Is the sample *representative*? There are really two questions involved here:

   a. Is the sample *typical* (random, unbiased, or selected on the basis of relevant variables)?

   b. Is the sample *large enough*?

The relation between these two subquestions is interesting. If *one example* is perfectly typical, then it is a large enough sample; on the other hand, if the sample is large enough to include the entire class, then it is necessarily typical. Of course, these are only hypothetical cases since we never know if a single instance is perfectly typical, and if we had a sample that was, in fact, the entire population, we would not be generalizing. Even if we had surveyed the entire class at a given point in time, we are usually interested in generalizing about that class in the future. Since the membership of most classes is constantly changing, we still would not have the entire class to which we want to generalize. Consequently, in practice the adequacy of a generalization is determined by the balance between the *size* of a sample and its *typicality*. Just what this balance is depends on the *variability* of the members of the class. Thus, we must ask the fifth question before the fourth can be answered adequately:

5. Is the *variability* of the class adequately represented in the sample?

One reason a sample of one case is inadequate is that any conclusion drawn from it would rest on the assumption that there is *no* variability within the class. Furthermore, with only one case we have no basis for deciding how much variability there is within the class. Even a sample drawn at random might not be typical if it were too small to represent the variability of the class.

One way to check on variability is to draw a fairly large sample and break it into subsamples. If the generalization is confirmed in some subsamples but not in others and if the variability between subsamples is too great, we may have to conclude that even the total sample is not large enough to represent the variability of the class. Another way to handle variability is to decide what *subclasses* within the larger class are likely to contribute to variability. The various polling agencies that attempt to predict voting percentages in elections on the basis of sampling have decided that it is important to sample at random from within certain subclasses based on educational level, income, and age, for example. To the extent that the important subclasses are identified and randomly sampled, the problem of variability is reduced.

The scope of the generalization and its accuracy also limit the range of acceptable variability. If the generalization is universal (all the members of the class have the characteristic), then *any* variability is unacceptable. If the generalization is less than universal but specifies some acceptable limits (between 50% and 60% of the class have the characteristic, or there is a .50 to .60 probability that a member of the class has the characteristic), then too much variability in the sample might lead us to conclude that the percentage of the total class having the characteristic might fall outside the acceptable range even though the sample percentage happens to fall within that range.

Obviously, what constitutes acceptable sample size in relation to sample variability is going to be an educated guess based on common sense, unless one is willing to apply the mathematical criteria available in treatments of statistical inference and sampling procedure. I do not propose to do that.

Collections of Examples: Statistics

Beyond the problems involved in generalizations, summarizing collections of examples by the use of statistics has its own difficulties. Shortly after the nationwide 55-mile-per-hour speed limit was imposed, an editorial on station KCBS in San Franciso charged that the California Highway Patrol was ticketing passenger cars but largely ignoring trucks and buses. On March 5, 1974, Commissioner Pudinsky of the CHP responded by saying, among other things: (a) the CHP gave more tickets to truckers in 1973 than ever before, and (b) they had issued twice as many tickets to truckers up to that point in 1974 than during the same period in 1973.

Those figures were obviously designed to make a big impression, and at first glance they do. The problem is that we still do not know how many tickets the CHP was giving to trucks or how that number compared to the number given to passenger cars. For all we know from what Pudinsky said, the CHP may have reached its previous all-time high by giving ten tickets to truckers in 1968, set the new record by giving twelve in 1973, and doubled that rate by giving 24 during January and February of 1974.

I also read a newspaper report that 98% of all cases of venereal disease are passed among friends, and only 2% of the cases are communicated (there's that word again) by prostitutes. Obviously it's safer to patronize a prostitute? It may be, but the statistics do not prove it, because we do not know what proportion of all sexual activity involves prostitutes. For instance, if prostitutes account for only 1% of all sexual activity, but 2% of all VD, one would be well advised to save his money.

Not too long after the EPA gasoline mileage report was issued, Mazda came out with an ad saying that its gas mileage was among the top 25% "of all cars sold in the U.S." But a quick check of the EPA report showed that Mazda mileage was far from being among the top 25% of all *makes* of cars sold in the United States and was, in fact, the worst of all the foreign "economy" cars.

One of the greatest books for examples of statistical sophistry is an interestingly written paperback by Stephen K. Campbell, *Flaws and Fallacies in Statistical Thinking.*[2] I cannot begin to do justice to the book but a quick review of the major problems mentioned is certainly worth the space. Under "Some Basic Measurement and Definition Problems," Campbell points out that in 1955 New York City had a population of anywhere from 1,910,000 to 13,630,000, depending on how one defined "New York City," whereas London's population ranged from 5,200 to ten million based on the same criteria. Among the "Far-Fetched Estimates" he cites is Mark Twain's projection on the basis of the rate at which the Lower Mississippi was being shortened by silt deposits that by about the year 2640, give or take 20 years, Cairo, Illinois, and New Orleans would be the same city.

On the topic of averages, he emphasizes the differences among mean (arithmetic average), median (point where 50% of all values fall below and 50% above), and mode (most frequent value). I have an example: What is wrong with a town 90% of whose population is on welfare when its "average" annual income is $100,000? Answer: Nothing, if it has a population of ten, one of whom is a millionaire.

Under "Ignoring Dispersion," Campbell quotes Lord Justice Matthews, "When I was a young man practicing at the bar, I lost a great many cases I should have won. As I got along, I won a great many cases I ought to have lost; so on the whole justice was done."

The most disturbing point is that statistics do not have to come from *anywhere* or mean *anything* to convince the average person 75% of the time. Try it sometime. It's a great party game. Into a discussion of the relative safety of compacts and full-size cars, drop a line such as: "Statistics show that 78.3% of all fatal accidents involve small cars." How often do you think someone will ask you where that percentage came from or what a "small" car is? Right. Less than 2.7% of the time.

In short, anytime you hear a speaker say something that begins, "The average American citizen ..." or "Over 73% of the time ..." you can bet there is at least an 87% chance you are about to be taken.

What is the difference between stereotyping and generalizing? Do generalizations that are produced in the "scientific laboratory" escape the dangers of stereotyping? Whenever we refer to groups of people with the word "most"—that is, most professors, most parents, most hippies, most 18-year-olds, what disservice do we do to individuals in the group who are not part of the majority? And even to those who are? And even if we have facts supporting our generalizations?

CONTINGENCY

By contingency reasoning I mean reasoning based on the observation that two or more events occur in some fairly dependable relationship. Such reasoning includes both "sign" and "cause." Sign reasoning is the easier of the two because the reliable, dependable occurrence of two events in some relationship makes each one a sign of the other *by definition*. However, one may conclude too quickly that one event is a sign of another, which produces "superstitious" behavior. On the other hand, some contingency relationships are difficult to detect. I have often marveled at the brilliance of the first person, whose name is unrecorded, who realized the relationship between sexual intercourse and pregnancy, considering the length of time that intervenes. At any rate, there are some rules that apply to contingency reasoning.

If a sign relationship is reliable, we assume that causality is involved, but we do not know the nature of that causality; that is, we do not know whether A causes B, B causes A, or some third factor C causes both, or a more complex causal chain or loop is operating. Thus, night and day are perfectly correlated, but one does not cause the other. Causal generalizations imply something more, and they will be discussed later. For the moment, remember that all the criteria I have mentioned as applicable to generalization are applicable to sign and causal generalization.

There are, however, some additional criteria that apply specifically to sign and causal generalization:

6. Were there *control conditions* in which the hypothesized sign or cause was absent (or present) to a lesser degree?

7. Were the conditions *comparable* in all respects except for the presence or absence of the hypothesized sign or cause?

8. If there are only certain conditions under which the sign or causal relationships are hypothesized to operate, are those conditions adequately represented?

Some additional criteria apply only to *causal* generalizations:

9. Are the nature and direction of the causal relationship clearly specified?

Sometimes the hypothesized effect will occur *if and only if* the hypothesized cause has occurred. In addition, there are instances in which the effect will *always* occur if the hypothesized cause has occurred. This is the most restrictive case. Sometimes the effect will occur as a result of some other cause as well, so it may occur even in the absence of the hypothesized cause. Finally, other conditions or "causes" may be necessary in order for the hypothesized cause/effect relationship to hold, so that the hypothesized cause may sometimes occur without being followed by the hypothesized effect.

Any causal relationship can be described in these terms, even if it is quite complex, involving multiple causal chains and loops. These complexities need not always be specified, but they do provide additional information that may be useful in subsequent effect-to-cause or cause-to-effect reasoning, or they may provide additional ways of evaluating the adequacy of the generalization:

10. Has the hypothesized cause been *manipulated*? If not, the hypothesized cause/effect relationship may be only a sign-significate relationship.

11. Does the hypothesized cause *precede* the effect? A "yes" answer to this question does not *establish* causality, but a "no" answer certainly eliminates it. In a causal loop, incidentally, the "effect" may both precede and follow the "cause," since they are mutually causal.

12. Have you eliminated all the possible *third factors* that might be causing both the hypothesized "cause" and "effect"?

Sign reasoning, reasoning from cause to effect, and reasoning from effect to cause are not themselves part of any process of generalization. They are the application of sign and causal generalizations to specific cases. We use such reasoning constantly in everyday life. We hear thunder and conclude that, since thunder is a sign of approaching rain, it is probably going to rain. We note that the cigarette butts in an ashtray are Bull Durham tailor mades and conclude that Seth must have been there, since he smokes that peculiar brand of cigarette. In both cases we are using *sign* reasoning. We reason that, since civil disobedience leads to disrespect for the law, illegally blocking traffic on Van Ness Avenue in San Francisco to protest policies at the Presidio will lead to disrespect for the law. This involves reasoning from *cause to effect*. We reason that, since the streets are wet, it must have rained, and use reasoning from *effect to cause*.

Such reasoning is limited by the universality and complexities of the generalization with which one begins. Thus, civil disobedience may lead to disrespect for the law only under certain conditions, and wet streets may be caused by rain or by a street sweeper. Such forms of reasoning are especially useful in the pursuit of *hypothesis*, which I will consider next.

HYPOTHESIS

An hypothesis is an *explanation* of data already available. These explanations seem to make use of generalization and deduction, applying them to specific configurations of data. One criterion by which the adequacy of an hypothesis can be judged is the extent to which it accounts adequately for the data at hand. A second criterion is the extent to which it makes specific, testable predictions regarding data not yet available and the extent to which those predictions are confirmed. Often more than one hypothesis is capable of explaining the available data and making successful predictions. One who is interested in evaluating a given hypothesis will make a serious search for these rival hypotheses. Assuming they are equally capable of accounting for the existing data, he or she will try to identify circumstances in which they will generate contradictory predictions. By testing these predictions, he or she will eliminate all the competing hypotheses except one. The survival of a given hypothesis does not "prove" its "truth"; the process is only analogous to the evolutionary concept of "survival of the fittest." In practice, such hypotheses do seem to evolve in the sense that they make predictions that are disconfirmed, after which they must be revised to account for the new data, from which revisions are generated new predictions that are also tested. Sometimes the only remaining hypothesis will be disconfirmed at such a basic level that it cannot be revised, in which case it is abandoned and new hypotheses must be devised. If two rival hypotheses seem to account equally well for all the available data and if testing them against one another is impractical, the tendency is to accept the simpler of the two (that is, the one requiring the fewest inferences, especially the fewest *inductive* inferences).

The general process, then, consists of the following steps:

1. Collect data.
2. Provide an hypothesis to explain the data.
3. Generate specific predictions from the hypothesis.

4. Test these predictions.
5. Revise the hypothesis to account for any disconfirmed predictions.
6. Generate new predictions from the revised hypothesis.
7. Test these new predictions.
8. Continue this process until it becomes more practical to adopt a rival hypothesis that is simpler or accounts more adequately for the available data.

Obviously, hypotheses tend to become more complex as they are revised, until at some point it becomes more appropriate to describe them as "theories." Sometimes complex hypotheses or theories that began as attempts to explain different sets of data come to "overlap" in that they generate similar predictions in certain cases. This is an unusual advantage of this sort of reasoning, since the theories then become mutually supportive.

One of the best books for someone interested in the process of hypothesis is *The Psychology Experiment* by Anderson.[3]

TESTIMONY

We use these methods of induction constantly in everyday life, although we do not usually apply such formal, systematic rules to the process. We gather examples and store them as part of our images of the world. We note certain regularities among those examples—people with shifty eyes seem to be untrustworthy, blondes have more fun, newspaper reporters seem to be politically liberal, that particular sound in a car means the water pump is going bad—and conclude that certain characteristics are signs of others. We speculate about the possible causes involved in such sign relationships: maybe there are so many accidents at that intersection because that tree blocks the stop sign; maybe I feel so sleepy when I come back from skiing because of the change in altitude. For these cause/effect hypotheses, we make predictions that we test using alternative plans: Maybe the reason my eyes burn at night is because I'm allergic to something; I think I'll take an allergy pill tonight and see if it makes any difference. From individual hypotheses we build theories: Well, since the allergy pill worked, I must be allergic; maybe that's also why I'm so tired and cough so much.

But in addition to reasoning by comparison/generalization, contingency, and hypothesis, we use a fourth major type of induction: reasoning from testimony. Testimony does not have a very good reputation among logicians either, but the fact is that people use it, and if they did not, they would have problems. It is simply impossible for everyone to be an expert on everything, to know everything he or she needs to know to deal with the world. So in many cases we are forced to rely on experts: professional mechanics, income-tax consultants, attorneys, and the like. The trick, of course, is to know who is actually an expert and which experts can be trusted not to take advantage of us:

1. He is or was in a position to observe the facts.
2. He is or was capable of observing, in the sense of:
   a. being physically capable,
   b. being intellectually capable,
   c. being psychologically or emotionally capable,
   d. being sensitive to the facts in question, and
   e. having had experience in making such observations.
3. He is motivated to perceive and report accurately, in that he:
   a. has nothing to gain by deceiving, and
   b. has goals similar to or compatible with your own;
4. He has reported accurately in the past on this and other topics.
5. He is responsible in the sense of being in a position to be held accountable for the testimony.

Now, since I presented the message model at the beginning of this chapter, I can point to another important reservation regarding testimony in light of that model. This reservation is that speakers use the opinions of others in more than one way: sometimes as *testimony* and sometimes as mere *approval*. Take the hypothetical example of a television commercial showing Roger Fastback, star of the Detroit Rocker Arms, extolling the virtues of Greaseless Kid Stuff hair spray. Now what in the name of Nirvana do I care if Roger Fastback likes Greaseless Kid Stuff? He probably doesn't know Greaseless Kid Stuff from Shinola, and after charging head first into the line that many times he probably should be putting silicon or Teflon on his head anyway. The advertiser is not using Fastback to *testify* as an expert to the causal relationship between the plan of using Greaseless Kid Stuff and the valued outcome of having attractive or durable hair. Rather, the advertiser is assuming that the famous Fastback is himself a value in his own right, and he is trying to associate him directly with the plan by means of an *approval* relationship, hoping the listener's liking for Fastback will transfer to the plan of using that particular hair spray.

It is easy to confuse testimony with approval, but they are very different. As I have already said, the only sound reason for adopting a proposed plan is that the plan will produce valued outcomes. Roger Fastback is not a valued outcome, and using Greaseless Kid Stuff will not produce him anyway.

Let's take another example, just to confuse matters a little further. Suppose the membership chairman for the local Rotary Club tells you that you ought to join Rotary because your boss belongs. What kind of argument is that? It may be a very good one. If your boss is the type of person who is impressed by that kind of thing and if you want to impress your boss, the argument makes perfectly good sense. Your boss is not being used to testify to the values of joining Rotary, nor is he being used in a relationship of mere approval. What the membership chairman is saying is that the proposed plan will produce valued outcomes, and that is what communication decisions are all about. Now that sort of plan may also wreak havoc with your self-image if you do not approve of kissing up to the boss, but that is just another outcome you will have to take into consideration.

Testimony is a strange case. Its most legitimate use is as a substitute for direct experience. We rely on testimony when we do not have the opportunity or ability to make our own observations, and that is its clearly legitimate use. But *observation* and *inference* are so closely related, and statements involving inference sometimes sound so much like statements of fact, that most listeners accept testimony as a substitute for other types of inference. Consequently, testimony is frequently used as a substitute for deductive inference, comparison, contingency, and hypothesis, so that it can be used to establish relationships of categorization, contingency, and similarity. Since it is so effective and versatile and since it is so easy to find "experts" to testify to most anything, it is little wonder that persuaders use it so frequently. However, *when substituted for inference,* testimony serves much the same function as a crutch between the ears.

CATEGORIZATION: INCLUSION AND EXCLUSION

Eventually one has to apply generalizations to specific cases. I may know that, in general, police dogs are likely to bite, for instance. For that generalization to be useful, I have to know that the animal in front of me is a police dog and is therefore likely to bite. That is the essence and function of this sort of reasoning—to make general, abstract information practical and useful by determining how it applies to the instance at hand.

This kind of reasoning is based on the inclusion of specific instances within general categories or the exclusion of those instances from general categories. That may sound a little strange, since most people are not aware that is what they are doing. Usually they do it too quickly to be aware of what they are doing. But let's take a look at the police dog example. First, I draw a circle representing "all dogs that are likely to bite" (Figure 7-1). Then within that circle I draw another representing "police dogs" (Figure 7-2). Finally, I place an "X" to represent this specific dog within the circle representing "police dogs." In doing that I *necessarily* also place the "X" in the circle representing "all dogs that bite" (Figure 7-3).

FIGURE 7-1

FIGURE 7-2

FIGURE 7-3

That is an essential characteristic of this kind of reasoning, which is also frequently termed "deductive." It will (if used properly) produce conclusions that are exactly as true as its premises. Another way of saying it is that the conclusion necessarily follows from the premises. As they say in computer language, "GIGO"—garbage in, garbage out. If the premises are not true, the deduction can be perfectly valid, and the conclusion will be perfectly untrue. Consequently, one cannot prove anything about "reality" by deduction alone because the premises, insofar as they bear any relationship to experience, have to be provided by one of the other forms of reasoning I have already discussed. What I want to prevent, however, is the wasting of good premises by drawing invalid conclusions—the dreaded SIGO, meaning "steak in, garbage out."

First, let's see how deduction relates to the model for persuasion I have been using. Deduction can be described in terms of a syllogism, which contains three elements: a major premise, a minor premise, and a conclusion. To diagram a syllogism in terms of the Toulmin model, one substitutes the minor premise for the datum, the major premise for the warrant, and the conclusion for the claim. Thus one argument might go:

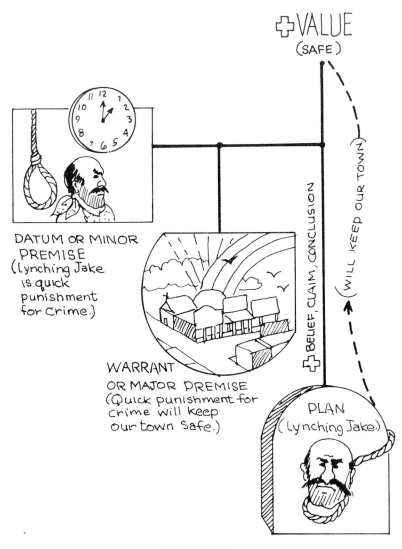

DATUM OR MINOR
PREMISE
(Lynching Jake
is quick
punishment
for crime.)

WARRANT
OR MAJOR PREMISE
(Quick punishment for
crime will keep
our town safe.)

FIGURE 7-4
The relationship between a syllogism and the Toulmin model.

Quick punishment for crime will keep our town safe.
Lynching Jake is quick punishment for crime.
Lynching Jake will keep our town safe.

In the model of persuasion I have been using, that argument would be diagrammed as in Figure 7-4.

This type of syllogism is called "categorical." The "conditional" syllogism uses a different form. For example:

If this mob hangs Jake, they will be arrested.
This mob is going to hang Jake.
This group is going to be arrested.

The third, and final, type of syllogism is the "disjunctive":

Either we will hang Jake, or we will be overrun by criminals.
We are not going to hang Jake.
We are going to be overrun by criminals.

The rules for the various forms of syllogisms are too numerous and complex to be treated here. Beardsley does an excellent job of explaining them, so you might refer to his book if you are interested.

SUMMARY

Several types of reasoning and evidence are used to support the basic cause-to-effect claim that the speaker's proposed plan or policy will result in valued consequences.

Comparison and generalization constitutes one such type of reasoning. It depends on the similarity relationship mentioned earlier. Speakers may use *single examples* (or a limited number of examples) to allow listeners to better visualize specific instances of general conditions that they claim exist, or they may use *extended examples* (analogies) for the same purpose. Larger *collections of examples* are necessary, however, to establish a generalization. In order to provide sound basis for generalization, such collections of examples must: (1) be drawn from a *clearly defined class or set*, (2) have in common some *clearly defined characteristic*, (3) be used in support of a generalization the *scope of which is clearly specified*, (4) be *representative* of the class or set (that is, typical and of adequate size), and (5) be adequately *variable* to represent the variability of the class or set. One way of summarizing collections of examples is by means of *statistics*. Although statistics are definitely convenient, the fact that they are numbers frequently gives them an aura of accuracy, finality, and unquestioned authority that may conceal fallacious reasoning of various sorts too numerous to list.

Contingency reasoning proceeds by applying causal or sign generalizations to a specific instance. In addition to the tests of generalization in general, both sign and causal generalizations require (6) *control* conditions, (7) *comparability* of control and test conditions, and (8) *adequate representation* of all relevant conditions. In addition, reliable causal generalizations require (9) specification of the *nature* and *direction* of the causality, (10) *manipulation* of the hypothesized cause and subsequent observation of the hypothesized effect, (11) *time precedence* of the cause (before the effect), and (12) elimination or identification of possible *third factors*. These are rules for sign and causal generalization. Application of the generalization to a specific instance requires that the specific instance be reliably identified as a case of the sign or causal generalization and cast into some acceptable form of deduction, discussed later.

Hypothesis is a process of reasoning that attempts to provide an explanation for existing data, generates specific testable predictions, tests those predictions, revises the original explanation if the predictions are disconfirmed, generates new predictions from the revised explanation, tests the new predictions, and continues until it becomes more practical to adopt a rival explanation.

Testimony involves the citation of a presumed authority in support of beliefs a speaker wishes to establish as "facts." To be acceptable, it ought to be more than mere approval of a speaker's proposal by a well-liked person. Rather, the presumed authority should (a) have had *opportunity* to observe the "facts," (2) be *capable* of observing, (3) be *unbiased*, (4) have a reputation for accuracy, and (5) be responsible (or accountable) for his or her testimony.

Categorization (or deduction) rests on the principle of exclusion and inclusion and can be cast into *a syllogism*, which applies a generalization to a specific instance, placing the specific instance inside or outside of the category to which the generalization applies. Three forms of syllogism are recognized: the *categorical* ("All A is B" or "No A is B"), the *conditional* ("If A then B"), and the *disjunctive* ("Either A or B").

ILLUSTRATIVE SPEECH

The speech by Abraham Lincoln from which the following excerpt is taken has been widely heralded by critics as one of the most carefully reasoned examples of political oratory available. It is generally referred to as his "Cooper Institute Address" because it was delivered at the Cooper Institute in New York City on February 27, 1860.

The issue to which he explicitly addressed himself was whether slavery ought to be allowed in the Federal Territories. The policy he explicitly proposed was relatively straightforward: the Republican Party ought to continue its efforts to outlaw slavery in the Territories as it was already outlawed in the "free states," should tolerate it as a fact of life in those Southern states in which it already existed, but should continue to denounce it as morally wrong.

However, there was a "hidden policy" Lincoln was attempting to advance, which should not be ignored, because it helps to explain why the speech was so carefully reasoned and so devoid of the backwoods witticisms and occasional flamboyance that characterized his earlier public addresses. Plainly put, Lincoln wanted to be the Republican candidate for President. To accomplish that, he had to convince relatively reserved Eastern Republicans that he was "Presidential timber" rather than "backwoods timber," that he was a reasonable, intelligent, sophisticated person who would be the best spokesman for the Republican position. Many historians believe the speech accomplished that purpose admirably; that is, it may have been the event that contributed most to his nomination and subsequent election.

This excerpt from the speech is carefully reasoned in one respect because it proceeds along the lines of a syllogism:

The 39 signers of the Constitution understood better than we whether the Constitution prevents the Federal Government from outlawing slavery in the Territories.

The 39 signers of the Constitution understood that the Constitution *does not* prevent the Federal Government from outlawing slavery in the Territories.

Therefore the better understanding is that the Constitution does not prevent the Federal Government from outlawing slavery in the Territories.

Actually, rephrased specifically and correctly as a *categorical* syllogism, this should read:

Major Premise: The interpretation held by those who signed the Constitution is the correct interpretation of the Constitution with respect to Federal control of Territorial slavery.

Minor Premise: The interpretation held by those who signed the Constitution was that the Federal Government can control slavery in the Territories.

Conclusion: The correct interpretation of the Constitution with respect to Federal control of Territorial slavery is that the Federal Government can control slavery in the Territories.

As you can see from the speech, Lincoln took the first premise from a statement by Senator Stephen A. Douglas, the well-known and outspoken leader of the opposition to outlawing Territorial slavery. Actually, I have taken some liberty with the language of the premises in order to clarify and condense it. In fact, Lincoln began with a statement by Douglas that was somewhat less precise and arrived at his first premise by defining the terms of that statement.

It then remained for Lincoln to establish the second premise, since Douglas obviously believed exactly the opposite. As you can see, he did so by examining the voting records of as many of the 39 original signers as had voted upon the issue in any form—23 by his count, 21 of whom voted so as to indicate they believed the Federal Government *could* prohibit slavery in its territories.

Now suppose we cast this into the model described in Chapters Six and Seven. The *policy* recommended by Lincoln was "Maintaining the position that the Federal Government can render Territorial slavery illegal." The *valued consequence* to which he related this policy was "Republicans remaining consistent with the Constitution." This was an especially valuable consequence for Republicans at this time, since they were frequently accused of being radicals devoted to the abolition of slavery by any means, Constitutional or not. The *claim* that Lincoln advanced, then, was "Maintaining the position that the Federal Government can render Territorial slavery illegal *will result in* Republicans remaining consistent with the Constitution." The *datum* that he offered to support his claim was: "[A majority of] the thirty-nine signers of the Constitution understood that the Constitution does not prevent the Federal Government from outlawing slavery in the Territories." That datum was related to the claim by the *warrant* derived from Douglas' statement: "The thirty-nine signers of the Constitution understood better than we whether the Constitution prevents the Federal Government from outlawing slavery in the territories."

However, since this datum was in dispute, it was in reality a "datum-claim," so Lincoln had to provide further data and a common warrant to support it. Those supporting data were the recorded votes of 23 of the 39 on the principle of Federal control of slavery in the Territories. The common supporting warrant was: "These votes, taken together, constitute a majority of the thirty-nine voting in favor of Federal control of Territorial slavery." All that can be diagrammed as shown in Figure 7-5.

With respect to advancing his "hidden policy," Lincoln also demonstrated an *implicit* claim that "Nominating Lincoln as the Republican candidate for President will result in the Republicans fielding a candidate who is intelligent, reasonable, knowledgeable in the law, and an able spokesman for the Republican position." Republicans, in fact, adopted that policy; Lincoln was elected; the South seceded from the Union;

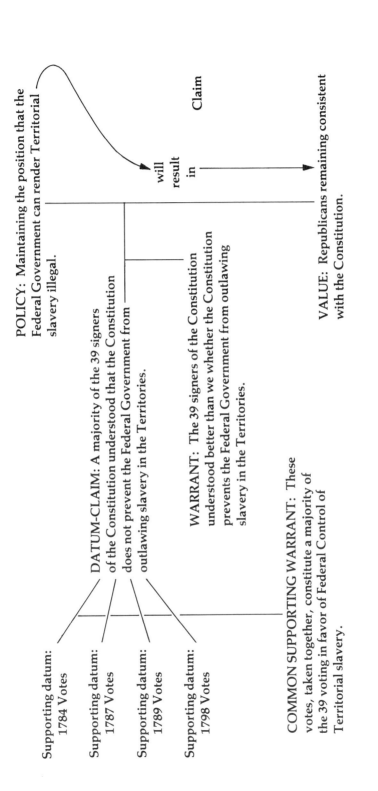

FIGURE 7-5

and the War Between the States began. Such are the results of reasoning too well.

The Cooper Institute Address
Abraham Lincoln
(excerpt)

Mr. President and fellow-citizens of New York: The facts with which I shall deal this evening are mainly old and familiar; nor is there anything new in the general use I shall make of them. If there shall be any novelty, it will be in the mode of presenting the facts, and the inferences and observations following that presentation. In his speech last autumn at Columbus, Ohio, as reported in the *New York Times*, Senator Douglas said: —

Our fathers, when they framed the government under which we
live, understood this question just as well, and even better, than we
do now.

I fully endorse this, and I adopt it as a text for this discourse. I so adopt it because it furnishes a precise and an agreed starting-point for a discussion between Republicans and that wing of the Democracy headed by Senator Douglas. It simply leaves the inquiry: What was the understanding those fathers had of the question mentioned?

What is the frame of government under which we live? The answer must be, "The Constitution of the United States." That Constitution consists of the original, framed in 1787, and under which the present government first went into operation, and twelve subsequently framed amendments, the first ten of which were framed in 1789.

Who were our fathers that framed the Constitution? I suppose the "thirty-nine" who signed the original instrument may be fairly called our fathers who framed that part of the present government. It is almost exactly true to say they framed it, and it is altogether true to say they fairly represented the opinion and sentiment of the whole nation at that time. Their names, being familiar to nearly all, and accessible to quite all, need not now be repeated.

I take these "thirty-nine," for the present, as being "our fathers who framed the government under which we live." What is the question which, according to the text, those fathers understood "just as well, and even better, than we do now"?

It is this: Does the proper division of local from Federal authority, or anything in the Constitution, forbid our Federal Government to control as to slavery in our Federal Territories?

Upon this, Senator Douglas holds the affirmative, and Republicans the negative. This affirmation and denial form an issue; and this issue—this question—is precisely what the text declares our fathers understood "better than we." Let us now inquire whether the "thirty-nine," or any of them, ever acted upon this question; and if they did, how they acted upon it—how they expressed that better understanding. In 1784, three years before the Constitution, the United States then owning the Northwestern Territory, and no other, the Congress of the Confederation had before them the question of prohibiting slavery in that Territory, and four of the "thirty-nine" who afterward framed the Constitution were in that Congress, and voted on that question. Of these, Roger Sherman, Thomas Mifflin, and Hugh Williamson voted for the prohibition, thus showing that, in their understanding, no line dividing local from Federal authority, nor anything else, properly forbade the Federal Government to control as to slavery in Federal territory. The other of the four, James McHenry, voted against the prohibition, showing that for some cause he thought it improper to vote for it.

In 1787, still before the Constitution, but while the convention was in session framing it, and while the Northwestern Territory still was the only Territory owned by the United States, the same question of prohibiting slavery in the Territory again came before the Congress of the Confederation; and two more of the "thirty-nine" who afterward signed the Constitution were in that Congress, and voted on the question. They were William Blount and William Few; and they both voted for the prohibition—thus showing that in their understanding no line dividing local from Federal authority, nor anything else, properly forbade the Federal Government to control as to slavery in Federal territory. This time the prohibition became a law, being part of what is now well known as the Ordinance of '87.

The question of Federal control of slavery in the Territories seems not to have been directly before the convention which framed the original Constitution; and hence it is not recorded that the "thirty-nine," or any of them, while engaged on that instrument, expressed any opinion on that precise question.

In 1789, by the first Congress which sat under the Constitution, an act was passed to enforce the Ordinance of '87, including the prohibition of slavery in the Northwestern Territory. The bill for this act was reported by one of the "thirty-nine"—Thomas Fitzsimmons, then a member of the House of Representatives from Pennsylvania. It went through all its stages without a word of opposition, and finally passed both branches without ayes and nays, which is equivalent to a unanimous passage. In this Congress there were sixteen of the thirty-nine fathers who framed the original Constitution. They were John Langdon, Nicholas Gilman, Wm.

S. Johnson, Roger Sherman, Robert Morris, Thomas Fitzsimmons, Abraham Baldwin, William Few, Rufus King, William Patterson, George Clymer, Richard Bassett, George Read, Pierce Butler, Daniel Carroll, and James Madison.

This shows that, in their understanding, no line dividing local from Federal authority, nor anything in the Constitution, properly forbade Congress to prohibit slavery in the Federal territory; else both their fidelity to correct principle, and their oath to support the Constitution, would have constrained them to oppose the prohibition.

Again, George Washington, another of the "thirty-nine," was then President of the United States, and as such approved and signed the bill, thus completing its validity as a law, and thus showing that, in his understanding, no line dividing local from Federal authority, nor anything in the Constitution, forbade the Federal Government to control as to slavery in Federal territory.

No great while after the adoption of the original Constitution, North Carolina ceded to the Federal Government the country now constituting the State of Tennessee; and a few years later Congress ceded that which now constitutes the States of Mississippi and Alabama: In both deeds of cession it was made a condition by the ceding States that the Federal Government should not prohibit slavery in the ceded country. Besides this, slavery was then actually in the ceded country. Under these circumstances, Congress, on taking charge of these countries, did not absolutely prohibit slavery within them. But they did interfere with it—take control of it—even there, to a certain extent. In 1798 Congress organized the Territory of Mississippi. In the act of organization they prohibited the bringing of slaves into the Territory from any place without the United States, by fine, and giving freedom to slaves so brought. This act passed both branches of Congress without yeas and nays. In that Congress were three of the "thirty-nine" who framed the original Constitution. They were John Langdon, George Read, and Abraham Baldwin. They all probably voted for it. Certainly they would have placed their opposition to it upon record if, in their understanding, any line dividing local from Federal authority, or anything in the Constitution, properly forbade the Federal Government to control as to slavery in Federal Territory.

In 1803, the Federal Government purchased the Louisiana country. Our former territorial acquisitions came from certain of our own States; but this Louisiana country was acquired from a foreign nation. In 1804, Congress gave a territorial organization to that part of it which now constitutes the State of Louisiana. New Orleans, lying within that part, was an old and comparatively large city. There were other considerable towns and settlements, and slavery was extensively and thoroughly intermingled with the people. Congress did not, in the Territorial Act, prohibit slavery; but they did interfere with it—take control of it—in a more marked and extensive way than they did in the case of Mississippi. The substance of the provision therein made in relation to slaves was:

1st. That no slave should be imported into the Territory from foreign parts.

2d. That no slave should be carried into it who had been imported into the United States since the first day of May, 1798.

3d. That no slave should be carried into it, except by the owner, and for his own use as a settler; the penalty in all cases being a fine upon the violator of the law, and freedom to the slave.

This act also was passed without ayes or nays. In the Congress which passed it there were two of the "thirty-nine." They were Abraham Baldwin and Jonathan Dayton. As stated in the case of Mississippi, it is probable they both voted for it. They would not have allowed it to pass without recording their opposition to it if, in their understanding, it violated either the line properly dividing local from Federal authority, or any provision of the Constitution.

In 1819-20 came and passed the Missouri question. Many votes were taken, by yeas and nays, in both branches of Congress, upon the various phases of the general question. Two of the "thirty-nine"—Rufus King and Charles Pinckney—were members of that Congress. Mr. King steadily voted for slavery prohibition and against all compromises, while Mr. Pinckney as steadily voted against slavery prohibition and against all compromises. By this, Mr. King showed that, in his understanding, no line dividing local from Federal authority, nor anything in the Constitution, was violated by Congress prohibiting slavery in Federal territory; while Mr. Pinckney, by his votes, showed that, in his understanding, there was some sufficient reason for opposing such prohibition in that case.

The cases I have mentioned are the only acts of the "thirty-nine" or of any one of them, upon the direct issue, which I have been able to discover.

To enumerate the persons who thus acted as being four in 1784, two in 1787, seventeen in 1789, three in 1798, two in 1804, and two in 1819-20, there would be thirty of them. But this would be counting John Langdon, Roger Sherman, William Few, Rufus King, and George Read each twice, and Abraham Baldwin three times. The true number of those of the "thirty-nine" who I have shown to have acted upon the question which, by the text, they understood better than we, is twenty-three, leaving sixteen not shown to have acted upon it in any way.

Here then, we have twenty-three out of our thirty-nine fathers "who framed the government under which we live," who have, upon their official responsibility and their corporal oaths, acting upon the very question which the text affirms they "understood just as well, and even better, than we do now"; and twenty-one of them—a clear majority of the whole "thirty-nine"—so acting upon it as to make them guilty of gross political impropriety and wilful perjury if, in their understanding, any proper division between local and Federal authorities, or anything in the Constitution they had made themselves, and sworn to support, forbade the Federal Government to control as to slavery in the Federal Territories. Thus the twenty-one acted; and, as actions speak louder than words, so actions under such responsibility speak still louder.

Two of the twenty-three voted against Congressional prohibition of slavery in the Federal Territories, in the instances in which they acted upon the question. But for what reason they so voted is not known. They may have done so because they thought a proper division of local from Federal authority, or some provision or principle of the Constitution, stood in the way; or they may, without any such question, have voted against the prohibition on what appeared to them to be sufficient grounds of expediency. No one who has sworn to support the Constitution can conscientiously vote for what he understands to be an unconstitutional measure, however expedient he may think it; but one may and ought to vote against a measure which he deems constitutional if, at the same time, he deems it expedient. It, therefore, would be unsafe to set down even the two who voted against the prohibition as having done so because, in their understanding, any proper division of local from Federal authority, or anything in the Constitution, forbade the Federal Government to control as to slavery in Federal territory.

The remaining sixteen of the "thirty-nine," so far as I have discovered, have left no record of their understanding upon the direct question of Federal control of slavery in the Federal Territories. But there is much reason to believe that their understanding upon that question would not have appeared different from that of their twenty-three compeers, had it been manifested at all.

For the purpose of adhering ridigly to the text, I have purposely omitted whatever understanding may have been manifested by any person, however distinguished, other than the thirty-nine fathers who framed the original Constitution; and, for the same reason, I have also omitted whatever understanding may have been manifested by any of the "thirty-nine" even on any other phase of the general question of slavery. If we should look into their acts and declaration on those other phases, as the foreign slave-trade, and the morality and policy of slavery generally, it would appear to us that on the direct question of Federal control of slavery in Federal Territories, the sixteen, if they had acted at all, would probably have acted just as the twenty-three did. Among that sixteen were several of the most noted anti-slavery men of those times—Dr. Franklin, Alexander Hamilton, and Gouverneur Morris—

while there was not one now known to have been otherwise, unless it may be John Rutledge, of South Carolina.

The sum of the whole is that of our thirty-nine fathers who framed the original constitution, twenty-one—a clear majority of the whole—certainly understood that no proper division of local from Federal authority, nor any part of the Constitution, forbade the Federal Government to control slavery in the Federal Territories; while all the rest had probably the same understanding. Such, unquestionably, was the understanding of our fathers who framed the original Constitution; and the text affirms that they understood the question "better than we."

But, so far, I have been considering the understanding of the question manifested by the framers of the original Constitution. In and by the original instrument, a mode was provided for amending it; and, as I have already stated, the present frame of "the government under which we live" consists of that original, and twelve amendatory articles framed and adopted since. Those who now insist that Federal control of slavery in Federal Territories violates the Constitution, point us to the provisions which they suppose it thus violates; and, as I understand, they all fix upon provisions in these amendatory articles, and not in the original instrument. The Supreme Court, in the Dred Scott case, plant themselves upon the fifth amendment, which provides that no person shall be deprived of "life, liberty, or property without due process of law"; while Senator Douglas and his peculiar adherents plant themselves upon the tenth amendment, providing that "the powers not delegated to the United States by the Constitution" "are reserved to the States respectively, or to the people."

Now it so happens that these amendments were framed by the first Congress which sat under the Constitution—the identical Congress which passed the act, already mentioned, enforcing the prohibition of slavery in the Northwestern Territory. Not only was it the same Congress, but they were the identical, same individual men who, at the same session, and at the same time within the session, had under consideration, and in progress toward maturity, these constitutional amendments, and this act prohibiting slavery in all the territory the nation then owned. The constitutional amendments were introduced before, and passed after the act enforcing the Ordinance of '87; so that, during the whole pendency of the act to enforce the Ordinance, the constitutional amendments were also pending.

The seventy-six members of that Congress, including sixteen of the framers of the original Constitution, as before stated, were preeminently our fathers who framed that part of "the government under which we live," which is now claimed as forbidding the Federal Government to control slavery in the Federal Territories.

Is it not a little presumptuous in anyone at this day to affirm that the two things which that Congress deliberately framed, and carried to maturity at the same time, are absolutely inconsistent with each other? And does not such affirmation become impudently absurd when coupled with the other affirmation, from the same mouth, that those who did the two things alleged to be inconsistent, understood whether they really were inconsistent better than we—better than he who affirms that they are inconsistent?

It is surely safe to assume that the thirty-nine framers of the original Constitution, and the seventy-six members of the Congress which framed the amendments thereto, taken together, do certainly include those who may be fairly called "our fathers who framed the government under which we live." And so assuming, I defy any man to show that any one of them ever, in his whole life, declared that, in his understanding, any proper division of local from Federal authority, or any part of the Constitution, forbade the Federal Government to control as to slavery in the Federal Territories. I go a step further. I defy anyone to show that any living man in the world ever did, prior to the beginning of the present century (and I might almost say prior to the beginning of the last half of the present century), declare that, in his understanding, any proper division of local from Federal authority, or any part of the Constitution, forbade the Federal Government to control as to slavery in the Federal Territories. To those who now so declare I give not only "our fathers who framed the government under which we live," but with them all other living men within the century in which it was framed, among whom to search, and they shall not be able to find the evidence of a single man agreeing with them.

Now, and here, let me guard a little against being misunderstood. I do not mean to say we are bound to follow implicitly in whatever our fathers did. To do so would be to discard all the lights of current experience—to reject all progress, all improvement. What I do say is that if we would supplant the opinions and policy of our fathers in any case, we should do so upon evidence so conclusive, and argument so clear, that even their great authority, fairly considered and weighed, cannot stand; and most surely not in a case whereof we ourselves declare they understood the question better than we.

If any man at this day sincerely believes that a proper division of local from Federal authority, or any part of the Constitution, forbids the Federal Government to control as to slavery in the Federal Territories, he is right to say so, and to enforce his position by all truthful evidence and fair argument which he can. But he has no right to mislead others, who have less access to history, and less leisure to study it, into the false belief that "our fathers who framed the government under which we live" were of the same opinion—thus substituting falsehood and deception for truthful evidence and fair argument. If any man at this day sincerely believes "our fathers who framed the government under which we live" used and applied principles, in other cases, which ought to have led them to understand that a proper division of local from Federal authority, or some part of the Constitution, forbids the Federal Government to control as to slavery in the Federal Territories, he is right to say so. But he should, at the same time, brave the responsibility of declaring that, in his opinion, he understands their principles better than they did themselves; and especially should he not shirk that responsibility by asserting that they "understood the question just as well, and even better, than we do now."

But enough! Let all who believe that "our fathers who framed the government under which we live understood this question just as well, and even better, than we do now," speak as they spoke, and act as they acted upon it. This is all Republicans ask—all Republicans desire—in relation to slavery. As those fathers marked it, so let it be again marked, as an evil not to be extended, but to be tolerated and protected only because of and so far as its actual presence amongst us makes that toleration and protection a necessity. Let all the guaranties those fathers gave it be not grudgingly, but fully and faithfully maintained. For this Republicans contend, and with this, so far as I know or believe, they will be content . . .

Chapter Seven References

1 Beardsley, M. C. *Writing with Reason: Logic for Composition* (Englewood Cliffs, N.J.: Prentice-Hall, 1976).
2 Stephen K. Campbell, *Flaws and Fallacies in Statistical Thinking* (Englewood Cliffs, N.J.: Prentice-Hall, 1974).
3 Barry F. Anderson, *The Psychology Experiment* (Monterey, Calif.: Brooks-Cole, 1971).

CHAPTER EIGHT
Search and Research

In preparing a speech you must find, evaluate, and prepare the material you will use in your explanation or persuasive appeal. I am going to assume that you have studied your audience and analyzed your topic so that you have a fairly good idea of the sort of supporting material you need. You have chosen a topic you believe will interest your listeners; you have narrowed that topic to a specific thesis or central idea, you have divided the speech into an appropriate number of major divisions or arguments; and you have some idea of how your explanation or reasoning will proceed. Now you are ready to look for the information that will make you an expert in this specific, limited area, the information that will cause your listeners to attend to your speech and make them feel they have profited from doing so.

Because the problems are very practical ones, they call for some quite specific and even prescriptive advice. The procedures I will recommend are not derived from abstract theory. Rather, they have been distilled from the experience of speakers who have confronted the same problems and have devised efficient and effective ways of dealing with them.

GATHERING INFORMATION

One question that arises immediately is: What kind of notes should I take? I will try to answer that question as specifically as possible.

Sometimes you will find statements that you want to quote directly and exactly. When you do, copy them—directly and exactly—with quotation marks around them so you will know later they are someone else's words and not your own, or photocopy the page and glue the quote to a card later. Other material you will want to paraphrase in your own words. If you do that, try your best to avoid changing the meaning. The usual reason for paraphrasing is to shorten a quote that is too long to use in your speech. Similarly, you may want to write a brief summary of an entire article. You may want to copy only statistics, or you may want copies of tables, figures, or pictures. The photocopying machines in the library are put there for that purpose.

Whether you record a direct quote, a paraphrase, a summary, statistics, tables, figures, or pictures, *always record the complete reference*. For an article, that should include the name(s) of the author(s), the title of the article, the title of the magazine in which it is published, the date, the volume number, the inclusive pages of the article, and the specific page on which the item you have recorded appears. For a book, you need the name(s) of the author(s), the title of the book, the publisher, place of publication, date of publication, and the page numbers. If the article appears in a book rather than a magazine, you need the title of the article and the name(s) of the editor(s) of the book as well. You may as well record the library call number of a book in case you want to go back to it. If they are available, you should also record the qualifications of the author(s). You *may* need any or all of these as you prepare your speech, and it is really frustrating to have to know something, refer to your notes, and discover it is not there. Then you have to make another trip to the library, perhaps only to discover that the book has been checked out. For a speech, record the name of the speaker, his or her qualifications, the time and place of the speech, and perhaps something about the audience and occasion. For a personal conversation or interview, record the name(s) and qualifications of the other person(s), the date, the time, and the place. If it is from a letter, keep the letter.

It may sound trivial and mechanical, but it is a good idea to take notes on small, stiff index cards (3″ x 5″, 4″ x 6″, 5″ x 8″) rather than on large, flimsy sheets of paper. You may be reading from your notes during your speech, and you may be nervous. If your hand is shaking. it is not nearly as noticeable when you are holding an index card. Index cards are also easier to handle and less distracting while you are speaking. Oh, yes—choose index cards large enough that you do not have to write on the back. It is also distracting to your listeners and confusing to you to have to constantly flip cards. The photocopies? If possible, glue them to index cards.

Beyond the question of how to take notes, it is the question of where to look for information that seems to be most puzzling to students. The first place to look is in your own head. If you have chosen a topic that really interests you, you probably also know quite a bit about it. You may even know more than you think you do. Take the time to list what you know. The more you think about it, the longer your list will grow. Try also to think of where your information came from, because that may suggest places to look for more information now that you want to do some serious research. Have you read newspaper or magazine articles on the topic, or noticed it mentioned in some book? Have you talked to someone who seemed to know a lot about it? Have you heard it mentioned by one of your professors in a lecture or in a television special? Try to retrace your steps the way you would if you had left your coat somewhere but did not know where. Then return to the sources of your information and see if you can find more.

The second place to look is among resource persons. Do you have friends who know something about the topic and who might be able to tell you where else to look? Are there faculty members who are specialists in the area? Two of my recent students wanted to do a class project demonstrating how people react when others get too close, and they were surprised to discover that one of the leading authorities on the topic was on the psychology department faculty. He seemed happy to help them and gave them quite a bibliography on the subject. Specialists are usually delighted to find students who are genuinely interested in their specialities. God knows we spend enough time sitting in our offices wondering if anyone outside our tight circle of colleagues really cares about what we are studying. So ask around. Look in your college catalog. You may not turn up anyone with a national reputation in your area, but your resource person does not have to have a national reputation to give you a great deal of help.

Local businesspeople, local agencies, or local politicians can help, too. Look in the yellow pages of your telephone directory, the local newspaper, or call your city or county offices to find people you might talk to.

You might find someone elsewhere in the state—on another university campus, in your state government, or in business in a large city nearby. You may find they are surprisingly accessible. Many universities have telephone lease lines that connect the university offices with the rest of the state, or with even larger areas. If you locate someone in another city in the state, especially on another campus, your professor might let you use the lease line to interview that person. If not, even a short telephone call at your own expense might be more than worthwhile. If all that fails, you might even write a letter.

Next, check some familiar sources. You or your friends might have textbooks covering your topic. You might be able to find specialty magazines that would help you. For instance, there is a store called Bollinger's in Pueblo, Colorado, where I went to high school, that has a tremendous variety of candy, newspapers, magazines, and paperback books. I did a great deal of research there for themes and speeches that were required in some of my high school classes. Look in *TV Guide* to see if there are any television news specials coming up which might be relevant. A really good dictionary is an excellent source of concise information.

There may be agencies on your campus that will be willing to help. Look in your campus directory for a teaching resources center, audiovisual center, or educational television center. They may have slides, videotapes or audiotapes, film strips, or other useful materials. If not, they may be able to steer you to someone who does, perhaps a professor who has worked on a similar project for a course. The editor of your campus newspaper or the director of your campus radio station may recall news or feature stories relevant to your topic. There may be a campus organization interested in the area.

Off-campus agencies may help, too. The editors of the local newspapers and news directors for local radio and television stations are possiblities. Government, industry, and independent agencies such as the

Heart Association, Common Cause, the Department of Agriculture, the U.S. Chamber of Commerce, the National Organization for the Reform of Marijuana Laws (NORML), and the like have pamphlets and brochures they will smother you with if you give some indication of being interested.

I have deliberately omitted mentioning the library so far because it is so obvious and I know you are aware of it. But suppose we consider it now. You may have wandered around the library before, becoming really frustrated and discouraged. It is one thing to go to the library reserve desk and check out a book a professor has required you to read. It is quite another thing to try to find something there on your own. One place to start is the reference section. Choose a good encyclopedia and look under your topic. But do not stop there. Try to think of all the terms and subtopics under which you might find relevant information, and check them out as well. Articles in good encyclopedias will be signed; that is, they will have initials at the end. Those initials will be translated into a *name* somewhere else in the encyclopedia, and the author's qualifications may be given. If not, find the latest edition of *Who's Who in America* and look under that person's name. If he or she is famous enough to be writing an encyclopedia article, chances are good the name will be there. Remember where you found *Who's Who*, because you will probably want to come back to it to check out other names.

While you are in the reference room, try to think of what other books might be there that would help you. The annual almanacs such as *Information Please* and the *Statistical Abstract of the United States* can be useful. By all means, consult one of the reference librarians. You will find them helpful and knowledgeable on a variety of topics.

Find the *Reader's Guide to Periodical Literature*. Begin with the latest volume and work back, checking all the terms you can think of that might be relevant. You will find at least the most recent issues of the magazines and periodicals to which it refers in the periodicals room. Earlier issues will probably be bound and located somewhere else. Most libraries have a separate section for government documents and pamphlets.

At this point you can begin to use a trick that will make your list of sources balloon. Some of the articles you will find in the *Reader's Guide* will contain footnotes and bibliographies. Find the most recent of such articles and pick out the footnote and bibliographical items to which they refer. Then go to those sources and find *their* footnotes and bibliographies, and so on. You will soon find you have more information than you can use, so you will have to begin to be selective.

Next you might go to the card catalog to look up your topic and all the related terms you have been collecting. Record the call numbers of specific books so you can locate them, but look also for call numbers that are frequently repeated. Then go to that area of the library and look through the stack for other titles that seem relevant. When you find a book, remember again that you can use it not only for specific information on your topic, but also to find additional sources by checking its footnotes and bibliography.

Scholarly journals are not generally indexed in the *Readers's Guide to Periodical Literature*. They are indexed in publications specific to the academic discipline with which they are concerned. There is no way I can tell you about all of them, so let me give you an example. In my area, two of the most useful publications are *Psychological Abstracts* and the *Annual Review of Psychology*. The first is an index of articles related to psychology. It is published every three months, and it includes an abstract or brief summary of each article. The second is published annually, but a given topic area is reviewed only every few years. Each review article covers the research published during the years since the previous review. Most academic disciplines have similar indexes and annual reviews. If your topic falls under biology or engineering, ask a biology or engineering professor what they are. Ask also what journals are likely to contain material on your topic. Then you can look at the tables of contents of the most recent issues of those journals that may not have been indexed yet. Once again, you are looking for the most recent article dealing with your topic, because a recent article will contain footnotes and bibliographies of previous articles. The authors' qualifications may or may not be given in the journals themselves, and they may or may not be listed in *Who's Who in America*, but there is a good chance they will be listed in *Who's Who in America Colleges and Universities* or *American Men of Science*.

Newspapers present a special problem because they are not thoroughly indexed. Most libraries have copies of the *New York Times* and several other major newspapers, although they may be on microfilm. There is an index to the *New York Times,* so if the event was one of national significance, you can probably locate it there. Once you know the date on which a particular story broke, you can find it in other newspapers as well, and you can find editorials dealing with that event a day or two later. If you do not find it in the *Times* index (if it is an event of only local significance, for example), you will have to recall the date or find someone who does recall the approximate date of the major events relating to your topic. Then you will have to hunt. If your library does not have copies of a particular newspaper, the office of the newspaper itself will keep copies, again probably on microfilm.

EVALUATING YOUR MATERIAL

Chapter Seven is useful when it comes times to decide which material you are actually going to use in your speech. First, the information and any inferences your sources make should be reliable. That must be decided largely on the basis of the reliability of the sources themselves. The list of questions to ask about a source appears in Chapter Seven. In addition, there are some other questions you can ask:

1. Is the information from a given source internally consistent; that is, are your source's statements consistent with one another?
2. Do your sources agree with one another?
3. Is your information consistent with things that are common knowledge or that you know from personal experience?

Second, your own reasoning and that of your sources should be logical and should not make inferences not justified by the information. Tests of various types of reasoning are discussed throughout Chapter Seven.

Third, even if your information is reliable and your reasoning logical, it may not interest your listeners, or it may not appeal to motives that are important to them. Try it on a few of your actual listeners or people like them, and then use your own judgment.

Fourth, your material may not be *clear*. Any material you use should help your listeners understand what you are trying to say. If it does not, out it goes. Again, try it on a few of them before you decide.

Fifth, your material should be directly relevant to your thesis or purpose. It may be very interesting, or you may really like it for some reason, but if it is not directly relevant it will cause more trouble than it is worth by muddling your organization and confusing and distracting your listeners from the point you are trying to make.

PREPARING YOUR MATERIAL

Finally, you must actually prepare your material for presentation. Your definitions, individual statistics, testimony, examples, comparisons, and contrasts will be presented orally, so each one should simply be prepared in some form that will remind you of what you are going to say about it. There are two basic considerations: (a) If your notes are too short, you may forget what you are going to say or you may be nervous because you are afraid you are going to forget what you are going to say. (b) If your notes are too long you will begin to sound like you are reading, you will pay too much attention to them and not enough to your audience, and the papers on which your notes are written will be so large or so numerous they will distract your audience. A good rule of thumb is that each idea should be written on a separate card and you should use nothing larger or more flimsy than a 5-inch-by-8-inch index card.

A little more must be said about audiovisual materials, however. Such materials can be a real help in clarifying your explanation. They should be chosen with that purpose in mind; that is, do not use a visual aid just because you have heard that every good speech should have one, and do not choose a visual aid *primarily* for its dramatic effect. To do so is to run the risk of appearing too self-consciously dramatic or of allowing the visual aid to distract listeners from your explanation rather than enhance it.

A girl in one of my speech classes once gave a speech to explain—ah— let's see, I *think* she was explaining how to sew a pants suit, with special attention to pattern-fitting. At any rate, she wore her visual aids and removed them piece by piece during the speech, turning each piece inside out to show how the pattern related to the suit itself. By the end of the speech, she was wearing only a bikini, and the attention of the class was not exactly riveted on what she was saying. As you can imagine, I can vividly recall her visual aids, but I recall only vaguely something about pinning the pattern to the material.

Similarly, another student giving an explanation of karate concluded the speech by removing his shirt and shattering a two-by-four placed across two concrete blocks. Splinters went all over the classroom. I suspect the students in both cases were more interested in enhancing their egos than in enhancing their explanations.

With that word of caution, suppose we consider the many types of visual aids available to you, and the special considerations applicable to each.

Objects, Models, and Demonstrations

If you plan to explain how something works, or if some object plays a central part in your speech, it may be a good idea to bring the object itself to class so that you can point to it and manipulate it. Some common-sense considerations apply here. The object you want to explain may be so small, or have parts so small, that it can only be seen by a few people in the first row or two. If so, it would probably be better to make or find an enlarged model of the subject, or to draw an enlarged diagram. A pocket calculator or digital watch are obvious examples. An object may be so large it will be difficult to get into the classroom, in which case a model or diagram will be more satisfactory. Sometimes the object may be the right size, but its working parts may be concealed. Some automobile transmissions or motorcycle engines may be the right size for display, but a cut-away model or diagram might be more visible.

This problem of visibility (or audibility) is an important consideration in all types of visual aids. A good rule is: If you are not sure, try it. Have a friend or two stand or sit as far from you as the last row of your audience and see if they can see the object or model clearly. Remember that this test is not foolproof, because in the actual speaking situation the people in the last row will be trying to look around the heads of the rest of the people in the audience. Consequently, you may want to devise a way to elevate the model or object so everyone can see it. Or you might consider standing in the middle of the room instead of at the front, if that is approved by your professor. You will have a special problem if you choose that option: You will not be able to face all your audience at any one time. The better solution is to seat your listeners in a semicircle, if possible, and then make sure the visual aid is large enough to be seen by everyone.

The object or model should be as simple as possible, containing only such parts as will clarify your explanation. If you are only going to explain some parts of the object or model, it might be a good idea to arrange it so the other parts are removable. In that way the audience can see how the whole object fits together, but after you remove the irrelevant parts they can concentrate on those you want to explain.

Some similar considerations apply to demonstrations. They must be visible. Do not try to demonstrate a process requiring hand movements so small they cannot be readily observed by everyone. Sometimes a demonstration will require you to lie down as, for example, a demonstration of skiing conditioning exercises might. If so, do not lie down on the floor, because few people will be able to see you. Use a desk, or a table high enough to be seen by everyone.

That example suggests a further consideration. You may find it difficult to speak while you are doing the demonstration, because you may have to turn away from the audience, or get yourself into an awkward position, or it may make you short of breath. The anxiety of facing an audience will make you a little short of breath anyway, so that a few calisthenics, for instance, might put you out completely. If so, get someone else to *do* the demonstration for you while you talk about it. In some cases that will also make your listeners less likely to suspect you are on an ego trip, and you are less likely to get on one.

A special word of caution here: It is seldom advisable to bring animals into the classroom for demonstrations unless they are accustomed to performing before audiences. An animal that is very docile and cooperative in private can become very excited and/or obstinate in public and could effectively sabotage an otherwise well-planned speech. Besides, they sometimes create health and slipping hazards, especially when excited.

Next, try to keep your demonstration as simple as possible. Demonstrations can easily become too complicated to be easily understood, and they can also run on longer than you expect, extending an assigned five-minute speech into ten or fifteen minutes. Time your demonstration, preferably in the presence of some other people. The demonstration that occupies five minutes when you are by yourself can take much longer in the presence of other people. On the other hand, if you are nervous about it and start to hurry, it might take much less time.

Be sure your demonstration will *work*. Rehearse it before other people, and rehearse it in the room where you will present it. Such small matters can create such embarrassing moments: the cord may not reach the outlet, or you may drop a test tube, or the floor may be slick, or you may not be able to get that bolt loose, or the thread you used in the sewing machine may suddenly insist on getting tangled. Sometimes I think machines get nervous in public, too; at least they do not perform very well there. It is a good time to remember Murphy's Law: if anything can go wrong, it will. So be prepared for it.

Finally, use some common sense as to what kinds of demonstrations are legal and appropriate. If you have any doubts, talk to your professor about it. A friend of mine still talks about the student who blew a hole in the rear wall of a classroom while he was demonstrating how to break down a shotgun which was supposedly unloaded. Stories about student speeches dealing with artificial insemination of animals and the conversion of stallions to geldings are rampant among speech professors. Somewhere, sometime, I am sure someone has given a demonstration speech on contraceptive devices. Some professors and some classes might feel some versions of such a speech would be appropriate, but I am sure you can visualize demonstrations on that topic which would have all manner of repercussions. I know one student who brought a great deal of unpleasantness down on his head by demonstrating how to roll a joint. Of course, he had to use real grass because tobacco does not roll like marijuana, right? Wrong. He could have used tea. Do not do anything illegal or potentially dangerous or embarrassing, no matter how loose your professor and your classmates seem to be. If in doubt, ask.

Graphic Art Displays

You may find it impossible to bring an object or model to class or you may want to explain a process that cannot be demonstrated in the classroom, so you may want to draw a diagram or chart instead. Your statistical evidence may give more impact in the form of graphs, tables, or charts. After reading the preceding section, you could probably write this one yourself, because the considerations are so similar. But let me take the time to be specific.

The first consideration is visibility. Make your graphic displays *big*. Little 8-1/2-inch-by-11-inch sheets of notebook paper just will not make it. If you are going to use diagrams, use large sheets of poster board. Think in terms of feet, not inches. Use dark lines and heavy lettering.

"Magic Markers" or crayons are good for the purpose. Ball-point pens or even felt-tipped writing pens will not do—they may be good for writing on bathroom walls, but you will not be standing that close. If possible, have them made by someone who is moderately artistic. If not, use the kind of plastic lettering or drawing aids you can get in the art and engineering section of the bookstore. Be careful about using colors. Most colors do not show up as well as black on white at a distance. Above all, try them. Stand back as far as your furthest listener will be and see if you can read them easily. Get independent opinions from some of your friends. That should make it clear very quickly that you should not try to show pages from books, magazines, and newspapers.

Second, your displays should be as simple as possible. I probably said enough about that in the previous section. You can get an idea of why simplicity is important by comparing some of the illustrations in this book. If a display is too simple, a picture will not be required. On the other hand, it is easy to reach the upper limit of useful complexity.

Third, consider how you are going to display your graphics. They can be taped to a wall or chalkboard, if they are taped securely enough that they do not fall down. A poster display stand will give a really professional appearance if you can borrow one from the art, theater, or audiovisual department. You are taking a real chance if you try to prop a poster on the table with books. It is almost guaranteed to fall down.

I have been talking as if graphics had to be displayed as posters, although there are a variety of other means available. If they are not too complicated, you can draw them on the chalkboard. Some professors and textbook authors advise that such drawings be done as you speak. I do not agree. I have never yet encountered an inexperienced speaker who could handle that well. It is very difficult to draw on the chalkboard and still talk to an audience. I would advise coming to class a little early and putting your drawing up before your speech. That may not be possible, of course, because someone else may want to use the board, too. In that case forget the chalkboard and try something else.

For example, you might consider making photocopies of your graphics and distributing them to your listeners before the speech. There are some problems with that, so you should probably ask your professor before you do it. One problem is that your listeners may study your handouts instead of listening to your speech. You could ask them to leave them turned face down until you are ready to use them, if you can do that gracefully. Another problem is that you may want to point to parts of a chart or diagram, and you cannot do that if each person has his own copy. If your presentation requires pointing, choose a different alternative.

That alternative might be to project your graphics onto a screen. You can probably borrow both the screen and projector from your campus audiovisual center with your professor's approval. Try to schedule this well in advance of your speech so you can be sure of getting the equipment. Also be sure to become familiar with the projector if you are going to operate it. It is probably better to have someone else operate it so you do not have to worry about it during your speech. If you do that, get your operator to rehearse with you so you can be certain he or she knows how to operate the projector and when to change graphics.

You have at least three alternative types from which to choose: opaque, transparency, or slide projectors. The opaque type requires the least preparation, since it will project drawings from paper or material directly from books, magazines, or newspapers. Unfortunately it also projects the poorest images onto the screen. Transparencies will produce a better image, and are not difficult to make. However, they do require some extra preparation, since you will have to put your graphics onto a special transparent material. It is probably worth the extra work, because it makes possible the use of "overlays" to superimpose one graphic on another. If you have access to a 35-millimeter camera with a copying lens, stand, and lights, you can photograph your graphics for use in a slide projector. That approach can produce a very clear image and opens the way for some interesting special effects, but it requires some work and technical knowledge on your part or on the part of someone you con into doing it for you.

Finally, let's consider the kinds of graphics you might use. You might want to use a diagram or picture of an object that is too large or too small or the internal parts of which are not visible. You might want to use a diagram or flow chart of a process such as the assembling of an automobile on an assembly line. You may be able to find such illustrations in an encyclopedia, a textbook, a magazine article, or a book such as *How Things Work*. For some explanations, you may want to display a map of your library, perhaps, or a weather map.

Or you may want to display your statistics in some sort or graph. There are three common types: bar graphs, line graphs, and circle or "pie" graphs. The pie graph is especially useful for displaying percentages, the bar graph for making comparisons among categories, and the line graph for making comparisons over time.

Electronic and Photographic Media

If you have the equipment at your disposal, you can produce audiovisual aids with a great deal of realism and animation. One of my students gave a report on the differences between "restricted" and "elaborated" language in children. She located audiotapes of children describing cartoons, and chose some tapes to illustrate each kind of language.

Another student played brief segments of taped conversations and asked the other students to guess the context in which each conversation was taking place. You can use audiotapes for similar purposes. If you do, be sure to get recordings of good quality and play them back on a machine with adequate power and speakers for a room as large as your classroom. Otherwise you may have to deal with a frustrated and irritated audience. Do not *substitute* the tapes for a large part of your speech; your professor and classmates probably will not look favorably on that.

Another student prepared a report on intense and obscene language. He obtained videotaped footage of the 1968 Democratic Convention in Chicago in which protesters goaded the police into rioting by the use of obscene language and gestures. You may be able to obtain videotapes and a playback unit from your campus educational television center, department of mass communication, audiovisual center, or teaching resources center. Videotape machines are becoming quite common on university campuses. You may even be able to borrow a portable video-tape camera and recorder to make your own tape. Two of my students did, photographing the reactions of students studying in the library when someone else sat down next to them. If you do that sort of thing you had best clear it with your professor and any other authorities who might be concerned.

A videotape camera has one advantage over a movie camera in that you do not have to wait for film to be developed. On the other hand, the recorders and playback units are harder to find than movie cameras and projectors. If you do not have access to videotape equipment, you can make equally effective film strips and 35-millimeter slide presentations. I have seen really effective student film strips and slides depicting littering, incidents of sexism, and high-pressure sales pitches, for example.

The real problem with such audiovisual materials is that you may become so enthralled with the audiovisual presentation that you forget you are giving a speech. The electronic and photographic media should be used only in longer speeches, and you should be careful that they *contribute* to your speech rather than *become* your speech. Ask your professor how extensively you may use such material in any given speech.

Most of this section has concentrated on the use of supporting material in *explanation*. Part of the reason is that the previous chapter dealt with motives, reasoning, and evidence that constitute supporting material in persuasion, so not much needs to be added. But another, more important consideration is that *clear explanation* is the foundation of persuasion. If you can *explain* clearly and vividly your reasons for believing a given proposition, and if those reasons appeal to the motives of your listeners, you really will not have to do anything more in order to persuade them. In fact, anything more you might do would be ethically questionable. Remember from the first chapter that my approach to communication is based on the assumption that listeners should be maximally aware of the bases for their decisions. Clear explanations can produce that sort of awareness.

SUMMARY

When gathering information it is important to take complete and accurate notes, preferably in a form that will allow you to use them as you speak. The search should begin with your own knowledge and continue through experts, textbooks, magazines, reference books, and audiovisual materials available to you, through agencies and organizations interested in your topic, and through a good library. Once there, you may consult books and staff in the reference section, the *Reader's Guide to Periodical Literature*, specialized and/or scholarly indexes to journals and magazines, the card catalog, newspapers (especially the *New York Times* index), and the bibliographies in any books or articles you find as you go along.

In evaluating your material use the criteria for "testimony" listed in Chapter Seven; check your sources for internal consistency, agreement with one another, and agreement with your own and common knowledge; check your own inferences and those of your sources against the tests of reasoning and evidence; and check the interest value, clarity, and relevance of your material.

In preparing your materials for presentation, a number of rules apply. Notes should be neither so sparse as to strain your memory nor so large and numerous as to be distracting. Audiovisual materials should be chosen for their clarifying effect, not merely for their dramatic effect. Objects, models, and demonstrations should be visible, audible, simple, comfortable, workable, legal, and sensible. Graphic art displays should be visible, simple, sturdy (secure), and may make use of a variety of visual media. Electronic and photographic media open new possibilities for realism if used imaginatively, but do not substitute them for your speech.

CHAPTER NINE
Structure and Sequence

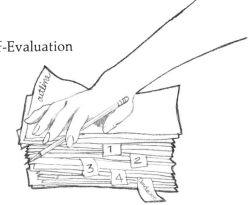

The difference between public speaking and other forms of communication is probably most evident when one considers the problems involved in planning the *structure* of a public speech. In most forms of communication the structure *develops* as the communication event unfolds.

In face-to-face conversation, for example, the participants take turns speaking, so that the conversation takes whatever turns the participants wish. They are free to change topics, and they have the opportunity to ask questions of one another if they do not understand. There is no need to *plan* the conversation before it begins. In fact, conversations frequently take turns that none of the participants anticipate.

Formal group discussions and business meetings have a planned structure or agenda, but that structure seldom goes beyond a specification of the major topics for consideration. Furthermore, if the group decides the agenda is not meeting its needs, members can amend it by spending more time on some items than on others, discarding some items altogether, adding new items, or discarding the agenda entirely.

This is not nearly so true of public speaking, however, because a public speech is basically a *monologue*. Listeners have some opportunity for feedback, of course, but those opportunities are generally limited to certain subtle forms of nonverbal communication, because conventions of American culture, at least, do not favor the audience interrupting the speaker. The advantage is that the speaker presents his or her ideas in their (hopefully) coherent entirety without having them fragmented into a confused and confusing jumble. But that advantage carries a penalty; the speaker must anticipate audience needs and structure the speech in advance to deal with those needs, because listeners cannot very well tell him or her what they do not understand or what they refuse to accept. If listeners fail to understand or accept a crucial part of the message, the entire speech may go awry since the speaker may not learn of the error until the end of the speech.

Consequently, the structure of public speeches requires careful planning. This planning is primarily a matter of anticipating audience needs as the speech develops and of structuring the speech so that it meets those needs as they arise. This is largely a matter of empathy. The source must try to imagine himself or herself in the position of the receiver, to imagine what the receiver will be thinking and feeling at each point in the message, and what the receiver would like to ask or say if free to do so.

The earlier parts of this book have been designed to provide a basis for such empathy. If you are aware of the general principles of communication, aware of the differences among people, and aware of the means of support and explanation, you are well on your way to putting yourself in the place of an audience, even when the audience can give you only limited feedback or no feedback at all. You can usually determine how successfully you have empathized by asking some people who are similar to your prospective audience to listen to your speech or read your paper before you present it. But the empathetic ability I hope you have developed must be applied to this specific problem of speech organization and sequencing.

The remainder of this chapter will be divided into two parts. The first will consider how the *internal* structure of speeches can be organized to accomplish these subordinate purposes on the way to achieving the primary purpose of informing or persuading. The second recognizes that sometimes more than one speech is required to achieve a speaker's purposes and that a given speech occurs in the context of other speeches; therefore, some consideration must be given to the ways in which speeches in sequence affect one another.

INTERNAL STRUCTURE

Organizing a speech is a task you will perform as a speaker. As a listener you may see ways speeches might have been organized more effectively. As a listener you may seek to impose organization on disordered informative speeches so you can better understand them. As a listener you may use the organization of persuasive speeches as a clue to what speakers are trying to do to you and how they are trying to do it. Consequently, as a listener you certainly should not forget what you will learn about organization. But it is in your role as a speaker that skill in organizing speeches will be most crucial, and it is that role in which I wish to address you in this chapter.

Purpose and Structure

Methods of organizing speeches differ considerably depending on whether the speaker's primary purpose is only to inform or whether it is also to persuade. Recall that, in terms of McGuire's analysis described in the introduction to this part of the book,[1] speakers whose primary purpose is only to inform must make certain their listeners *attend to*, *comprehend*, and *retain* the message. Speakers who also intend to persuade must bring their listeners to *yield* to the message and *act* (or intend to act) on it as well.

Each of these five subservient purposes entails different organizational considerations and strategies. Sometimes strategies that will serve one purpose well are not well-suited to another, so that the speaker must make intelligent artistic choices.

The organization itself should not become so noticeable as to be distracting. A speech can be overorganized so that audience understanding depends on following too many complex turns and inter-dependencies, or more time is spent in introduction, transition, and conclusion than is spent in explanation or argument.

Despite these various purposes and the potentially conflicting considerations and strategies that accompany them, at least one general statement can be made before we proceed to specifics: *Good organization follows naturally from the material; it aids attention, comprehension, retention, yielding, and action without becoming noticeable and distracting.*

Suppose we think first about some of the considerations involved in choosing a structure, survey some of the standard structures available, see how outlining can be used to impose a specific structure on material, and consider the functions of the specific organizational devices of introductions, transitions, and conclusions.

Some Structural Considerations

Different considerations apply to each of the five subservient purposes.

Attention   Regarding attention, there are at least three considerations: (1) To capture listener attention, some interesting material ought to be provided at the very beginning of the speech. However, since attention cannot be merely captured and securely caged while the speaker goes on about other business, (2) one ought to try to decide where the attention of the audience is likely to lag and put material of interest at those points. (3) Some method ought to be used to bring listeners to a peak of attention during the conclusion of the speech.

Comprehension   Regarding comprehension there are a number of additional considerations:

(4) Explanation of some parts of the material will depend upon explanation of other parts. Definitions of basic terms are usually necessary at the outset if those terms will be used later in the explanation. Similarly, there may be basic and relatively simple concepts that must be explained first because their understanding is necessary to the understanding of more complex concepts to come later. For example, it is useful for the listener to know about the composition of the atmosphere before encountering an explanation of combustion and useful for the listener to understand combustion before coming upon an explanation of the production of carbon monoxide. On the other hand,

you may want to explain an overriding or very inclusive concept at the outset and then explain its component concepts; you might, for example, define "atmospheric pollution" in general and then explain the various types or causes.

It may be possible to take advantage of knowledge the audience already has. You may be able to begin with what they know and lead them gently into the unknown. If they know about something very similar to what you are going to explain, it may help to describe the similarities and then explain the differences.

(6) Remember that the most difficult explanation should come when your listeners are best able to cope with it. That will probably be near the beginning of the speech, after allowing a brief warm-up. It is probably best, if it can be arranged, to follow the explanation of basic terms and concepts with the part of the explanation you consider to be most difficult.

Retention   Enhancing retention of the information involves three further considerations:

(7) The research indicates fairly clearly that the first and last parts of a speech are better remembered than is the material in the middle, all else being equal. There is a strong suggestion that the first part of a message is remembered *longer* than the last part. Consequently, the material might reasonably be arranged so that the most important information comes early, the next most important comes late, and the least important comes in the middle.

(8) If the speech is divided into parts and if the audience knows what they are and understands how they relate to one another, they will be better able to remember the information. Not at all incidentally, this will also facilitate initial understanding if they learn of the divisions at the beginning of the speech. The psychological principle is well established and easy to demonstrate. To call San Quentin Prison from my office phone, I would have to dial 914154541460. That number would be rather difficult to remember, even for someone addicted to calling San Quentin every day. However, it is much simpler to remember if one understands that the number consists of 9 to get an outside line, 1 to reach the direct distance dialing equipment, 415 to reach the San Francisco area, 454 to reach the San Quentin exchange, and 1460 to reach the prison. Thus, the number is easier to remember when written 9-1-415-454-1460, especially for someone familiar with the idiosyncrasies of Ma Bell. Since digit span difficulty increases up to a practical maximum of about seven (plus or minus two) digits or items for the general population, the general rule is that the number of major divisions in a message and the number of subdivisions under each major division should be balanced so as to be as few as possible, generally in the range from two to four. I say "balanced"

because if there are fewer major divisions, there are likely to be more subdivisions, and vice versa.

(9) It is a good plan to remind the listeners at times of what you have said and of what you have yet to say. These internal summaries ought to occur at least between the major points in the body of the speech, and a summary ought to be provided in the conclusion.

Acceptance   The considerations related to the purpose of achieving acceptance (yielding) are even more complex:

(10) If a speaker tells the listeners at the outset that his or her purpose is to persuade them to accept a position which is at that point unacceptable to them, they may prepare themselves to reject his arguments and may refute each one in turn. This is especially true if the speaker is somewhat unattractive to the audience for one reason or another or if they are especially opposed to his or her point of view. If the audience likes the speaker and if the position advocated is not too different from their own, they may be gratified that he or she values their opinions enough to want to persuade them. In that case he or she will probably be more successful in stating the thesis, purpose, and major arguments clearly at the outset of the speech and proceeding to support each argument in turn. However, a speaker not so favored may gain acceptance more easily by presenting the arguments as if they were primarily informational, *leading* the audience instead of *pushing* them to accept the conclusions. The audience may move to the speaker's position without ever being told what they *should* believe.

This is closely allied to (11): the speaker may well begin with those propositions that the audience already accepts and lead them as gently as possible to accept those they initially reject. This can be done in successive small steps from their initial position to one the speaker hopes they will accept, or their initial beliefs can be used as premises that lead logically to the conclusions. In either case the speaker avoids the unattractive appearance of attempting to impose beliefs on others.

(12) A further question is whether the strongest arguments should be placed first or last. Obviously one should not use *weak* arguments, but the arguments will differ in effectiveness. I have already suggested that the strongest arguments will be best remembered if they are placed *either* first or last. If a speaker's credibility is not extremely high, it will probably raise that credibility to begin with a very persuasive argument. Once credibility is established, the audience may not be so hostile to the rest of the speech. On the other hand, if credibility is not in question and if the speech is short enough that one can depend on having the listeners' attention at the end, it may be advantageous to build to a climax near the end. This arrangement is especially useful if opposing arguments are

going to be expressed by another speaker immediately afterward. The opposing speaker will have a more difficult job if that strongest argument is fresh in the minds of the audience.

(13) A persuasive speech can generally be viewed as a *solution to a problem*. The speaker will usually demonstrate some reason for a change and demonstrate that the proposal is indeed a solution. However, there are two possible approaches: one may demonstrate that problems exist, describe the proposal, and demonstrate that the proposal will solve the problem; or one may describe the proposal and then demonstrate its advantages over the existing system. A major consideration is whether the audience is likely to be initially hostile to the proposal. If they are, it is probably better to emphasize the severity of the problems at the outset. Otherwise, it may be more effective to present the proposal first and then dwell upon its advantages, especially if there are no glaring problems in the present system.

(14) Another consideration concerns the point at which one undertakes to refute opposing arguments. If the speaker has reason to believe that the listeners are preoccupied with opposing arguments before the message, dealing with the opposing arguments immediately will probably produce more acceptance. Otherwise they may not pay much attention to attempts at constructive persuasion. What he may want to avoid at this point, however, is introducing opposing arguments that the audience has never encountered or reminding them of objections that would not be salient if they were not mentioned. The objections refuted at the outset, for greatest acceptance, will be only those of which the receivers are already quite aware and which might interfere with their attention to the constructive part of the message. Objections they might think of later are probably more effectively dealt with after the constructive argument has been presented and, hopefully, after one has secured from them some sort of commitment to the proposal.

(15) Should you cite the source of information before or after the information is presented? If the credibility of the source of the information is higher than your own, cite the source first; otherwise give the information and then cite its source. Research seems to indicate that if the audience knows the source before they encounter the information, their opinions of the source will influence their acceptance or rejection of the information, but their opinions of the source have little effect if they hear the information first.

Action   Finally we come to three approaches to consider when you want the listeners to perform some action:

(16) This probably calls for a clear, overt appeal for some specific action, most reasonably at the end of the speech.

(17) Recalling the discussion of the effects of commitment, it seems clear that getting listeners to commit themselves to the desired action verbally and publicly at the end of a speech will make it more likely that they will later actually perform that action. Of course, this is exactly the opposite of what listeners want if they are concerned about making critical decisions, since a public commitment will make it more difficult for them to respond freely and objectively to subsequent information.

(18) Closely related is the need to warn listeners that they may encounter arguments intended to dissuade them from performing the action and to show the weaknesses of those potential arguments (or at least refute *some* of the possible arguments). This concept of forewarning will be considered in more detail in the section dealing with the ways in which speeches in a sequence affect one another.

Some Standard Structures

It is important to consider the speaker's overriding purpose as we confront the various alternative structures available. The speaker whose primary purpose is to *inform* will deal with noncontroversial "facts," creating *new beliefs* for the listeners on the assumption that they will accept those beliefs if they only attend, comprehend, and retain them. Consequently, he or she will choose those speech structures that best *fit the material and adapt it to what the listeners already know.*

The speaker whose primary purpose includes *persuasion* may be dealing with controversial *beliefs* ("questions of fact"), *questions of value*, or *questions of policy*. To deal with values, he or she must deal with beliefs and in proposing policies must treat both beliefs and values. Consequently, he or she will choose structures that will not only *present the material coherently but will also facilitate listener acceptance* of that material.

Informative structures   Some of the available structures are generally considered to be useful in explanation because they do not make explicit provision for listener acceptance. They may be used to persuade as well as inform, but not necessarily so. (I will have more to say about that in a moment.)

(1) *Chronological* structures are those in which the material is described in a time order. A past event, for instance, may be described in the order in which it occurred. A process may be described in the order in which it ordinarily occurs or, for "how-to-do-it" speeches, in the order in which it should be performed. If a speaker chooses a chronological structure, it indicates that he believes the order is important to his listeners' understanding the event or process.

(2) *Flashback* structures are sometimes used to create dramatic effect and thus to create interest and attention. You have probably encountered this structure in short stories, novels, movies, and dramatic television programs. Sometimes it is important for a speaker's narration of an event to build to a climax. But events do not always occur in a climactic order. In a typical crime drama, for instance, if the audience were presented with a description of events in the order in which they occurred, they would know who was guilty long before the end of the narrative, and the suspense would be resolved too early. Much of the narrative might be anticlimactic. In describing the events leading up to the bombing of Pearl Harbor, you might decide that some of the earlier events are more important (perhaps more puzzling or mysterious) than the bombing itself, especially since your listeners would already know the *end* of the narrative. In that case it might be reasonable to use the flashback structure. Note, however, that this structure almost invariably complicates comprehension by disrupting the actual sequence of events, so that the gain in audience attention must be considerable to justify its use.

(3) *Ascending and descending* structures are similar, except that the order is based on some dimension other than time. Such descriptions may proceed from least to most important (or vice versa), from largest to smallest (or vice versa), from most to least colorful (or vice versa), or in order on any dimension the speaker considers important to listener understanding. Choice of such a structure, of course, implies that the speaker believes both the dimension and the order of progression contribute to clarity, and the choice commits the speaker to maintaining and completing the chosen ordering.

(4) *Spatial* structures may be used to describe objects, physical structures such as buildings or bridges, geographical areas, or anything else in which spatial representation is the important consideration. The ordering may follow any spatial dimension: near to far, left to right, low to high, east to west, inside to outside, and the like. Sometimes spatial and chronological orderings will happily coincide, as in the description of an assembly line, a road race, or the progress of a storm across the United States, for example.

(5) *Causal* structures are to be preferred when chains of causality are most important to listener understanding. You might use the *cause-to-effect* order when you know listeners are interested in the future consequences of some present condition. I have used it in describing the likely effects of adopting new communication technology, such as two-way cable television or computer-assisted communication. The *effect-to-cause* order might be used by a speaker who believes listeners are interested in the causes of present conditions such as the energy shortage or inflation. Either may be useful in explaining a process, as long as the

causal relationships are of primary importance to the explanation. Sometimes—even frequently—causal structures coincide with chronological and spatial structures and reinforce one another to the advantage of clarity.

(6) *Reflective* or *inductive* structures may be used when it seems advantageous to encourage listeners to arrive at general principles or conclusions on their own rather than being provided with explicit statements of those principles or conclusions. (The explicit statements will probably be provided near the end of the speech, of course.) Both empirical research and the experience of competent speakers suggest that such structures make comprehension more difficult. However, they have the advantage of inviting listeners to participate more actively in the reasoning process; they must expend some effort rather than listening passively as they are "spoon-fed." It is fairly well established that active participation facilitates learning and that the expenditure of effort makes the products of the effort seem more valuable. Consequently, although these structures make *comprehension* more difficult, they are likely to produce increased *retention*. Obviously, then, they should be used in cases in which comprehension is easier to achieve than retention. Such structures are also especially useful if the speaker wants to explain the issues involved in a controversial question, but for one reason or another does not want to advocate a specific position—that is, when he or she wants to explain rather than persuade.

(7) *"Topical"* structures are those formed out of, or dictated by, some peculiarities of the material to be discussed. They are generated by the internal structure of the material. Again, describing the issues involved in a controversial question may not lend itself to other structures, which is one possible instance when a topical structure may be used, perhaps combined with reflective or inductive structure. A speaker trying to explain why people sometimes become profoundly depressed, for instance, might decide to discuss *psychological* and *physiological* explanations of depression. The individual explanations (the answers to the question why?) lend themselves to the effect-to-cause structure, but the topics of major divisions come from somewhere else—specifically, from the nature of the material. A speaker discussing the general concept of depression might want to discuss *who* is depressed, *when* they are depressed, what the *consequences* may be, and what one can *do* about it. Again, those divisions are *not* generated by any of the other structures I have discussed. Rather, they are topics that make sense only because of the nature of the matter under consideration. In fact, the "topical" structure is just one of those "et cetera" categories all lists must have as a place to put cases that do not fit anywhere else.

Persuasive structures   Persuasive speeches advocate controversial beliefs ("facts"), values, and/or policies.* Some writers believe these three types of propositions require different types of analysis that yield different types of speech structure. In an earlier chapter, however, I expressed the opinion that persuaders always try to get their listeners to *do* something: sometimes to change their beliefs or values and sometimes to perform overt (observable) actions or to be prepared to perform such actions. Furthermore, I have pointed out that changes in beliefs and values always have at least the potential to produce changes in overt actions. Consequently, I am going to discuss persuasive structures as if they are always designed to support a proposed change in the listeners' *policies*: sometimes proposed changes in the policy of maintaining their beliefs, sometimes in the policy of maintaining their values, and sometimes in the policies governing their overt actions.

As we consider the available persuasive structures, it should become clear that one of the most important decisions speakers have to make is *when* to tell listeners what they are advocating. That decision will frequently have implications for their choice of message structure. The rule is easy to state but more difficult to apply. *The more hostile an audience is to a speaker's proposal, the more likely they are to reject it and the supporting arguments if they hear it early in the speech.*

Now, regardless of the persuasive structure a speaker chooses, he or she can *always* state the proposal in the introduction. On the other hand, most (not all) of the structures allow the speaker to postpone stating his proposal until late in the speech, even until the conclusion. In some cases the speaker may not state it at all. Still, some of the available structures are especially useful to speakers who know their listeners will initially strongly oppose the proposal and who consequently want to postpone revealing it. Obviously speakers in such situations will want to give special consideration to such structures.

This approach may sound very manipulative and unethical. Isn't it always to the listeners' advantage to know the speaker's proposal? Isn't it unfair for the speaker to take advantage of the listeners by concealing it? My answer is, *not necessarily*. It is to the listeners' advantage to maintain open minds to the speaker's arguments, to postpone closure until they have heard all the evidence. A mind that is bound, closed and locked like

---

*Some writers add a fourth type of persuasive proposition, writing about propositions of definition, fact, value, and policy. Propositions of definition can be controversial, of course, but I believe that on closer inspection they prove to be either propositions of belief ("fact") or policy. In arguing about the definition of *rhetoric*, for instance, one might argue either that *rhetoric* does mean (is generally used to mean) "discourse devoid of significance," or that it *should* be used to mean "the art of informing or persuading." The first would be a proposition of belief ("fact"), and the second a proposition of policy.

a diary is less useful than a loose-leaf mind in which the pages are securely in place but capable of being changed. A critical decision is not facilitated by being hypercritical of everything a speaker has to say. Of course, one's mind ought not to be so open that anyone can come along and dump trash into it on the pretext of being purely informative, but if hearing a speaker's proposal is going to produce such bias in a listener that he or she is incapable of distinguishing between trash and treasure, that person may be better off not hearing it immediately. Obviously, this is a difficult area in which to make sweeping ethical pronouncements, and I am going to decline to do so. Now, however, let's consider some persuasive structures from which a speaker may choose.

(8) All the *informative* structures I have described can be used as persuasive structures as well. Someone speaking in favor of capital punishment might use a chronological narration of an event such as the Manson cult murders. A speaker urging reform of mental hospitals might find a spatial description of a ward at such a hospital most persuasive. Arguments can be arranged in ascending order to achieve emotional impact. One can point out the causes of present undesirable conditions when calling for a change or can point to the likely effects of present or proposed policies. Use of reflective or inductive structures can lead listeners to conclusions the speaker wants them to arrive at, or a speaker might argue three or four "topics" or issues that arise out of the peculiar nature of a specific controversial question. Because these structures may be used for purely informative purposes, they do not in and of themselves reveal a speaker's persuasive purpose. Thus, they are especially useful when the speaker wants to delay announcing a position to a hostile audience.

(9) The *need–plan, problem–solution,* or *disease–remedy* structure is a classic persuasive sequence; in a sense it is the norm from which the others depart. Using it, you proceed by dealing in turn with the "stock issues" to be argued in a proposition of policy. First, you demonstrate that there is a *need for a change* from the present policy. Then you present a proposed *plan* for change, explain how the *plan will meet the need* or solve each of the existing problems, mention any *additional advantages* the proposed plan may have beyond solving the problems mentioned, and then *refute* objections to the plan you believe the listeners may have already heard or may hear in the future. If the proposed plan involves some specific future overt action on the part of the listeners, you try to secure their active *commitment* to that action in the conclusion. As you can easily see, this structure does not allow for subtlety. In using it, you begin laying your cards on the table from the opening of your speech; in fact, you lay them out in order within suits so that the other players can more easily appraise your hand. The result is a very coherent persuasive message, one in which you say, in essence, "I have very sound arguments here which I believe will bear the test of

objective scrutiny." If the audience responds with objectivity, a well-reasoned critical decision will result.

(10) Monroe's motivated sequence is so closely related to the need–plan or problem–solution structure that it may be a mistake to discuss them separately.[2] It consists of a sequence of steps: an Attention Step, a Need Step, a Satisfaction Step, a Visualization Step, and an Action Step. A speaker is advised to get the attention of the listeners, present them with a need, suggest a plan for satisfying the need, help them to visualize how the plan will work, and then try to get them committed to action. Arnold says, "When used for persuasive purposes this sequence is, of course, but an outline of the *psychological stages* that are advisable when using the problem–solution pattern. The names Monroe attached to his 'steps' ... identify *effects to be accomplished* at various stages of communication."[3] Personally I do not like the idea that getting attention is a "step" or a "stage." The same is true of *visualization*, if that word is applied too literally and specifically. Ideally listeners will be attending and visualizing throughout the speech. With that reservation, however, the motivated sequence does seem to be at least a useful way of thinking about the problem–solution structure.

(11) The *comparative advantages* structure is another straightforward approach to be used when there is no "crying need" for a change. The present system may be limping along without serious problems, but the speaker may believe there is room for improvement. Consequently, he or she first describes a proposed plan and then proceeds to demonstrate that the plan has more advantages and fewer disadvantages than the present system.

(12) The *elimination of alternatives* structure is sometimes used because there is no "present system" or because everyone agrees the present system is inadequate. For example, a speaker proposing a particular location and structure for a bridge, if everyone agrees a bridge is needed, really does not have a "present system" to deal with. What he or she needs is a list of the competing locations and structures in order to explain why each is unsatisfactory, culminating with a description of the advantages of his or her own proposal. It is important to be certain that all the possible (or at least all the practical) alternatives are included. One of my students gave a speech arguing that Truman did a good thing in deciding to bomb Hiroshima and Nagasaki since "the" alternative (invasion by ground troops) would have prolonged the war and produced many Allied casualties. However, she neglected to mention another alternative—dropping an atomic bomb on an uninhabited island as a demonstration for the Japanese. If such omissions are pointed out, they can be embarrassing to a speaker. If they are not pointed out, they can result in listeners making a choice among one set of alternatives when better alternatives are available.

(13) The *mock problem-solving* structure incorporates the elimination of alternatives. In this approach the speaker first *surveys the problems*, then *lists the possible solutions*, then *evaluates each solution* in turn, and finally *advocates one solution*. A "real" problem-solving approach, of course, is one in which the problem solvers are open-mindedly searching for a solution to a set of problems. I call this a "mock" problem-solving approach when used by a persuader because the persuader, by definition, already has one solution he or she wants to advocate.

Outlining

After a structure has been chosen, it will probably be helpful to apply that structure to your specific topic by constructing an outline. This helps to make certain that: (a) the divisions are clear, (b) the divisions are easy to understand, (c) the divisions are more or less equal and each contains about the same amount of time or space to cover as every equivalent division, (d) the divisions under a single head are mutually exclusive, in that they do not overlap, (e) the divisions under a single head are comprehensive, in that they cover all the material to be expected under that head, (f) all the divisions under a given head are actually related to that head and to one another, (g) all the divisions under a given head are actually subordinate to that head, (h) the divisions under a given head are parallel to one another both logically and in the way they are worded (with respect to voice, number, person, tense, sentence structure, and the like).

I will not attempt to prescribe any specific outline form. I will offer two examples. The first is a relatively acceptable sentence outline of an informative speech using chronological structure to explain how to perform a process. Since the speech was never presented, I cannot report on its effectiveness. That may be just as well.

> THESIS: Approaching the corner correctly, choosing the best line, and steering with the accelerator are necessary to drift a sports car through a simple corner at maximum speed without wiping out.
>
> DEFINITIONS: (As necessary for the audience)
>   I. Approaching the corner correctly involves braking, shifting, and placing the car correctly on the road.
>   A. Correct braking is begun as late as possible, but completed before entering the corner.

B. Correct shifting involves use of the tachometer and gearbox.
   1. Lugging and overrevving are avoided by paying close attention to the revolutions per minute indicated by the tachometer.
   2. Usable power is maintained by choosing the lowest gear you will use in accelerating out of the corner, so that the engine will be operating above its torque peak but well below its power peak.
C. Correct placement involves locating the car at the outside of the curve, pointed at an angle toward the inside.

II. The best line begins and ends at the outside of the curve and approaches the inside at a point near the apex, which depends on the location of the straightaways.
   A. If the straightaway precedes the curve, the best line is found by braking late and cutting the corner after the apex so as to maintain speed as long as possible.
   B. If the straightaway follows the curve, the best line is found by braking early and cutting the corner before the apex so as to gain speed for the straightaway as early as possible.
   C. If there are no straightaways at either end, or straightaways at both ends, the best line is a compromise between (A) and (B).

III. Steering when the car is in a four-wheel drift or power slide is accomplished primarily by use of the accelerator, using the steering wheel for minor corrections. (A car is drifting when it is sliding sideways at an angle to the road with the front end pointed toward the inside of the curve and the front wheels pointed toward the outside.)
   A. In a drift, accelerating will slide the rear wheels further out, increasing the slip angle of the car and forcing it toward the inside of the curve.
   B. In a drift, decelerating will decrease the slip angle, forcing the car toward the outside of the curve.
   C. In a drift, too much acceleration will force the rear wheels out too far, causing the car to spin.

CONCLUSION: The novice racing driver who knows how to set a car into a corner and steer it through the correct line by delicate use of the accelerator has only one thing to remember: if all else fails, aim for the hay bales.

This second example is an outline of a speech intended to be persuasive as well as informative. It uses the need-plan or problem–solution structure but does not include an appeal for commitment to a specific course of action. Obviously, the outline is for a speech longer than those you are likely to give in class.

THESIS: We should all support a comprehensive system of compulsory national health insurance.

I. There is a need for such a system.

    A. Medical expenses are capable of rendering almost anyone unable to pay.

        1. Few families can meet the cost of serious medical illness without outside help.

        2. Each year a sizeable number of families incur medical expenses exceeding their entire annual incomes.

        3. Medical costs are rising much faster than the cost of living in general.

        4. Low-income families are those least likely to have voluntary insurance coverage for catastrophic illness.

        5. Even those families who do have voluntary medical insurance usually have limited coverage for catastrophic illnesses.

           a. Some medical insurance plans limit the length of a hospital stay for which they will pay.

           b. Sometimes medical insurance plans limit the total dollar amount of their liabilities.

    B. Those who are unable to pay still receive medical care through charity, absorption of their unpaid bills in increased prices, or government relief.

        1. Voluntary charity accounts for a small percentage of medical expenses not covered by insurance or direct payments from patients.

        2. The fact that doctors and hospitals charge their losses from the indigent onto the cost of the care of the solvent sick accounts for a large proportion of medical expenses not paid by insurance or by the patients who incur them.

        3. Government relief already accounts for a large proportion of medical expenses not paid by insurance or by patients who incur them.

C. These present methods of payment are disadvantageous.
　　1. Each of the methods has its own peculiar disadvantages.
　　　　a. Charity
　　　　　　(1) is inefficient in terms of a cost/benefit ratio,
　　　　　　(2) is undependable,
　　　　　　(3) is so degrading and embarrassing it is frequently refused,
　　　　　　(4) is essentially regressive since tax-deductible contributions to charity are most advantageous to those in high-income brackets.
　　　　b. Absorption of unpaid bills in higher medical prices
　　　　　　(1) contributes to inflation,
　　　　　　(2) compels people to pay higher prices at times when they can least afford it, and
　　　　　　(3) is partially regressive in that it hits hardest those who are barely able to pay.
　　　　c. Government relief
　　　　　　(1) is a hodge-podge patchwork of federal, state, and local programs, and
　　　　　　(2) except for Medicare, it covers only those who are on relief.
　　2. The methods taken together have some general disadvantages.
　　　　a. There is a lack of coordination among the three methods.
　　　　b. The cost is high because of duplication of services, facilities, and administration.
　　　　c. Those who are willing to do so are allowed to forego medical insurance coverage, taking a calculated risk knowing that their medical expenses will be paid somehow.

II. The following plan constitutes a comprehensive program of compulsory medical insurance.
　　A. Everyone will be required to contribute premiums to a federal health insurance program to maintain a basic level of coverage on him (her) self and dependents.
　　B. The premiums will be graduated according to ability to pay.
　　C. An office of health insurance will be established to collect these premiums and make payments to doctors, hospitals, and laboratories.
　　D. This office of health insurance will have the power to regulate medical prices for participating doctors, hospitals, and laboratories.

    E. Patients who wish will be free to obtain supplemental private insurance coverage, to contract with nonparticipating doctors, hospitals, and laboratories, and to obtain at their own expense medical service beyond those provided by the federal program.

    F. Patients will be allowed to forego paying their federal premiums if they obtain satisfactory coverage from private insurance companies.

III. This plan will solve the problems mentioned, in that

    A. The program will eliminate the specific disadvantages of charity, since

        1. it will be more efficient,

        2. it will be more dependable,

        3. it will be available to everyone equally without admission of indigence, and

        4. it will be a progressive rather than a regressive assessment.

    B. The program will eliminate the specific disadvantages of absorption of unpaid bills in higher medical prices, since

        1. it will be anti-inflationary in that basic medical prices will be regulated,

        2. costs will be paid when people are healthy rather than when they are sick, and

        3. it will be a progressive assessment.

    C. The program will eliminate the disadvantages of government relief, since

        1. one federal agency and program will consolidate the present patchwork,

        2. everyone will be covered.

    D. The program will eliminate the general disadvantages, since

        1. it will provide coordination of payments which the present three methods do not provide.

        2. it will eliminate the cost of duplication of services, facilities, and administration,

        3. it will require contributions from everyone according to his ability to pay.

IV. The plan has the following advantages in addition to solving the problems mentioned:

    A. It will provide individuals with a greater sense of security.

    B. It will allow individuals to feel they are providing for their own medical expenses.

    C. It will improve the quality of medical services in impoverished areas.

V. The plan avoids the typical charges of those who oppose federal medical programs, in that:
  A. it will not interfere in the patient–doctor relationship;
  B. it will not impose government control over medical practice, only over medical fees, and then only in the case of participating doctors, hospitals, and clinics, and then only in the case of certain medical procedures;
  C. it will not lead to excessive use of medical facilities, since only basic and necessary medical procedures will be covered; and
  D. it will not lead to the destruction of free enterprise in the field of health insurance, since private insurance companies will be free to compete with the government program.

Communicating the Structure

Once you have chosen a general structure and translated the material into that structure by dividing it and arranging it in a sequence appropriate to the structure, the remaining problem is to indicate that structure to the audience without being too obvious and clumsy about it. The basic procedure is to indicate the structure in the introduction, use transitions to let the audience know when you are moving from one point to another, and summarize the major points in the conclusion.

This procedure is designed to achieve the greatest *comprehension*. Considerations involving *acceptance*, especially, may call for modifying the initial statement of structure to make it less explicit, thus avoiding alienating an audience by presenting the proposal before they are ready for it. Introductions and conclusions are used to achieve purposes other than communicating structure, of course, and I will mention those other purposes in the course of the discussion.

Introductions Actually, introductions serve a multitude of purposes in addition to that of clarifying organization. You can try to make the audience like you and respect your opinions sometimes by the use of humor, almost always by emphasizing areas of agreement and, when possible, by allowing them to discover the "credentials" that qualify you to discuss the topic, if you can do this without giving the impression of bragging. The introduction is also the first point at which you can try to capture the attention and interest of the listeners, but you do not "capture" it in the sense that it can be securely caged and then left alone. Instead, you will have to use devices to gain attention at the outset of the speech and devices to maintain it throughout. Arousing audience curiosity and demonstrating the relevance and importance of the topic or proposal are two of those devices most often used in the introduction.

It is also the point at which you can introduce such background material and definitions as the audience will need to understand the remainder of the speech. In an explanatory speech it is probably best to state the *thesis* in the introduction. The thesis is a one-sentence summary of the entire speech. In a persuasive speech the thesis is the statement of the position that you would like the listeners to accept. As I pointed out before, it is not as effective to state the thesis of a persuasive speech in the introduction if the listeners will be so hostile to it as to interfere with their acceptance or rational evaluation of the arguments that follow. The same is true of the statement of the purpose. Its appearance in the introduction will probably clarify an informational speech, but it may interfere with acceptance and reasonable evaluation of a persuasive speech. Finally, the major divisions of the speech may be somehow indicated in the introductions, except in a persuasive speech in which a statement of major arguments will often put a hostile audience on the defensive.

Transitions   Transitions are always important, but they are especially important in the case in which a persuader has chosen to forego the statements of thesis, purpose, and major divisions. The intent in such a case is to *lead* the audience to a conclusion, and the transitions serve as the signposts by which they are led. Probably the worst transition is "Now I am going to my second major point," but the next worse is "Let us consider, secondly . . . ." Of course, you will find them in profusion throughout this book, but hopefully you will be more imaginative than I have been.

Transitions, or at least the points at which they appear, are also good places for interest and attention material. Of course, the entire speech should be interesting, but just in case the audience is not electrified and totally enthralled, the points of transition offer themselves as convenient places to pay some extra attention to attention.

Conclusions   The conclusion can serve at least two functions; it can *summarize* and *provide a climax* for the speech. Too often the message dies at the end of the body, and the conclusion becomes merely an obituary. Instead, the most effective conclusion is one that brings the listeners to a peak of attention and interest at the same time as it summarizes the major points. You should look for ways to prevent the speech from giving the appearance of ending; it should, instead, remain open, inviting the audience to become involved with its material. Question-and-answer sessions are one standard, but not very imaginative, means of allowing the audience to become actively involved. You should search your material carefully to find others especially appropriate.

The conclusion of a *persuasive* speech will almost certainly be more effective if it contains an appeal for a *specific, immediate,* and *committing* action. If the audience will actually do something at the conclusion of the speech, they will later feel obliged to justify having done it and will help persuade themselves even after the speech is over. It is much more effective if the action taken is one that would be difficult to justify on any grounds other than rational agreement with the speaker, so that the audience cannot later rationalize away their commitment. Beyond the advantage of helping to commit the listeners, there is some evidence that such an appeal will cause them to have greater respect for the speaker. Apparently they view a speaker who makes an appeal for action as a "doer," not merely a "talker," perceiving him or her as more sincere and active than if there were no such appeal.

There is one case in which the appeal for commitment may well come earlier in the speech, however. If the speaker has chosen to put the constructive arguments first and then refute opposing arguments, the appeal for commitment might reasonably come after constructive argument and before refutation. The procedure is to persuade the listeners, get commitment, and then innoculate the listeners against counterarguments that might come later. After commitment he is less likely to catch some of the disease as a result of the innoculation.

SEQUENCING OF SPEECHES

Sequencing and timing of messages is important whenever an audience encounters a series of messages, whether those messages are all from the same source or from different sources. Messages can affect each other directly. They can affect each other as a result of having common sources. They can serve as mediators that allow sources to affect each other. And in combination with feedback they provide the means by which one audience can affect a source, modifying that source's subsequent messages to other audiences.

Forewarning or Immunization

It appears that audiences can encounter messages on opposite sides of a question and encounter them in fairly close succession without the first influencing the second to any appreciable extent. That is true if they merely hear or read the messages. However, if the receivers *commit* themselves in some way after the first message or if they are *forewarned* that counterargument will follow, then they are likely to be less responsive to a second message contradicting the first.

Most of the research dealing with forewarning has been done by William McGuire or by someone testing his theories.[4] Forewarning and refutations seem to become more effective if the receivers have some time between the first and second messages. McGuire theorizes that forewarning acts as a sort of "innoculation," and receivers need some time to construct "belief defenses" against the countermessage. It is interesting that forewarning appears to work just as well if the arguments that the receivers later encounter are not even those mentioned and refuted. In fact, it seems to work best if some of the arguments encountered have actually been refuted and some have not. Furthermore, the effect seems to be enhanced if the speaker can get the listeners to actively participate in constructing refutations for counterarguments. A speaker taking full advantage of our knowledge to this point would say something like this:

> Look, you're going to run into arguments on the other side of this question. I'll tell you what some of them are and what's wrong with some of them, but I wish you'd help me think up refutations for some of the others. Also, since I can't begin to tell you what all the opposing arguments may be, try to keep alert to what's wrong with any new arguments you may hear.

Although the effectiveness of most types of persuasion decreases as time passes, the effectiveness of this sort of immunization appears to *increase*. There are two important qualifications. One is that there is some evidence listeners who are forewarned may begin changing their beliefs in the direction of the counterattack apparently so that the counterattack will not be so disparate from their own opinions. Getting strong commitment from the listeners *before* they are forewarned will reduce that effect. The second caution is that refutation seems to be far more effective if it comes *before* the counterattack rather than afterward.

Messages Affect Sources

When the same source produces two or more messages, an audience aware of the preceding messages will respond to the one at hand in a way that depends at least in part upon what they thought of the others. If the earlier messages caused the audience to perceive the sources as less credible, their suspicions regarding speaker credibility will be reflected in a reluctance to accept what he or she says now. Furthermore, messages the listeners have encountered from other sources will affect their responses to the one at hand to the extent that the previous messages are relevant and salient. Their reaction to the message at hand will also affect their responses to the present source and his or her future messages. It is not entirely a matter of getting there first; reputation and subsequent persuasive effectiveness can suffer even if one speaks *before* a more respected speaker. This chaining can continue from speech to speech and speaker to speaker longer than anyone cares to observe.

Audiences Affect Other Audiences

Finally, one audience can interact with another when they encounter the same speaker. The speaker states opinions before the first audience. They use whatever feedback channels are available to them to indicate that they like some of what the speaker says and dislike the rest. He or she is likely to drop or underemphasize what they disliked and increase the emphasis on what they liked when speaking to the next audience. The first audience has affected what the second hears, and they, partly as a result of what they have heard, will affect subsequent speakers and speeches. Again, the chain is endless. Audiences are not "passive." They work actively to change the opinions of speakers they hear, to change speeches those speakers produce in the future, which change future audiences so they respond differently to subsequent speakers.

Sequencing in Practice

I have said elsewhere that communication is a social disease with no known cure. Given these complicated effects of speeches upon one another—forewarning effects, commitment effects, effects of prior, intervening, and subsequent refutation on the credibility of a speaker, and the effects of audience feedback on a speaker's own opinions, which he or she, in turn, transmits to other audiences—it is easy to see that it is also a highly contagious (communicable?) social disease. The speaker who is so naive as to ignore all these effects of speeches in sequence, who fails to consider what previous speakers have told the listeners and what subsequent speakers will tell them, is going to be constantly surprised at audience reactions during and after his or her speeches.

Sophisticated speakers will take the trouble to find out what previous messages the listeners have encountered that are relevant to their topic, and will take the time to deal with those previous messages in their own speeches. They may find that they can build upon information and opinions the listeners have acquired from previous messages, or they may find that they must correct erroneous information or refute prior opinions contrary to their own. Whatever they find, they will gain a better idea of how to support and structure their own speeches.

Furthermore, sophisticated speakers will take the time to try to anticipate future information and opinions to which listeners may be exposed and will take the trouble to prepare listeners for those subsequent encounters, whether such encounters will reinforce or contradict their own speeches. Sometimes this "anticipation" will take the form of pure conjecture, but sometimes they may speak to groups that schedule their meetings far enough in advance that speakers can actually find out who or what will follow their speeches. That will be important if they want the effects of their speeches to endure and will be even more important if they ever speak to the same group again.

Finally, sophisticated speakers will be aware that the audience to which they are preparing to speak will produce feedback that will affect their own opinions, perhaps more than they will affect the listeners'. Speakers should be prepared to take that risk. It is, after all, a perennial risk when speakers and listeners expose themselves to one another.

Public deliberation should be considered a mutual exposure of consenting adults aware of the risks involved in the encounter.

SUMMARY

In most communication formats, structure develops as the communication event proceeds and is a product of the interactions among the participants. However, because of the restrictions placed on listener feedback, the speech structure in public speaking must be preplanned to anticipate and deal with listener responses and needs as they develop. Effective preplanning of speech structure depends heavily on the speaker's anticipatory empathy.

The internal structure of speeches depends considerably on whether the speaker's purpose is only to inform or is to persuade as well. Structural considerations for informative speeches include the need for: (1) getting initial attention, (2) maintaining attention, (3) concluding with peak attention, (4) building later explanations on earlier ones, (5) taking advantage of what the audience already knows, (6) putting difficult explanation where the audience is best able to cope with it, (7) putting the most important explanation first or last, (8) making listeners aware of major divisions, subdivisions, and orderly progression, and (9) providing internal and concluding summaries.

Beyond these considerations, persuasive speeches introduce the following considerations for producing listener acceptance and action: (10) delaying revelation of thesis and purpose until listeners are prepared for them, (11) beginning with those propositions or arguments the listeners are most likely to accept, (12) placing strongest arguments first or last, (13) sequencing problem and solution effectively, (14) placing refutation advantageously, (15) citing sources at appropriate times, (16) concluding with an appeal for action, (17) obtaining commitment at an advantageous time, and (18) forewarning and innoculating listeners with respect to future counterarguments.

Some standard structures for informative speeches are the: (1) chronological, (2) flashback, (3) ascending or descending, (4) spatial, (5) causal, (6) reflective or inductive, and (7) topical. Some persuasive structures are: (8) any of the informative structures, (9) need–plan, problem–solution, or disease–remedy, (10) motivated sequence, (11) comparative advantages, (12) elimination of alternatives, and (13) mock problem-solving.

Outlining is helpful in planning structure because it allows one to make certain divisions that are: (1) clear, (2) easy to understand, (3) more or less equal but not overlapping, (4) comprehensive, (5) properly related, (6) properly subordinated, and (7) properly coordinated or parallel.

Introductions, transitions, and conclusions are devices for keeping listeners aware of the structure and sequence of the speech—where you are going, where you are, and where you have been—as well as performing certain other important functions. Since any speech is likely to be one of a sequence of more or less related messages, it is important that you be aware of the effects of forewarning or innoculation, the effects of messages on sources, and the effects of one audience upon another.

ILLUSTRATIVE SPEECH

It is impossible to illustrate all the possible structures for informative speeches, of course. What I have done instead is to choose a single example of clear and effective structure: Karl Menninger's speech, "Healthier Than Healthy" (see Chapter Five). Menninger's speech contained four major divisions, which he terms "observations." Although he did not state his major divisions in the introduction, he did tell the audience to expect four, and then he stated and elaborated on each in turn. Note also how logical the sequence of divisions is—they build on one another until the speech climaxes in the fourth and most important division.

The speech of Vera Micheles Dean, "Anti-Westernism: Cause and Cure," is an example of the *problem–solution* structure mixed with the *elimination of alternatives* structure. The speech was delivered at the conference of the National Association of Women Deans and Counselors in Cleveland, Ohio, on March 21, 1959.

Notice how Ms. Dean identified the problems and described a specific policy for solving those problems. She did not explain *how* the plan would solve the problems after she presented it; instead she spent some time explaining the causes of the problems so that, when she described the plan, its provisions would appear to match and eliminate those causes. Instead of mentioning possible *objections* to the plan she mentioned *alternatives* to it and explained why they would not work. She apparently felt the advantages of the plan lay in its solutions to the problems, and she apparently did not feel the need to obtain commitment from her listeners since there were no "additional advantages" nor "action appeal" sections in the speech. Although this speech did not follow the specific steps of the problem–solution structure described in this chapter, it did constitute an excellent adaptation of that structure, incorporating some of the "elimination of alternatives" structure as well.

Anti-Westernism Cause and Cure *
Vera Micheles Dean

In Cuba, one of our Latin American neighbors, Fidel Castro denounces the United States. In Iraq, until 1958 an active member of the Baghdad pact, crowds jeer at an American diplomat, and a Communist-dominated regime comes to power. The mayor of Manila, speaking on Edward R. Murrow's *Small World* TV program, tells us why we are losing friends in Asia in terms so bitter as to befit a foe rather than a friend of the United States.

As these and other incidents are reported from around the globe, Americans ask themselves: Why are these non-Western peoples against the West—and particularly why are they against the United States? What is anti-Westernism? And how can it be cured?

So deeply is the West imbued with the sense of benefits it has conferred on the non-Western areas in the past, and is ready to confer in the future, that we find it difficult to believe anti-Westernism can exist and flourish without the help of communism. Yet, this is the harsh reality we must face in Asia, the Middle East, and Africa if we are not to fall prey to perilous illusions.

The Russians did not need to lift a finger, fire a gun, or spend a single ruble to foment anti-Westernism in Egypt or Saudi Arabia, in Indonesia or Jordan. It's in the air. It is deeply imbedded in the consciousness of peoples who have lived under the rule of Britain, France, or the Netherlands, not of Russia. True, the Russians capitalize with marked success on a sentiment against the West which corresponds to their own, but they did not in the first place create it. This sentiment can exist and

*From *Representative American Speeches: 1959-1960*, ed. Lester Thonssen (New York: H. W. Wilson Co., 1960, pp. 116-122; and William J. Dean).

has existed apart from communism—just as some plants need no soil or fertilizer to remain alive. In fact, anti-Westernism was a sturdy plant in Russia itself during the nineteenth century under the czars, long before the Bolsheviks came on the scene.

But, if these manifestations in Russia were not initially a product of communism, were they an exclusive product of Russia's historical development? Is the anti-Westernism we see today in other areas of the world just a carbon copy of that practiced in Russia? Would it vanish if the West could discover some magic formula for eliminating Russia or sealing it off from the rest of the world?

The answer, disappointing as it is for the West, must be in the negative. From New Delhi to Cairo, from Jakarta to Karachi and Nairobi, men and women who have never read Marx, Lenin, or Stalin, and who often abhor what they know of Russia, are in the grip of the same emotions and ideas which fan the as yet unfinished controversy between Westernizers and Slavophiles in Russia. Their anti-Westernism, like that of the Russians, is an explosive mixture of contradictory reactions inspired by rising nationalism.

Non-Westerners admire our material achievements—the fruits of modern science and technology. They long to have their own peoples benefit by these fruits, to which they feel entitled by reason of living in the twentieth century; this is the essence of what has been well called the revolution of rising expectations. But they realize, with a poignancy which no Westerner, however sympathetic, can possibly understand— because like intense fear or joy it cannot be expressed in rational terms but must be experienced to be known—that their own countries are poor and retarded, ridden with disease and ignorance. The contrast between what they see around them, in Egypt or Indonesia, and what they painfully wish to achieve is so staggering as to fill them with a sense of hopelessness and frustration. Instead of trying to escape from this state of mind by tackling the nearest practical job, no matter how modest it may be, they are likely to vent their feelings of disappointment against the West, making it the scapegoat for all the ills from which they and their countrymen suffer.

The situation becomes all the more painful—for non-Western peoples and for the West—where the rulers, today or in the recent past, are or have been Westerners who may well have concentrated on their own interests such as the building of strategic facilities or the development of resources needed by Western industry, rather than on improvement of the economic, social, and political conditions in the areas under their control. Then the anti-Westernism which is found even in independent nations such as Japan becomes dangerously aggravated by anticolonialism and, since the foreign rulers are representatives of white nations, also by racialism. To all these feelings must be added the fear of some, who want to maintain ancient political and religious customs, that the impact of the West will destroy the fabric of the nation's traditional life. They want to oust all Westerners before this horrifying prospect has come to pass.

We, however, are particularly puzzled by the tendency of the non-Western nations to denounce Western colonialism yet say little or nothing about the colonialism of the USSR. Here again Russia's past experience is much closer to that which Asia, the Middle East, and Africa are now undergoing than is the experience of the Western nations. Russia itself was a relatively backward nation as late as the 1920's. It, too, both wanted to learn from the West yet feared its impact on institutions and on national security.

This does not mean, and should not be interpreted to mean, that the Asian and African countries accept Russia without criticisms or qualms. They are aware of the dangers of eventual pressure from Moscow. They are not enthusiastic about Russian dictatorship—although, being often accustomed to authoritarianism at home, they are less repelled by it abroad than the nations of the Atlantic community, where democrary is—more or less—an old story. Russia was not invited to the Afro-Asian conference at Bandung in 1955, presumably because it is a Eurasian, not an Asian or African, country. But Russia's experience in modernizing its economy and in making the difficult transition from ancient times to the nuclear age within a third of a century is of intense interest to all non-Western areas, which feel that they have more to learn, in a practical way, from a country far closer to their current problems and experiences than from such advanced nations as the U.S.A. and Britain. This sense of affinity with Russia—economic and social if not always political—on the part of non-Western peoples of diverse religious faiths, political traditions, and international aspirations constitutes our most difficult hurdle in our efforts to find a cure for anti-Westernism.

This cure canot be found by denouncing communism, by demanding that the non-Western nations abandon all contacts with Russia and Communist China, or by threatening to cut off aid unless they agree to join our side. Such moves would merely reinforce their hostility to and suspicion of the West and cause them to strengthen rather than weaken their still tenuous bonds with Moscow.

As in the case of some other troubles, the most promising remedy is the hair of the dog. The cure for anti-Westernism is Westernization, but it cannot be forced on peoples by military pressure or financial handouts. Nasser in Egypt or Nehru in India, like the Japanese after 1867 or the Russians after 1917, must be free to take the initiative in accepting or rejecting what the West has to offer. They must be free to pick and choose those features of our development they think best adapted to their own particular needs.

The essence of anti-Westernism, in Czarist Russia as in the USSR and other areas, is resistance to the assumption, which the West makes as a matter of course, that our civilization is superior to the civilizations of other regions and represents a norm which should be the ideal goal of Asians, Arabs, and Africans. When Glubb Pasha, upon reaching London after his expulsion from Jordan, was asked what it was the West had done wrong, he said that, while the West had committed mistakes, it had also done much good but that its main error is its "superciliousness" toward the non-West. If the West is to succeed, it must learn to restrain its natural feeling of pride in its own achievements—a feeling which, when transposed to non-Western lands, looks and sounds like arrogance—and display modesty in offering to improve the conditions of Egyptians or Indians.

We must, moreover, constantly bear in mind that, as a matter of historical fact, many of these today economically underdeveloped countries had achieved a high type of civilization and culture when our own ancestors were still relative savages. It is no wonder, then, that they think they have something to preserve.

Nor is it enough for us to point out that the Communist powers now practice the imperialism which the Western nations are in process of relinquishing. For Asia, Africa and the Middle East, colonialism and imperialism have been associated with the West, and symbolized by the unequal treatment accorded by whites to non-whites. What Russia does in Eastern Europe, repugnant as it may be to all non-Communists, is regarded as a conflict between white peoples. The situation changes, however, when non-whites try to subjugate and repress non-whites, as shown by the sharp reaction in Asia against Communist China's actions in Tibet.

What then, can the United States do to counter Soviet influence? First, we must renew our efforts to facilitate orderly self-determination for those peoples who are still under colonial rules. This does not mean that all will benefit by achieving independence overnight but that we should show genuine concern for their desire to rule themselves in at least a limited form—perhaps, for a stated period of time, under the supervision of the United Nations.

Second, when we advocate independence, we must accept the fact that independence includes the right for a free nation to choose its own course in world affairs. We must stop criticizing those of the non-Western nations which, like India or Burma, choose neutralism in preference to membership in one or other of the military blocs that have emerged out of the cold war.

Third, we must look at foreign aid not merely as a weapon in the cold war. We must understand that it is in our national interest to give aid to the underdeveloped countries, even if communism did not exist, in order to improve economic and social conditions in the world community of which we are a part. Once we realize that the goal of foreign aid is not just to defeat communism but to advance the development of non-Western areas, then we should think of long-term aid of a more substantial character than we have undertaken in the past. Economists calculate that we could and should allocate $3 billion a year during two or three decades for economic, as distinguished from military, aid. This figure may seem large, but it is less than 1 percent of our national income.

Fourth, we must realize that foreign aid cannot be considered apart from foreign trade. The non-Western nations have no desire to become permanent pensioners. They do not just want to receive handouts; they want to stand on their own feet and gain self-respect. But they can do this only if they can repay the long-term loans we may make to them. And this they can do only if they can sell their products in Western markets. This means that we and our allies must rethink the character of world trade.

And, finally, we must learn that relations with the non-Western nations, if they are to be successful, have to be a two-way street. We have much to offer in terms of democratic procedures and technological skills, but we can greatly enrich ourselves by sharing their contributions to the world's cultural heritage through religion, philosophy, art, literature, and music.

This five-point program may sound like a tall order. But no one who has faith in the American way of life can believe that we are unable to meet Russia's challenge for peacetime competition in the non-Western World. As the *New Yorker* said about the world domination dreams of the Nazis when Germany conquered France in 1941: "We, too, can dream dreams and see visions."

Chapter Nine References

1 William J. McGuire, "Persuasion," in *Communication, Language, and Meaning*, ed. George A. Miller (New York: Basic books, 1973), pp. 242-255.

2 See Alan H. Monroe and Douglas Ehninger, *Principles and Types of Speech*, 6th ed. (Glenview, Ill.: Scott, Foresman, 1967), Chapter 16.

3 Carroll C. Arnold, *Criticism of Oral Rhetoric* (Columbus, Ohio: Charles E. Merrill, 1974), p. 129.

4 See William J. McGuire, "Inducing Resistance to Persuasion," in *Advances in Experimental Social Psychology*, Vol. I, ed. L. Berkowitz (New York: Academic Press, 1964).

PART TWO
QUESTIONS FOR SELF-EVALUATION

Speaking Objectives

Organization
1. Does your speech begin with an introduction suited to your purpose?
2. Does your introduction make provision for getting the initial attention of your listeners?
3. Will your introduction help your listeners like and respect you?
4. Does your introduction contain a clear statement of purpose? If not, do you have a good reason for omitting it?
5. Does your introduction contain a clear statement of your central idea or thesis? If not, do you have good reason for omitting it?
6. Does your introduction contain a clear organizational statement (statement of major divisions or arguments)? If not, do you have good reason for omitting it?
7. Does your introduction include all the definitions of terms and background information your listeners will need to understand your speech?
8. Is the sequence of your divisions logically planned?
9. Are your transitions clear and effective?
10. Do you have a conclusion?
11. Does your conclusion adequately summarize your speech?
12. Does your conclusion provide a climax which will bring your listeners to a peak of attention and interest and get them to take some specific action if that is your purpose?

Amplification and information
13. Is your information specific and concrete?
14. Is all your information relevant to your purpose and central idea?
15. Do you have enough information?
16. Is your information attributed to qualified sources or otherwise adequately tested for reliability?
17. Is your explanation clear?
18. Is your reasoning sound?
19. Is your material interesting?
20. Is your audiovisual material adequate to clarify your explantion?

Listening Objectives

Understanding and evaluating content and structure

1. Does the speaker's purpose appear to be only to inform or also to persuade?
2. If the speaker's thesis, central idea, purpose, and major divisions or arguments are stated in the introduction, does your initial agreement or disagreement make you want to prematurely, uncritically accept or reject the speech?
3. If the speaker's introduction does *not* contain such statements, are there any indications he or she may be deliberately concealing them?
4. If the speaker's introduction does *not* contain such explicit statements, can you provide them on the basis of transitions or your overall analysis of the speech?
5. If the speaker's purpose appears to be only to inform, which type of informative speech is it?
6. What methods of explanation and amplification is the speaker using?
7. Is the speaker's material or its structure and sequencing threatening your attention, comprehension, or retention?
8. If the material is creating such problems, can you help by relating the explanation and amplification to other information or experiences you have encountered?
9. If the speech structure and sequencing are causing problems, are there ways you can arrange it which will aid your comprehension and retention?
10. If the speaker's purpose appears to be to persuade as well as inform, which of your beliefs, values, plans, and policies is he or she trying to change?
11. If the speaker is trying to persuade you, what *specifically* is he or she trying to get you to do?
12. What physical, social, or internal consequences is the speaker explicitly claiming will ensue if you accept or reject the proposal?
13. Is the speaker suggesting implicitly that any other physical, social, or internal consequences will ensue? If so, does this reflect his or her unwillingness to state those implicit suggestions as explicit claims?
14. Are these consequences ones on which you want to base your decision?
15. Are there any consequences in addition to those the speaker mentions? If so, are there any reasons to believe the omissions are intentional?
16. Are the speaker's data related to the claims by adequate warrants; that is, does the reasoning used to relate the evidence to the claims meet the applicable tests for such reasoning?
17. Does the speaker leave unsupported any data or warrants you believe require further support?

18. Are the speaker's data or items of evidence attributed to reliable sources or, if not, do you know them to be accurate?

19. To what extent is the speaker depending on the likableness or general prestige of his or her sources rather than upon their qualifications to offer expert testimony on the specific matters in question?

20. Are there any other data or lines of reasoning you know of that are relevant to the speaker's claims? If so, do they hurt his or her cause? If so, are there reasons to believe the omissions are intentional?

21. Which type of persuasive speech structure is the speaker using?

22. Is there anything about that structure that might lead you to accept or reject the speaker's proposal uncritically?

23. If the structure is one that might produce uncritical acceptance, are there reasons to believe the speaker might have chosen the structure for that reason?

24. Does the speaker at any point attempt to get you to commit yourself to the proposal in ways which might prevent you from objectively evaluating future information?

25. Does the speaker at any point appeal for immediate action when it seems more beneficial to postpone action pending further investigation?

26. Does the speaker fairly describe and adequately refute important opposing arguments, or does he or she describe those arguments unfairly and/or try to prepare you to uncritically reject opposing arguments you may encounter in the future?

27. Have you previously encountered messages from this speaker or other speakers that are relevant to the present proposal?

28. Is there anything about those previous messages that might cause you to uncritically accept or reject the present proposal?

29. Is there anything about this present speech that might prevent you from objectively evaluating future messages from this speaker or future messages on this topic?

30. Has the feedback you have provided this speaker reinforced his or her speech behavior in ways that will be beneficial to his or her future listeners?

PART THREE

Speech Presentation

In these next two chapters you will have to be unusually careful to apply what you learn about public speaking to situations in which you function as a listener. Chapter Ten, especially, addresses the problems of speaking more directly than those of listening.

On the one hand, language and delivery are capable of affecting you as a listener in ways you may not be aware. A speaker's language and/or delivery may be offensive to you for reasons that are not immediately apparent; you may fail to attend to and thus comprehend and retain the message content even though it might be useful to you, or you might refuse to accept and act upon the speaker's proposals when they might in fact be beneficial. Conversely, a speaker's presentation may be so seductive that you fail to evaluate critically the reasoning and evidence or even, in extreme cases, become so enamored of the beauty of the language and the grace of the delivery that you fail to attend to the content.

On the other hand, a listener can gain a great deal from close scrutiny of a speaker's presentation. Even written language, which the writer has had time to compose and revise, can reveal motives and thought processes not otherwise evident, as certain types of literary criticism and linguistic psychoanalysis have demonstrated. Spoken language, since it is usually spontaneous, can be even more revealing. Nonverbal "leakage" of a speaker's true motives, emotions, level of attention, and interest in the audience can be a valuable source of information.

CHAPTER TEN
Language and Style

LANGUAGE GAMES, RULES, AND STRATEGIES

One way of thinking of speech in its verbal and nonverbal aspects is to compare it to a game based on rules and played by devising strategies that use or abuse the rules. As a listener, especially, you can profit from such an analogy in that you can learn to spot a speaker's verbal and nonverbal strategies whether or not the speaker is aware of them. Because the analogy has been pursued primarily by people interested in verbal language, this explanation will focus on verbal rules and strategies. The same approach is equally applicable to nonverbal communication, however.

Language is a game in that it operates by means of rules understood by its users who employ strategies to achieve certain goals. A member of one language community who finds himself in another language community will be at least as mystified as a person who plays only poker and finds himself suddenly in the midst of a bridge game. That is true even if the foreign speaker "knows" the language of the other culture.

Robin Lakoff, a linguist at the University of California, Berkeley, has provided a good example.[1] She points out that most foreigners are taught that *may* is generally a more polite form of address than *must*. And it frequently is. But suppose a hostess says to a Japanese guest, "You *must* have some of this cake." Is she being less polite than if she were to say, "You *may* have some of this cake"?

The native speaker of English knows that she is not—that *must* in this case is more polite than *may*, that to say, "You *may* have some of this cake" would, in fact, be mildly insulting. But how to explain that to the Japanese guest? One might say that the hostess' utterance really means "The humble baker of this poor cake begs you to try some in the hope that it will please you." But that is really not quite right; it is at least too formal and stilted and even a little silly. Yet Japanese honorifics—terms used by the Japanese to convey respect—sound just as foolish and are equally misrepresented when translated as "Humble speaker begs honorable American to taste some of this abominable tea."

When I say language is governed by rules, I am not referring to the "rules" of "correct" usage that you were taught in elementary school. Those rules are violated almost as frequently as they are followed and usually without any negative consequences as long as the speaker knows *when* and *where* they may be violated. As a matter of fact, there are many situations in which it is inappropriate to apply the rules of correct usage. For example, try converting the phrases "Put up or shut up" and "That's where it's at" into correct usage, and see how far it gets you in informal conversation. One of the important rules every native speaker of English knows is that precisely correct usage is inappropriate in informal conversation. No, the rules I am referring to are more complex, and to violate them brands the speaker as deficient in his or her understanding of the language.

Semantic Rules

Linguists generally distinguish among four levels of language study: the phonemic, syntactic, semantic, and pragmatic. Phonemic rules are concerned with the sounds of a language and how those sounds are combined. They are learned very early; the babbling of Chinese infants can be distinguished from that of American infants before they have reached the age of six months, simply because they have begun to use the sounds and sound combinations required in their respective languages long before they learn to speak.

Different sounds are significant in different languages. The best known example is probably the English distinction between *r* and *l*, a distinction that is insignificant in Japanese. The Japanese tendency to confuse words such as *rot* and *lot* is not due to an inability to pronounce the words. Rather, it is due to the fact that speakers of Japanese have not been taught to make the distinction. On the other hand, English speakers trying to learn Japanese tend to pronounce the Japanese words for *door* and *ten* identically, ignoring the distinction the Japanese make between two sounds that can only be poorly represented by the English "o" and "oo." I used to live in the town of Los Gatos, California, which is pronounced *Loss* Gatos by most of its residents, who simply do not distinguish between that and the Spanish pronunciation, which sounds more like Loze Gatos.

Syntax, too, is rule-governed, a fact that has been recognized for some time. Take the sentence "The bartender ejected the drunk." To produce such a sentence, one needs to know the following rules: (1) a sentence may consist of a noun phrase plus a verb phrase; (2) a noun phrase may consist of an article plus a noun; (3) a verb phrase may consist of a verb plus a noun phrase; (4) an article may be the word *the*; (5) nouns may be the words *bartender* and *drunk*; and (6) a verb may be the word *ejected*.

These six rules constitute a very limited grammar, of course, since they are capable of producing only two sentences: "The bartender ejected the drunk," and "The drunk ejected the bartender." By adding more verbs and nouns, one could quickly expand the number of possible sentences. Next, one might adopt rules for plurals and different verb forms and add rules for modifiers, such as adverbs, adjectives, and prepositional phrases. Eventually one would have to add rules for other sentence forms as well.

You can see from this simple illustration what linguists have been concerned with for the past few decades. They have been trying to explain what it is a person *knows* when he or she is said to "know" a language. They are trying to produce a limited set of rules by which one can form any acceptable sentence in a language and no unacceptable ones. That is a big job, since the number of acceptable sentences in a language is infinitely large.

Chomsky has argued that phrase/structure rules such as these describe only the "surface structure" of language and ignore the "deep structure" from which surface utterances are derived. He has proposed that there are "transformation" rules that speakers understand and use to relate surface structures to deep structures. Thus, a single deep structure can produce several acceptable surface structures, which are related by different transformational rules, or different deep structures can produce the same surface sentence by the application of different transformations.

The semantic level, the level at which we consider questions of "meaning," can also be viewed as governed by sets of rules. Imagine a speaker who tells an audience, "Friends, let's throw these crooks out of office." This utterance seems to imply that: (a) there are people present (the listeners) who meet certain criteria or rules for being addressed as "Friends"; (b) there are people previously mentioned in the speech who meet certain criteria for being labeled "crooks"; (c) these "crooks" presently occupy a position that meets certain criteria for being labeled "office" (the absence of the word *the* makes it clear "office" is a political position rather than a room); (d) the speaker believes the listeners are capable of removing the "crooks" from office; (e) the speaker wants the "crooks" removed from office; and (f) the listeners will be more likely to remove the "crooks" from office if the speaker suggests they do so.

If any of these conditions are not met, the listeners will perceive that something is semantically wrong with the utterance. They may not agree that they themselves meet the criteria for being addressed as "Friends"; they may not agree that the people previously mentioned meet the criteria for being labeled "crooks"; they may not believe they have the power to remove the "crooks" from office; and so on. Some of the things the utterance *presupposes* or *implies* are then not believed to be the case.

Of course, those are all *literal* implications of the utterance, and the utterance may be intended to be taken *figuratively*, in which case other rules apply. Condition (d) might be violated for the purpose of humorous irony if the speaker has in fact been pointing out that these listeners are politically powerless; conditions (b), (e), and (f) might be violated for the same purpose if the "crooks" were known to be friends of the speaker; conditions (b) and (f) might be violated if they were known to be friends of the listeners.

In fact, the utterance does violate one literal presupposition for the sake of metaphorical effect, but the metaphor is so old that you may not have recognized it. People cannot *literally* be "thrown out" of something that is not an *enclosure*, and a *political* "office" is not literally an enclosure, although the same word used in a different sense is, so the metaphor *is* consistent.

Pragmatic Rules and Strategies

Assuming that the speaker's utterance conformed to these semantic rules and that it conforms to phonemic and syntactic rules, the speaker could still have chosen some alternatives. She could have said, "Throw these damn crooks out!" or "Why don't you throw these fellows out?" She could have substituted some nonverbal symbols by saying "Here's what we ought to do with these crooks!" and then hooking her thumb toward the door or going through the motions of heaving or kicking some large object. All these alternatives are phonemically, syntactically, and semantically acceptable. In fact, there is a sense in which they all relate to the same "deep structure." But they are not equally *pragmatic*; that is, one may be more likely than the others to produce the desired effects.

Consequently, to fully understand the use of verbal and nonverbal symbols, we have to know something about pragmatic rules. Pragmatic rules are extremely subtle. They depend heavily upon the context of the utterance, and they are embedded in cultural norms and expectations. A foreigner may have learned the phonemic, syntactic, and semantic rules, but unless he has spent a great deal of time in the country where the language is sproken and the nonverbal symbols used, he is not likely to know these pragmatic rules. In fact, many are so subtle and specific that it is probably more appropriate to call them *strategies*.

Bowers and Desmond have referred to some strategies with the label "devious messages."[2] As an example, suppose a friend of yours says, "Are you going to the party at Blake's tonight?" and suppose you are not quite sure whether you are going to be able to make it or not, or whether you are going to want to make it. You might say, "I have an exam coming up tomorrow," which is not an outright "No," although that is clearly what it implies. It leaves you the option of showing up if you decide you are able to or want to. Public speakers frequently take advantage of rules that are assumed to be operating in such a way that they seem to say one thing, but leave their statements open to interpretation. Public officials become masters of the game of avoiding reporters' questions by giving them devious answers. Suppose, for example, the president has decided that it is absolutely necessary to impose price controls in a certain industry. He knows, however, that if he announced that fact before the price controls are actually imposed, the companies in the industry will rush to raise their prices before the advent of the controls. During the press interview a reporter asks the press secretary, "Does the president intend to impose any price controls?" The press secretary may answer, in all truthfulness, "There is no change in the president's position on price controls." Two days later, when the controls go into effect, he can explain by saying, "The president has always said that he would impose price controls as a last measure if runaway inflation should occur in any industry, and he considers that this particular industry is experiencing runaway inflation." Consequently, the press secretary was truthful when he said the president had made no change in his stand. But the answer was certainly devious, did not respond to the reporter's questions directly, and, in fact, took advantage of certain assumptions that we make about communication: namely, that the answers to questions will be direct responses to those questions. Clearly this is a pragmatic *strategy* based on pragmatic *rules*.

We know other kinds of pragmatic rules as well. For example, Susan Irvin-Tripp has produced a sort of flow diagram that illustrates the choices we go through in deciding how to address someone.[3] You have the task of introducing the speaker at a meeting. You know that she has a doctorate. You know that she is married. You know that she is a member of a women's liberation group. And you know that this is a fairly informal occasion. What are you going to call her? Are you going to call her Doctor Rogers? Mrs. Rogers? Jane? In making that decision, you will take into consideration a number of pragmatic rules that you understand perfectly well, although you may never have articulated them or heard them articulated before. You will decide, for example, whether status is important in this situation, and if so, whether her status is higher than yours or that of the listeners. You will try to decide whether she is enough older than you and the listeners that she requires a more deferential term of respect. You will try to decide whether it is important to indicate that you know she is married, or whether it is more important to show that you recognize her involvement in women's liberation. If you decide that this is not a situation in which status is important, because it is very informal, and if you decide that it is not important to recognize her educational level, her marital status, or her involvement with women's liberation and that she is well enough known to the listeners, you simply introduce her as "Jane." If you have chosen correctly— observed the characteristics of the situation accurately and applied the pragmatic rules correctly—you will achieve your purpose, in this case, to introduce her appropriately, without offending her. The purpose of understanding pragmatic rules is to achieve your goals in public deliberation in as effective a way as possible.

There are other areas, however, in which it is much more difficult to state specific rules. For example, a public speaker knows it is important to state ideas as clearly as possible, but it is impossible to sit down in an armchair and derive a set of rules, at least very specific rules, that will allow one to accomplish that objective. You may know, too, that the effectiveness of a public speech is to some extent determined by the intensity of the language used. In certain situations, profanity or obscenity will damage your credibility and make listeners less likely to accept what you have to say; in other situations profanity and obscenity are almost called for. This area is one in which one must first speculate about the probable effects of certain types of symbols and then test those speculations in actual situations. Some of the principles drawn from such speculation, from the practice of successful speakers, and from experimental testing are summarized.

STYLISTIC CHOICES

Given this foundation of language theory regarding the nature of language, the levels at which language can be studied, especially the concept of semantic and pragmatic rules, and the effect language has upon those who hear it, we can approach the more practical questions of what kind of language public speakers choose, or at least the considerations that affect those choices.

Assuming you speak the English language fluently, the choices you will need to make are *pragmatic* choices; that is, your job is to choose language on the basis of the ways it will affect the listeners. Generally it can be said that *the language of choice is clear, appropriate, dynamic, and aesthetically pleasing*. My job in this chapter is to define what I mean by those terms.

Clarity

A chapter titled "Gobbledygook" in Stuart Chase's book *The Power of Words* contains many excellent examples of language that is unclear even though it abides by the syntactic and semantic rules of English. One example is a famous statement by Franklin Roosevelt in a speech shortly after he had become president in the depths of the Great Depression. Roosevelt said, "I see one-third of a nation ill-housed, ill-clad, ill-nourished." If that were translated into standard bureaucratic prose, says Chase, it might read:

It is evident that a substantial number of persons within the continental boundaries of the United States have inadequate financial resources with which to purchase the products of agricultural communities and industrial establishments. It would appear that for a considerable segment of the population, perhaps as much as 33.333 [percent] of the total, there are inadequate housing facilities, and an equally significant proportion is deprived of the proper types of clothing and nourishment.

FDR could have made a big hit with that, couldn't he? Happily he had the good sense to know that his listeners did not want a demonstration of the extent of his vocabulary or the complexity of his syntax—they wanted to know what he was going to do about the economy.

Not all speakers have that sort of common sense. Similar to "bureaucratese" is this example of what Chase calls "pedagese" ("academese"):

Realization has grown that the curriculum or the experiences of learners change and improve only as those who are most directly involved examine their goals, improve their understandings, and increase their skill in performing the tasks necessary to reach newly defined goals. This places the focus upon teacher, lay citizen, and learner as partners in curricular improvement and as the individuals who must change, if there is to be a curriculum change.

The idea which someone has cleverly concealed in this wordstack seems to be, as Chase puts it, that "if we are going to change the curriculum, teacher, parent, and student must all help."

An example I have encountered in at least three sources is this supposed exchange of letters between a plumber and the National Bureau of Standards:

Plumber: I've found hydrochloric acid is very good for cleaning drains, and thought you'd like to know.
NBS: The efficiency of hydrochloric acid is indisputable, but the corrosive residue is incompatible with metallic permanence.
Plumber: I'm happy to hear I'm right.
NBS: We cannot assume responsibility for the production of toxic and noxious residues from hydrochloric acid, and suggest you utilize an alternative procedure.
Plumber: I'm glad to hear you folks are honest and aren't going to try to take credit for my discovery.
NBS: Don't use hydrochloric acid! It eats the hell out of pipes!

What is it that makes the difference between clear and difficult language? Well, it is easy to see some of the differences by looking at these passages. First, in two of the examples *the words are less common* in the unclear version. We commonly talk about how "using big words" destroys clarity; many uncommon words are also "big," but not necessarily so. However, it does seem to be true that most "big" words are uncommon. Big or small, unusual words seem to be very effective in keeping others from understanding what you are saying.

But the second example—the one regarding curriculum changes— really does not contain unusual words, unless you count "curriculum." It has different problems. The sentences are very long and complex and there are too many of them. Here a simple idea is puffed up beyond recognition, not by use of an unusual vocabulary, but by use of sentences that are too long, too complex, and too "redundant."

Long, complex sentences are just very difficult to process. An example of embedding might be: "The fat cat which my father left with the skinny old lady with the hungry look on her face never came back." Embedding phrases within phrases is one type of complexity. Just the use of many phrases and clauses, even if they are not embedded, makes sentences more difficult to understand. Passive sentences are also difficult. Consider the difference between "I see one-third of a nation, ill-housed, ill-clothed, and ill-fed" versus "One third of a nation, ill-housed, ill-clothed, and ill-fed is seen by me." Negative transformations, too, can badly complicate sentences: "No patient should be allowed to eat anything that cannot be completely processed before an operation begins." Now let's see—how many "nots" were there, and do they cancel one another?

It is difficult to decide whether the *redundancy* in the "curriculum" example is good or bad. Without the redundancy and repetition, the sentence complexity might be completely baffling; that is, the redundancy finally lets the idea escape from the tangle of syntax. But the redundancy itself becomes tiresome, so that if the complicated syntax didn't get you, the redundancy would. Sometimes stating the same idea several ways just serves to confuse.

Two of these examples use long and uncommon words. But there is a different kind of uncommon word that is also unclear: euphemisms or slang. Such words are used because speakers want to be "polite" and avoid emotion-laden words or because they want to be part of some in-group. For example, speakers will go out of their way to avoid saying someone "died." Instead, they say that person "passed away," "kicked off," "cashed in his chips," or "bought the ranch." Women are seldom "pregnant"; they are "pg," "in a family way," or "have one in the chute." Talking about sexual intercourse is especially difficult. *Of course* one cannot use the "dirty" words, right? "Having intercourse" or "copulating" both sound too clinical. So speakers talk about two people "getting laid," "making out," "playing house," "fooling around," or "sleeping together"—when sleeping is exactly what they are *not* doing. "Making love" is a popular term and is not too ambiguous, although it has done strange things to the meaning of the word "love." "Having sex" is about as straightforward as most speakers are likely to be, and that does not strike me as too bad a choice, although it seems too close to having potatoes. "Have some potatoes?" "No thanks, I just had sex." Ech.

One final problem I am going to mention—although there are certainly many more—is the case of unclear referents. This example is "noisy" because the referent is unclear: "The queen broke the bottle of champagne over her stern as she slid gracefully into the sea." Another example is "Whenever I get a cold I buy a bottle of whiskey and within a few hours it's gone." Or this one, which I encountered when I was working for a Denver detective agency that handled security at the Colorado State Fair: "Excuse me, have you found a handbag? When we got to the car, we discovered we had left my wife's behind." I restrained myself from saying "Considering your wife, Fella, it looks like you should have left more of it." But it took a great deal of self-control. Another example I encountered on a gravestone near Mammoth Cave, near the Kentucky/Tennessee line. The inscription on the gravestone went like this: "Sleep on, dear mother, sleep. Thy family mourns thy loss. Around thy silent grave we weep, all covered o'er with moss."

These, then, are some of the major enemies of language clarity: unfamiliar words, words with many syllables, long sentences, complex sentences (those with too much embedding, many phrases and clauses, passive constructions, and double negatives, for example), euphemisms, slang, excessive or insufficient redundancy, and unclear referents.

Appropriateness

Earlier in this chapter, I said that language should be *appropriate*. Keeping it appropriate is again going to be a test of your sensitivity and ability to empathize.

To the purpose   The first concern is that the language be appropriate to the purpose of the speech. If your purpose is to *inform* your listeners, then the function of language is to be clear and to keep the listeners' attention and interest without being distracting in itself. If the purpose is to get your listeners to perform some overt physical act, then the function of language may also be to get them aroused enough to act.

There are just some kinds of language you could use appropriately under certain circumstances but not under others. I recall reading in *Reader's Digest* several years ago—in the "Humor in Uniform" section, I believe—about an officer who was arrested by an M.P. who observed him running down the hall naked, chasing a young woman. He was charged with being out of uniform. His defense counsel, however, cited a part of the dress regulation that excuses an officer from being in uniform if he is "suitably attired for the sport in which he is engaged." The officer was acquitted.

To you   How can you clothe your speech in language suitable to the sport in which you are engaged? A second concern, beyond your purpose, is whether the language is suitable to *you*. The language you use in a speech ought to be within the range of language you are accustomed to using. It may be a little more elevated than your normal conversation, but not so elevated that you are uncomfortable with it. Your listeners will be very quick to recognize your discomfort and may interpret your stilted language as evidence of insincerity.

To the situation   The situation, too, places some constraints on a speaker's language. The language you will use in class is probably going to be a little different from the language you use in normal conversation. If you are invited to speak at your father's club when you are at home, or at a graduation ceremony, your language would differ even more, largely because of the different expectations listeners have about language in different situations. Your language still ought to be appropriate to you, but appropriate to you *in that situation*.

To the listener   Finally, language ought to be appropriate to one's listeners. The idea is to cause your listeners to *identify* with you and to *avoid alienating* them. Thus, you must return to audience analysis once again, but with a focus this time upon the kinds of language suitable to different audiences. You will be considering your listeners' personal characteristics, personality characteristics, opinions and policies, reference persons, reference groups, cohesiveness, commitments, your credibility with them, and their cultural assumptions and racial characteristics.

It is important to use language that is suitable to you but still similar to language your listeners are accustomed to hearing and, if possible, similar to language they themselves use. Listeners are quickly alienated by language that gives the appearance that the speaker is trying to ingratiate himself or herself with them, trying to be one of them. When you try to use the technical jargon or slang of a group to which you do not belong, it is all too easy to *mis*use it in such a way as to appear foolish and pretentious. You may deliberately try to use a different vocabulary and syntax when speaking to an audience less educated than yourself, which is very likely to make the listeners perceive you as "speaking down" to them. They are not likely to react very well to that, since it suggests that you do not think very highly of their intellectual abilities.

Dynamism

Another consideration is the appropriateness of your language intensity or dynamism. This consideration is an especially important one if you are trying to get your listeners to accept as well as understand your ideas. Recall that listeners tend to perceive opinions falling within their latitudes of rejection as being even more extreme than they really are. If your opinions differ quite a bit from those of your audience, you may be inclined to choose language they will consider very strong. Consequently, you ought to give some thought to where your audience is as you choose the language of your speech. That is especially true at the beginning of a speech. If you begin by using language that strongly condemns something they like or strongly praises something they dislike, before you have given your reasons, they may see you as irrational and emotionally unstable.

That might explain Bowers'[4] finding that listeners rejected intense language used *throughout* his speeches, whereas Bowers and Osborn[5] found their listeners reacted favorably when intense language was used only in their conclusions.

I believe one can think of language as ranging on a continuum from dull and plodding to lively and dynamic to intense to, perhaps, profane, obscene, or scatological. I am least certain of the upper end of that continuum: I am not sure whether profane, obscene, and scatological language is *necessarily* the most intense, or whether listeners *tend* to perceive it as unusually intense.

Be that as it may, one inevitably chooses language that varies from extremely dull to lively and dynamic to extremely intense. Language having different degrees of dynamism is chosen to the extent that it is appropriate. It is difficult to imagine when dull language would be appropriate; on the other hand, it is rather seldom that *extremely* intense language is appropriate. Between those two extremes you will have to exercise your common sense. The question I would like to consider now is: What makes language more or less dynamic?

Evaluative language Language is dynamic to the extent that it *evaluates* what it describes. Language that introduces evaluation into a description is also described as "loaded" language. Imagine that it has just been revealed that the director of a national "intelligence" agency once ordered the killing of the leader of an unfriendly government. In reporting the incident, various newspapers describe it as a "murder," a "killing," an "assassination," an "elimination," and a "neutralization." Could you guess, from the language of the descriptions, which newspapers support the director's action and which condemn it? All the words describe the same act, but they evoke very different responses, and they cause one to visualize different scenes.

Sartre has been one of the philosophers who has argued most convincingly that an act or event is exactly what it is until someone *names* it. The act the director ordered was not a "murder," or a "killing," or an "assassination," "elimination," or "neutralization." That act was what the director *did*.

In his book *1984*, Orwell has illustrated how powerful a force the *naming* of actions and events can be. In the society Orwell pictures, a new language—Newspeak—has been created by the state. Newspeak is a language in which it is impossible to criticize the state, because the only words for what the state does bear favorable connotations. The state propaganda agency, for example, is the Ministry of Truth, or "Minitrue" in Newspeak. In Newspeak, as in the slogan of the Party, "War is Peace, Freedom is Slavery, Ignorance is Strength."

What you as a speaker can distill from all this is that the *naming* of an act or event or idea is inevitably an *evaluation* of that act, event, or idea. The name you choose may be favorable, neutral, or unfavorable, but it is evaluative. Thus, if you were speaking about the act performed by the director of the intelligence agency in the present example, you would have at least two considerations as you chose an "appropriate" label for that act. The first consideration would be whether the label was *semantically* appropriate if you believed the act met the conditions under which the term *murder* is customarily applied—that is, if you believed the act was the intentional, malicious killing of another human being.

The second consideration would be whether the label was *pragmatically* appropriate. If your purpose were to cause your listeners to believe as you did, use of the term *murder* might not be the most effective way to achieve that. Instead, use of that term at the outset of the speech might alienate your listeners to the point that they would reject everything else you said. See Mark Antony's funeral speech from the play *Julius Caesar* at the end of this chapter as a case in point. "We have come here not to praise Caesar, but to bury him . . . "? Mark Antony did not accuse Brutus and his cohorts of "murdering" Caesar, although he believed they had. Instead, he repeated the words "Brutus is an honorable man . . . And so are they all, all honorable men . . ." after each of his examples. Those examples were chosen to illustrate the fact that Caesar was not about to set himself up as a dictator, as Brutus claimed, but instead had refused dictatorial powers when it was offered to him. As he cleverly built the evidence against Brutus, the contrast between that evidence and "honorable Brutus" became more and more obvious, until it moved to a climax more compelling than the direct accusation "murder" could have been.

Mark Antony chose not to use the word *murder* and instead made much use of the word *honorable*. His choice was made on pragmatic grounds, and it was pragmatically appropriate in that it achieved his purpose—the killing was avenged. But was his choice ethical? It was pragmatically appropriate but not semantically appropriate. If he believed Brutus was not honorable at all, but had in fact murdered a beloved leader for his own selfish gain, shouldn't he have said so? We tend to judge his *means* as ethical because we feel his *purpose* was ethical. But that is shaky justification.

My ethical judgments are no better than yours, and I do not intend to lay them on you. Chances are you will decide what is ethical communication behavior on the basis of the same ethical system you use to decide about other kinds of behavior. What I have to say about com- munication ethics I said in the first chapter: *Any communication device that reduces awareness to some extent prejudices humanity's chances for survival* The question then becomes: Would Mark Antony's listeners have been so alienated by his use of the term "murder" that it would have interfered with their conscious, rational, objective evaluation of his arguments? Perhaps, and perhaps not. Only Shakespeare knew for sure, and he is dead.

But public speakers constantly face the same dilemma when they have to choose between language that is semantically appropriate and that which is pragmatically appropriate. Furthermore, such choices are the most difficult speakers have to make, because this device of evaluative naming is the most devious a speaker has. Observers can check a speaker's reasoning and evidence, and they can even catch him or her appealing to unconscious motives, but it is much harder to argue with choice of words. Remember when Luke disagreed with the speaker who called the deaths in Second Mesa "murders"? Who was right? Someone else might have called them "suicides." After all, for a kid of sixteen to pick an argument with Fast Eddie seems to be fairly good evidence of a death wish.

Strong, active language   Dynamic language is also strong and active and can be achieved both by word choice and sentence construction.

Certain words cause listeners to visualize power and activity. You can find those words in Osgood's semantic atlas, but you can find them more easily in your own head.

Generally, words that picture a person *doing* something are more dynamic than are words that only describe a state of being. To say a woman is "striking" is more dynamic than saying she is merely "beautiful." To say "Her speech was forceful" seems less dynamic than "She spoke with force." But words that picture a person doing something *to* someone or something are more dynamic than those describing actions with no object. For teachers to "picket" is active, but for them to "picket the school board" is more active.

Verbs are not the only strong, active words. Nouns, too, can be dynamic, as when a person is described as "a shaker and a mover." Adjectives and adverbs such as "hot," "quickly," and "fierce" are dynamic. A "moving tribute" is more moving than a merely "emotional tribute."

Sentence structure also contributes to a feeling of strength and activity. Active sentences are more dynamic than passive ones. "Butch Cassidy shot the sheriff" is more dynamic than "The sheriff was shot by Butch Cassidy," even though the actions described are identical.

Sentence structure can even cause listeners to visualize specific types of action, at least specific rhythms. Short, choppy, "running" sentences can enhance the impression of short, choppy activity. Sentences of the "not only ... but also ..." variety can give the impression of a rising crescendo of activity. Antithetical sentences, "on one hand ... but on the other ...," give an impression of measured walking toward a goal.

Strong, active words and sentences are another part of my definition of dynamic language.

Concrete, specific language   Language that describes real people and events tends to be more dynamic. Suppose a newspaper editorial writer says "Voting patterns among Wisconsin's youth are changing rapidly." But he wants to make that rather dull, abstract statement come alive for his readers, so he adds something like this:

> One day last February, 22-year-old Jan Nordquist of Prairie-du-Chein paused at the top of the ski run, brushed her long blond hair out of her eyes, and told me, "I don't really reject my parents' political views. They were fine for their time. But we have to live in a world that changes every day. I'm not going to commit myself to any one political party today because it might not have the answers tomorrow."

As *evidence*, that single example is not worth much. But as a means of giving a reader or listener a lively audiovisual sense of the abstract concept of "changing voting patterns" it may be worth a great deal.

Vivid, sensory language   Language is more dynamic if it makes the listeners see, hear, taste, smell, and feel the experiences described. Let me try my hand at describing my feelings about working certain wards at a state hospital several years ago:

> They were called the "bedpan wards," and for good reason. They were not hospital wards, because there was no expectation that the "patients" would ever recover; instead they were waiting their turns to die. Opening the door was like walking into an animal's cage, and a poorly tended one at that. The stench of human excrement was like a physical force pushing me back; the sharp ammonia-like odor of urine penetrated into my sinuses and made my eyes water. The room was oppressively hot and humid. I felt the perspiration start on my forehead, the insides of my arms, the backs of my legs, and knew I would have to live with it for the full eight-hour shift. My clothes clung to me like a wet sheet. The paper on which I wrote stuck to my forearm, and my sweat smeared the ink. The room was dark, but I knew there were people there because I could hear their moans and incoherent mumblings. One old man repeated "Help me, help me . . ." in a low voice for hours, but he couldn't tell me how to help him. Another patient interrupted the endless monotony of her life by waiting until an unsuspecting new attendant came near her bed and then turning loose with a shriek which always made my heart jump in my chest. My lunch usually went only half-eaten on nights I was assigned to those wards, because I could not separate the animal smells from the taste of the sandwich. At the end of the shift I put my clothes in a plastic bag and considered burning them. I felt I never wanted to wear those shoes again. And as I felt the cleansing, refreshing shower wash away the unspeakable micro-organisms I was sure infested every pore of my body, I realized that I had been there only eight hours. To the withered, helpless inmates those sounds, those smells, that heat, and that darkness represented home—the last home they would ever know.

Suppose you are going to give a speech favoring a comprehensive plan of national health insurance. Wouldn't that passage be more useful than the flat statement: "Under the present system, many people are forced to live in state hospitals and nursing homes where they receive only minimal care"? It would be more useful because it would enhance your listeners' sense of empathy by helping them to see, hear, smell, taste, and feel the experiences such people have to tolerate.

Personal language   Personal language is more intense and dynamic because it makes listeners feel you are talking about or to them individually, not to some generalized other. Listeners are more likely to apply what you are saying to their own situation, to recall examples from their own experience, to actually prepare to *do* something. Your language is more personal when you use personal pronouns, when you talk about "you," "'me,'" and "we" instead of "one" or "a person." If you know your listeners well enough, you might even refer to them by name, and use as examples actual experiences you know they have had. The speaker trying to get Jake lynched was using very personal language when he said:

> If we ain't safe from murder we ain't safe from anything. What about the money from the cattle sale that ya have in the strongbox? Ya think it's safe fer one day if word gets round that we set a murderer free in this town? What are ya gonna do without it? How ya gonna pay the mortgage? Yer cattle ain't gonna be safe on the range. Ya'll be *wiped out!* Yer children are gonna be beggin' for food in the streets; yer wife and daughters are gonna be sellin' themselves to the miners in Central City and Cripple Creek to keep body and soul together!

As another example, suppose you want to really intensify the language of that speech favoring national health insurance, so you decide to bring it down to a really personal level. You might say something like this:

> We of the middle class are self-reliant. We pride ourselves on being able to pay our own way by honest industry. We can meet the normal medical expenses.
>
> But what would happen if your next medical checkup revealed the beginnings of multiple sclerosis—you found yourself destined to life as a cripple—could your parents pay for the care you would require? When you're actually teaching, what will you do when your child is feverish and in pain, but you can't keep your mind on how best to care for him because you keep thinking what it's going to cost?
>
> You may have seen classmates drop out of school to work because of illness in the family. You may have pitied families just like your own which were suddenly stricken by illness and forced into privation and hardship. Or when your brother was ill you

may have seen through your father's strained good humor to realize he was covering worry—worry about how the expense would be met.

You and I aren't secure from this threat. Someday we will have children to care for, and aged parents who, without us, will face the gray life of a nursing home or public institution. I don't want to pay premiums to a loan shark to conserve my child's health. I don't want my parents to while away their "golden days" of retirement in the crowded solitude of a state hospital, to die on a hard cot in a room full of strangers—and I don't think you want that either.

We all want to realize our full capacities, provide ourselves and our children with every opportunity for success—this should be every man's right—but some of us will never achieve it unless we act to protect ourselves from catastrophic medical expense.

That passage combined with the description of a state hospital ward may give you some idea of how evaluative, strong, active, concrete, specific, vivid, sensory, personal language works to produce dynamic and intense passages.

Metaphorical language   Metaphorical language can contribute to dynamism. If the context in which a word ordinarily occurs is one in which there is high emotional intensity and that word is transplanted into a new context, it seems to carry with it a part of the emotional intensity associated with the original context. Take the sentence "Would you lower yourself to vote for Reagan after he vetoed public welfare programs in California?" Now suppose I want to intensify that. I might say instead, "Would you *prostitute* yourself to vote for Reagan after he *strangled* public welfare programs in California?" The words "prostitute" and "strangled" are ordinarily used in the contexts of hired sex and violent death, both of which are emotionally charged. Their use in a political context transfers some of the emotional intensity from the old context to the new.

A more extended example appears in the earlier description of the Bowers and Osborne study of a language intensity, where a literal passage is transformed into an extended sex metaphor. But the use of the metaphor extends beyond *intensification* of language; metaphor is one of the devices that can be used to make language more aesthetically pleasing. Let me turn to that topic now.

Aesthetic Style

Beyond its clarity, its appropriateness, and its dynamism, there is a quality to the language of some speakers which makes that language something above the ordinary. Such language can best be described as artistic. Its artistry lies in the "well-turned phrase" and is easier to point to than to describe or analyze. Consequently, I am going to consider some types of artistic language, but I will rely most heavily on examples rather than description.

Not everyone can achieve the heights of eloquence, but certainly everyone can improve his or her use of language by being aware of some of the possibilities and using some imagination. I am going to write about some of the possiblities. You will have to provide the imagination.

Metaphor and simile   Metaphors and similes are probably the most frequently used figures of speech. Everyone uses them every day, but some people use them better than do others. When you ask someone, "Would you really stoop to that?" you are using a metaphor, because "stoop" is customarily (or was originally) used in a physical context; it was originally a rather specific physical action with no moral connotations. When you say, "He ran like a deer," you are using a simile. A simile is very like a metaphor. Both make comparisons. One difference is that a simile *announces* that a comparison is being made, whereas the comparison drawn in a metaphor is only implied. Furthermore, a simile usually makes a more limited comparison, whereas a good metaphor makes an extensive comparison between two entire contexts and invites further extension of the comparison. This second difference is rather coincidental, I think. A simile *can be* as extensive as a metaphor. "The man was a lion in the fight" is a metaphor; "The man was *like* a lion in the fight" is a simile. The difference is probably not all that important.

Dead and dead tired metaphors   Language is littered with the corpses of dead metaphors. There is a school of thought that holds that language *is* metaphor. I will not worry about that philosophical argument, but certainly most words can be traced back to metaphors. We speak of table "legs," for example. At one time that was a metaphorical comparison between what a chair stands on and what a human being stands on. There is a place called Table Mesa in Colorado. Actually there are probably hundreds of such formations in the Southwest. That is a redundant metaphor because, if it were translated totally into English, it would be "Table Table" or in Spanish "Mesa Mesa." Whoever named the hill "Table Mesa" probably thought he was creating a metaphor, not realizing the metaphor already existed.

Totally dead mataphors are no threat or problem for public speakers. They have become so much a part of the language that their original meanings have been forgotten. The word *sensible* originally meant "detectable by the senses." Modern synonyms for its original meaning might be *sensory* or *observable*. The word *attitude* is another. It originally referred to the angle at which a ship was proceeding or the angle at which it sat in the water. The *Oxford English Dictionary*, which is virtually a history of the English language, is a storehouse of dead metaphors.

A "storehouse"? *Storehouse* is another type of metaphor, and one with which public speakers need to be concerned. It is a cliche, which is a metaphor not yet quite dead, but sorely fatigued by overuse. Speakers are tempted to use cliches because they come easily, and the speaker either does not have time or imagination to come up with something better. Had I thought a little longer, I could have said the *OED* is a *graveyard* or *morgue* for dead metaphors, or that it is a rich archeological site for the excavation of dead metaphors.

I did a little better a few pages back near the beginning of this chapter. Look back at the first sentence after the example of "pedagese," the one that begins "the idea which someone has cleverly concealed in this wordstack . . . ." My first thought was to say "Looking for an idea in this passage is like looking for a needle in a haystack," but I rejected that because it was too obvious a cliche. Then I tried "The needle of an idea which someone has cleverly concealed in this haystack of words . . . ." That was a little better, but it still rested on the same cliche. So I finally decided on "an idea concealed in a wordstack," because it is a sort of a metaphor of a metaphor.

In the chapter on reasoning I was about to use the cliche "waving the bloody shirt" to describe emotional appeals when I realized just how much of a cliche it was. So I decided to go back to the roots of that cliche, and it eventually became the scenario for much of the chapter.

As you can see, it is difficult to avoid cliches. Sometimes you have to bite your tongue (oops, there goes another one) to keep from saying them. But most tired old cliches were once lively, powerful, young metaphors. It is now very tiresome to talk about a country being a "hotbed of revolution." The first time someone used it, it was a creative, exciting metaphor. It probably came from colonial days when starting a new fire with flint and steel was a pain. So people banked their fires at night, leaving a "hotbed" of glowing coals ready to burst into flames when new fuel was added the next morning. A beautiful new figure of speech. Now a tired, overused cliche.

You have watched this process yourself. "Right on!" was once a powerful metaphor when applied to something someone had just said instead of to a shot which had just hit the bulls-eye in target practice. It was especially appropriate when used in the revolutionary context of the Black Power Movement in the late 1960s. *Revolutionary* is another. The American Revolution was revolutionary, but it is overused when applied to a "new" detergent or deodorant.

Mixed metaphors and other confusions   You can invent imaginative metaphors. It just takes a little extra time and thought. Sometimes it is possible to organize a whole speech around a metaphor. But metaphors have to be *consistent*; they can become downright hilarious when they are mixed. Consider, for instance, this excerpt from a speech reportedly delivered in the British House of Commons:

> The British lion, whether roaming in the sand of the Near East or climbing the forests of Africa, will not draw in its horns or retire into its shell.

Or this, which brought down another house, this time the U.S. Senate:

> We pursue the shadow, the bubble bursts, and leaves but sackcloth and ashes in our empty hands.

Sometimes a metaphor can be inconsistent, not in context but in style, as in this example:

> I prefer champagne. When I drink it I get bubbly all over. I imagine myself far away on some midocean beach. I dream that I am lying alone nude on the soft warm sands. Then I see a tall handsome man walking toward me from a distance. When he reaches me he gazes lovingly into my eyes. Then he smiles and rises, goes into the sea and returns with two huge shells filled with beautiful pearls. He pours them over my quivering body and I feel bubbly all over, a divine sensation. But when I drink beer, I burp.

Some other examples are not exactly mixed metaphors, they just fall into some strange category we might label "Remember to Think What You Are Saying":

> The cup of our troubles is running over, and it is not full yet.

> Our country is overrun by absentee landlords.

> You're biting the hand that lays the golden egg.

> As an experienced anaconda hunter, I can tell you this: Don't ever let them get you into deep water—they'll drown you every time.

> As I look over the audience I see many faces I would like to shake hands with.

Climax   Another figure of speech you can use is to build your sentences as well as longer units in a climatic order, keeping the listeners' attention until you give them the outcome, just as you hold attention when telling a joke until you deliver the punch line. George Bernard Shaw has effectively parodied this style:

> In moments of utter crisis my nerves act in the most extraordinary way. When utter disaster seems imminent, my whole being is simultaneously braced to avoid it. I size up the situation in a flash, set my teeth, contract my muscles, take a firm grip of myself, and without a tremor, always do the wrong thing.

Like the punch line of a joke, the climax had better be worth all the suspense. Another problem may be that the speaker will get the items out of their naturally climactic order, and the result can be funny, as DeQuincey illustrates here:

> If once a man indulges in murder, he comes to think little of robbing; and from robbing he next comes to drinking and Sabbath-breaking, and from that to incivility and procrastination.

The periodic and the antithetic   Sometimes a speaker's sentences all sound alike in that they are short, choppy, and contain a subject, a verb, and an object. That may be clear, which is good, but it can become very boring after several minutes. There are at least two other sentence styles that sometimes fit the content better and certainly break up a repetitive style: the periodic and the antithetic. You might want to experiment with them.

A friend and I conducted an experiment comparing these three styles: the running, periodic, and antithetic. In preparing for the experiment my friend, Mike Leff, rewrote passages from one style into the two others. Suppose we take a look at one of those passages written in all three styles. Can you spot the differences? First the running style, which most people use most frequently:

> We need a more inclusive and consistent approach to morality. There are many who blast *Playboy* as immoral. They are outraged by dirty books and movies. They campaign against nudity. They protest the use of sex in the mass media. They fight sex education in the public schools. They condemn the exploitation of sex for profit. But these same people apparently see nothing immoral in prejudice and racist segregation. They are unconcerned about dirty air and water. They seem to ignore the plight of the poor who have inadequate housing and clothing. They are apparently untroubled by scenes depicting violence—murder, fighting, assaults, robberies,

and war. They often seem indifferent to the quality of education in schools that the children of the poor and minorities attend. They apparently see nothing wrong in the exploitation of war for their own personal profit.

As you can see, that style could become very boring if continued for several minutes. Instead, the same content might be rephrased into the periodic style, which builds a series of parallel phrases and then ends with a clause or verb phrase that ties them together. In the next example the second sentence is only quasi-periodic, but the third sentence is an excellent example of the style:

> We need a more inclusive and consistent approach to morality. There are many who blast *Playboy* as immoral, who are outraged by dirty books and movies, who campaign against nudity, who protest the use of sex in the mass media, who fight sex education in the public schools, and who condemn the exploitation of sex for profit. Yet, in respect to prejudice and racist segregation, in respect to dirty air and water, in respect to the plight of the poor who have inadequate housing and clothing, in respect to scenes depicting violence—murder, fights, assaults, robberies, and war—in respect to the quality of education in schools that the children of the poor and of minorities attend, in respect to the exploitation of war for their own profit, these same people express no concern and find nothing immoral.

This version certainly builds to a better climax than does the first. However, what it gains in variety and suspense, it may lose in clarity. That is not an unusual feature of the periodic style, and you may have to decide between them. The question is: Which do you need more at that point in the speech?

The third version is an example of the antithetic style. This style sets one element against another, emphasizing contrasts. Since contrast is the essence of this passage, this style seems to me to "fit" best. But judge for yourself:

> We need a more inclusive and consistent approach to morality. Many who blast *Playboy* as immoral apparently see nothing immoral in prejudice and racist segregation. Some who are outraged by dirty books and movies are unconcerned about dirty air and water. Some who campaign against nudity seem to ignore the plight of the poor who have inadequate housing and clothing. Many who protest the use of sex in the mass media are apparently untroubled

by scenes depicting violence—murder, fighting, assaults, robberies, and war. Those who fight against sex education in public schools often seem indifferent to the quality of education in schools that the children of the poor and the minorities attend. Some who condemn the exploitation of sex for profit apparently see nothing wrong in the exploitation of war for their own personal profit.

After you have become comfortable speaking before an audience, you can begin to think about varying your style by using different patterns. Do not write them out and read them or memorize them, but if you practice using them they will begin to come to you when you need them.

SUMMARY

Language can be viewed as a game played by sets of rules operating at phonemic, syntactic, semantic, and pragmatic levels. Rules at the *semantic* level specify the conditions under which utterances are meaningful and the conditions under which utterances are meaningful constitute their meaning. At the *pragmatic* level, rules are used to devise strategies for the effective use of language—strategies for being devious, for expressing and acquiring status, for achieving clear explanation and effective persuasion, among others.

To achieve the purposes of informing and persuading, language strategies must be clear, appropriate, reasonably dynamic, and aesthetically pleasing. To be *clear,* language should be free of unfamiliar words, words of too many syllables, long and complex sentences, euphemisms, excessive slang, excessive or insufficient redundancy, and unclear referents. It should be *appropriate* to the purpose, the speaker, the situation, and the listeners. Language is more *dynamic* when it is evaluative, strong, active, concrete, specific, vivid, sensory, personal, and metaphorical. Although *aesthetically pleasing* language is difficult to describe, it generally makes good use of a variety of stylistic figures, such as metaphors, similes, and climax and a variety of constructions including running, periodic, and antithetic styles.

ILLUSTRATIVE SPEECHES

Several of the speeches reprinted in this text provide excellent examples of the effective use of language. The speeches by Martin Luther King and Jonathan Edwards are especially forceful, in their own ways. The speeches by John Kennedy and Abraham Lincoln are models of reserved clarity in style.

To improve on those examples would be impossible. I have chosen three short speeches, however, that illustrate some additional stylistic concepts. The first of those was written by Shakespeare to be delivered by Mark Antony. You may recall that, in Shakespeare's play, Caesar had just been murdered by Brutus and his cohorts. The conspirators granted Antony permission to speak at Caesar's funeral, so long as he said nothing to stir the audience against them. Antony, however, was seeking revenge. He had to let his listeners know Caesar had been murdered and stir them to take revenge without explicitly revealing the murder or urging action. The result is a masterpiece of devious language. Try to pursue the analysis of the speech by asking what *semantic rules* Antony violates in pursuing his *pragmatic strategies*, particularly in his use of the word *honorable*. Do you think the violations are justified? Are they ever justified? Do you feel the same about the devious language employed by Nixon in his "Checkers" speech?

The second speech was delivered by the new Prime Minister, Winston Churchill, to the British House of Commons on May 13, 1940, in support of the following resolution he had just introduced:

> That this House welcomes the formation of a government repre-
> senting the unified and inflexible resolve of this nation to prosecute
> the war with Germany to a victorious conclusion.

Why has the style of this speech, which seems so straightforward with no apparent pretense to being "flowery" or embellished, been characterized as "striking, stirring, and noble"?

The remaining speech was unabashedly embellished, and appropriately so—it was delivered on a highly emotional occasion commemorating the dead. Frederick Douglass, black leader in the struggle against slavery, gave this speech on May 30, 1871, at Arlington National Cemetery. Its title, "Address for the Unknown Loyal Dead," seems self-explanatory.

How does the language of this speech give it its elevated, aesthetic style? In what ways is it "embellished"? Does it strike you as too "flowery" or "emotional"? Why do you suppose the example of the most embellished language style is a speech commemorating the dead? On what other occasions might similar language be appropriate?

Antony Speaks to the Citizens of Rome
William Shakespeare

Friends, Romans, countrymen, lend me your ears;
I come to bury Caesar, not to praise him.
The evil that men do lives after them;
The good is oft interred with their bones;
So let it be with Caesar. The noble Brutus
Hath told you Caesar was ambitious:
If it were so, it was a grievous fault,
And grievously hath Caesar answer'd it.
Here, under leave of Brutus and the rest—
For Brutus is an honorable man;
So are they all, all honorable men—
Come I to speak in Caesar's funeral.
He was my friend, faithful and just to me:
But Brutus says he was ambitious;
And Brutus is an honorable man.
He hath brought many captives to Rome
Whose ransoms did the general coffers fill:
Did this in Caesar seem ambitious?
When that the poor have cried, Caesar hath wept:
Ambition should be made of sterner stuff:
Yet Brutus says he was ambitious;
And Brutus is an honorable man.
You all did see that on the Lupercal
I thrice presented him a kingly crown,
Which he did thrice refuse: was this ambition?
Yet Brutus says he was ambitious;
And, sure, he is an honorable man.
I speak not to disprove what Brutus spoke,
But here I am to speak what I do know.
[Here Antony tells of Caesar's will, the citizens implore him to divulge its
contents, which inflames them more because Antony does so while
showing them Caesar's bodily wounds. He finishes his speech with:]
Good friends, sweet friends, let me not stir you up
To such a sudden flood of mutiny.
They that have done this deed are honorable:
What private griefs they have, alas, I know not,
That made them do it: they are wise and honorable,
And will, no doubt, with reason answer you.
I come not, friends, to steal your hearts:
I am no orator, as Brutus is;
But as you know me all, a plain blunt man,

That love my friend, and that they know full well
That gave me public leave to speak of him:
For I have neither wit, nor words, nor worth,
Action, nor utterance, nor the power of speech
To stir men's blood: I only speak right on;
I tell you that which you yourselves do know;
Show you sweet Caesar's wounds, poor poor dumb mouths,
And bid them speak for me; but were I Brutus,
And Brutus Antony, there were an Antony
Would ruffle up your spirits and put a tongue
In every wound of Caesar that should move
The stones of Rome to rise and mutiny.
[The citizens respond "We'll mutiny!"]

Blood, Toil, Tears and Sweat
Winston Churchill

On Friday evening last I received His Majesty's Commission to form a new Administration. It was the evident wish and will of Parliament and the nation that this should be conceived on the broadest possible basis and that it should include all parties, both those who supported the late Government and also the parties of the Opposition. I have completed the most important part of this task. A War Cabinet has been formed of five Members, representing, with the Opposition Liberals, the unity of the nation. The three party Leaders have agreed to serve, either in the War Cabinet or in high executive office. The three Fighting Services have been filled. It was necessary that this should be done in one single day, on account of the extreme urgency and rigour of events. A number of other positions, key positions, were filled yesterday, and I am submitting a further list to His Majesty to-night. I hope to complete the appointment of the principal Ministers during to-morrow. The appointment of the other Ministers usually takes a little longer, but I trust that, when Parliament meets again, this part of my task will be completed, and that the administration will be complete in all respects.

I considered it in the public interest to suggest that the House should be summoned to meet to-day. Mr. Speaker agreed, and took the necessary steps, in accordance with the powers conferred upon him by the Resolution of the House. At the end of the proceedings to-day the Adjournment of the House will be postponed until Tuesday, 21st May, with of course, provision for earlier meeting, if need be. The business to be considered during that week will be notified to Members at the earliest opportunity. I now invite the House, by the Motion which stands in my name, to record its approval of the steps taken and to declare its confidence in the new Government.

To form an Administration of this scale and complexity is a serious undertaking in itself, but it must be remembered that we are in the preliminary stage of one of the greatest battles in history, that we are in action at many other points in Norway and in Holland, that we have to be prepared in the Mediterranean, that the air battle is continuous and that many preparations, such as have been indicated by my hon. Friend below the Gangway, have to be made here at home. In this crisis I hope I may be pardoned if I do not address the House at any length to-day. I hope that any of my friends and colleagues, or former colleagues, who are affected by the political reconstruction, will make allowance, all allowance, for any lack of ceremony with which it has been necessary to act. I would say to the House, as I said to those who have joined this Government: "I have nothing to offer but blood, toil, tears and sweat."

We have before us an ordeal of the most grievous kind. We have before us many, many long months of struggle and of suffering. You ask, what is our policy? I will say: It is to wage war, by sea, land and air, with all our might and with all the strength that God can give us; to wage war against a monstrous tyranny, never surpassed in the dark, lamentable catalogue of human crime. That is our policy. You ask, what is our aim? I can answer in one word: It is victory, victory at all costs, victory in spite of all terror, victory, however long and hard the road may be; for without victory, there is no survival. Let that be realised; no survival for the British Empire, no survival for all that the British Empire has stood for, no survival for the urge and impulse of the ages, that mankind will move forward towards its goal. But I take up my task with buoyancy and hope. I feel sure that our cause will not be suffered to fail among men. At this time I feel entitled to claim the aid of all, and I say, "Come then, let us go forward together with our united strength."

Address for the Unknown Loyal Dead*
Frederick Douglass

Friends and Fellow Citizens: Tarry here for a moment. My words shall be few and simple. The solemn rites of this hour and place call for no

---

*The text for "Address for the Unknown Loyal Dead" is to be found in Frederick Douglass, *Life and Times of Frederick Douglass* . . . (Hartford, Conn.: Park Publishing Co., 1882), pp. 461–63. Presumably the text was supplied by Douglass himself.

lengthened speech. There is in the very air of this resting ground of the unknown dead a silent, subtle, and an all-pervading eloquence, far more touching, impressive, and thrilling than living lips have ever uttered. Into the measureless depths of every loyal soul it is now whispering lessons of all that is precious, priceless, holiest, and most enduring in human existence.

Dark and sad will be the hour to this nation when it forgets to pay grateful homage to its greatest benefactors. The offering we bring to-day is due alike to the patriot soldiers dead and their noble comrades who still live; for whether living or dead, whether in time or eternity, the loyal soldiers who imperiled all for country and freedom are one and inseparable.

Those unknown heroes whose whitened bones have been piously gathered here, and whose green graves we now strew with sweet and beautiful flowers, choice emblems alike of pure hearts and brave spirits, reached in their glorious career that last highest point of nobleness beyond which human power cannot go. They died for their country.

No loftier tribute can be paid to the most illustrious of all the benefactors of mankind than we pay to these unrecognized soldiers, when we write above their graves this shining epitaph.

When the dark and vengeful spirit of slavery, always ambitious, preferring to the rule in hell than to serve in heaven, fired the Southern heart and stirred all the malign elements of discord; when our great Republic, the hope of freedom and self-government throughout the world, had reached the point of supreme peril; when the Union of those States was torn and rent asunder at the center, and the armies of a gigantic rebellion came forth with broad blades and bloody hands to destroy the very foundation of American society, the unknown braves who flung themselves into the yawning chasm, where cannon roared and bullets whistled, fought and fell. They died for their country.

We are sometimes asked, in the name of patriotism, to forget the merits of this fearful struggle, and to remember with equal admiration those who struck at the nation's life and those who struck to save it,—those who fought for slavery and those who fought for liberty and justice.

I am no minister of malice. I would not strike the fallen. I would not repel the repentant, but may my "right hand forget her cunning, and my tongue cleave to the roof of my mouth," if I forget the difference between the parties to that terrible, protracted, and bloody conflict.

If we ought to forget a war which has filled our land with widows and orphans, which has made stumps of men of the very flower of our youth; sent them on the journey of life armless, legless, maimed and mutilated; which has piled up a debt heavier than a mountain of gold—swept uncounted thousands of men into bloody graves, and planted agony at a million hearthstones; I say if this war is to be forgotton, I ask in the name of all things sacred what shall men remember?

The essence and significance of our devotions here to-day are not to be found in the fact that the men whose remains fill these graves were brave in battle. If we met simply to show our sense of bravery, we should find enough to kindle admiration on both sides. In the raging storm of fire and blood, in the fierce torrent of shot and shell, of sword and bayonet, whether on foot or on horse, unflinching courage marked the rebel not less than the loyal soldier.

But we are not here to applaud manly courage, save as it has been displayed in a noble cause. We must never forget that victory to the rebellion meant death to the republic. We must never forget that the loyal soldiers who rest beneath this sod flung themselves between the nation and the nation's destroyers. If to-day we have a country not boiling in an agony of blood like France; if now we have a united country, no longer cursed by the hell-black system of human bondage; if the American name is no longer a by-word and a hissing to a mocking earth; if the star spangled banner floats only over free American citizens in every quarter of the land, and our country has before it a long and glorious career of justice, liberty, and civilization, we are indebted to the unselfish devotion of the noble army who rest in these honored graves all around us.

Chapter Ten References

1 Robin Lakoff, "Language in Context," *Language* (1971), 907–927.

2 Roger Desmond, private communication, 1977.

3 Susan Irvin-Tripp, "On Sociolinguistic Rules: Alternation and Co-occurrence," in *Directions in Sociolinguistics*, ed. John Gumperz and Dell Hymes (New York: Holt, Rinehart, and Winston, 1972), p. 219.

4 John Bowers, "Language Intensity, Social Introversion, and Attitude Change," *Speech Monographs*, 30 (1963), pp. 345–352.

5 John Bowers and Michael M. Osborne, "Attitudinal Effects of Selected Types of Concluding Metaphors in Persuasive Speeches," *Speech Monographs*, 33 (1966), pp. 147–155.

CHAPTER ELEVEN
Nonverbal Communication and Delivery

What we know about the effect of a speaker's delivery really comes from two sources. One of those sources is the scientific study of nonverbal communication, which is quite a recent development, most such research having occurred within the past 20 years. The other source is the distillation of speakers' experiences, which have been formalized and described by writers since well before the time of Christ. The output of the scientific study of nonverbal communication tends to be descriptive, theoretical generalizations. The output of the distillation of speakers' experience tends to be more prescriptive, usually consisting of specific suggestions as to how a speaker can be more effective in his or her delivery. I would like to take both approaches in this chapter. First, I will present a brief summary of the research in a variety of areas of nonverbal communication that relate particularly to public speaking and then turn to some more specific suggestions regarding delivery. You will probably find the first section more useful to you in your role as a listener and the second more useful in your role as a speaker.

RESEARCH IN NONVERBAL COMMUNICATION

Teachers and students of public speaking have vacillated between almost exclusive fascination with the speaker's delivery and studied ignorance of the topic. The excesses of the elocution movement in the nineteenth century, when every twitch of the finger and squeak of the voice was specifically defined and prescribed, led to a reaction against the teaching of delivery, which occupied easily the first half of the twentieth century. Now comes a sudden surge of interest in the study of "nonverbal communication," which bids fair to rival if not surpass the earlier interest in elocution.

Those who study nonverbal communication, however, are not very interested in *prescribing* nuances of voice, gesture, and posture during the speech act. Rather, they are interested in *describing* the various elements of nonverbal communication and the meaning transmitted by each element. The field is so young that few researchers have gone beyond attempts to describe the kinds of behaviors that seem to be communicating *something*; no one is very deep into the description of what it is that is to be communicated. If there is any advice to the speaker to be gleaned from the research to date, it would seem to be this: There are so many nonverbal communication channels, so many of which are not under the conscious control of the speaker, that one is almost bound to appear insincere if he or she tries to "fake" delivery. Awkward delivery can be smoothed out, and the speaker may learn to use gesture, vocal variety, and eye contact to maintain the attention of the audience.

Such things develop as beginning public speakers come to feel more at ease in speaking situations. They are helped along by the suggestions of friendly observers, or by the speakers' observations of themselves by some device such as videotape equipment or a full-length mirror. They are *not* learned by reading books such as this.

It is the communicator in his or her role as *listener* who can profit more by some knowledge of the language of nonverbal communication. It is not that the "naive" listener *misses* the nonverbal messages. If you are reading this book, you must have had at least 17 or 18 years practice in decoding nonverbal messages. The problem is that you are probably receiving more nonverbal messages than you realize, and you may be reacting to some of them without being fully aware of them. Furthermore, just as you learn to attach incorrect meanings to words, you may learn to attach incorrect meanings to nonverbal symbols and to react inappropriately. Some conscious attention to nonverbal communication should allow you to be more sensitive in this area.

Actually, the concern of this section is not so broad as the entire field of nonverbal communication. Nonverbal communication may include the study of tactilics (touch), aromatics (odor), objectics (objects and symbols), graphics (configuration of writing and printing), chronemics (timing), kinesics (body movement), and vocalics (nonverbal elements of vocalization), among others. Since this book focuses upon public deliberation, I will direct my attention in this section to those nonverbal communication symbols that accompany and most clearly modify face-to-face verbal interaction. We might label this focus the study of extra-verbal elements in public deliberation. At any rate, I will deal briefly with general appearance, kinesics, proxemics, and paralinguistics (or vocalics).

Most researchers agree that the nonverbal channels carry more social meaning than do the verbal channels.[a] If so, this is very important to the study of public deliberation. What has prevented it from being studied in any detail is probably the difficulty of isolating and describing its elements. Until quite recently most students of communication despaired of ever describing all the combinations of facial expressions, gestures, and vocal inflections, to consider only three of the numerous nonverbal channels. Furthermore, context seems to play an even more important part in nonverbal than in verbal communication, so that generalizations are even more difficult to make. Finally, the attempt of the elocutionists to teach nonverbal communication to speakers was such an abject failure that few speech experts saw any hope of applying knowledge about nonverbal communication even if it were available. Writers of recent textbooks have generally assumed that nonverbal behavior (or "delivery") is learned at a low level of awareness so that it is "second nature" and very difficult to teach.

The *reception* and *interpretation* of nonverbal cues are probably easier to teach and of at least equal importance. One is constantly called upon to make decisions on the basis of speeches—decisions that necessitate constant and usually rather quick evaluations of the trustworthiness of speakers and their information. Speech textbooks have customarily dealt with the tests of reasoning and evidence, so that the interested listener could use the verbal part of the message for such evaluation. Generally, evaluation of nonverbal cues has been ignored. The study of nonverbal communication still has not progressed to the point that it is possible to compile anything resembling a catalog of meanings. What is possible is to encourage you to be sensitive to the various nonverbal channels, with some suggestions regarding nonverbal cues you may miss and others you may misinterpret.

General Appearance

One study concluded that an "attractive" female student had more persuasive impact upon male students than did an unattractive female student.[b] Another seemed to indicate this was true regardless of the sex of the persuader and persuadee.[1] And one of these suggests that listeners are flattered and responsive when an attractive speaker reveals that she intends to try to persuade them, but they are put off when an unattractive speaker does the same.[2]

The area of "general appearance" probably should be divided between those matters of appearance that are physically fixed and those the speaker can manipulate. The listener who judges the credibility of speakers on the basis of their inherited physical attractiveness is basing his or her decision on an irrelevant and irrational factor; pretty people can be pretty stupid and pretty dishonest. Matters of dress and grooming are a little more complicated. The speaker has a choice in such matters, so they do communicate something. What the listener must decide is, first, what is communicated and, second, whether it is relevant to the speaker's credibility regarding the matter at hand. The employer who is a pushover for a suit and tie may discover to his or her dismay that even the village idiot can be trained to tie a Windsor knot, and the prisons are full of drug pushers who didn't think a narcotics agent would grow a beard and long hair.

Speakers must decide just how much they can manipulate their appearance for the sake of impression and still maintain self-respect. Listeners had best be aware that they can easily be misled by the speakers' attire and grooming; appearance bears no necessary relation to competence or trustworthiness. What listeners can look for are signs that speakers are using physical appearance in the service of communication. It may be important to decide what image they are trying to project in order to know what they perceive to be their role.

Kinesics

The field of kinesics can be most grossly divided into the study of facial and body movements. Ekman has contended that facial movements or expressions generally communicate the *type* of emotion an individual is experiencing, whereas body movements reveal the *extent* of the emotional intensity or level of arousal.[3] These are two channels to which listeners will become sensitive if they are to receive *all* the messages the speaker is sending. They are especially important precisely because speakers are often unaware of the messages they are carrying so that listeners, if they know something about the code, can gain insight into the uncensored feelings of speakers. As Hall puts it:

> All people communicate on several different levels at the same time but are usually aware of only the verbal dialog and don't realize that they respond to nonverbal messages. But when a person says one thing and really believes something else, the discrepancy between the two can usually be sensed. Nonverbal systems are much less subject to the conscious deception that often occurs in verbal systems. When we find ourselves thinking, "I don't know what it is about him, but he doesn't seem sincere," it's usually this lack of congruity between a person's words and his behavior that makes us anxious and uncomfortable.[4]

Types of kinesics   Not all nonverbal communication occurs at such a low level of awareness. Ekman and Friesen offer a breakdown consisting of five different types of kinesic behaviors, each developing somewhat differently and each operating at a somewhat different level of awareness.[5] *Emblems* are nonverbal acts that can be given relatively precise verbal definitions. They are learned and culture bound, actually an extension of the language. The crew of the *Pueblo* temporarily confounded their North Korean captors by raising their middle fingers in the well-known gesture of derision when they were photographed for propaganda purposes. The North Koreans, not familiar with this extension of the English language, publicized the picture widely, inadvertently reassuring Americans that the crew had not lost its spirit.

The gesture is an excellent example of an emblem, because of the preciseness of its meaning. Note that emblems are transmitted and received at a high level of awareness. They may contradict an oral message, but if they do, the contradiction is probably intended.

Illustrators accompany and complement the oral message. Their meanings are less precise and more dependent upon oral language, they are probably learned by imitation, and they are used at a high level of awareness. A speaker who holds his or her hands apart to indicate the length of an object is using an illustrator.

Affect displays are facial expressions that indicate emotional states. They probably originate in a combination of physiology and learning; that is, the coordination of facial muscles may be largely determined physiologically with little learning, but the relationship between the behaviors and the cues that evoke it are probably learned. Thus, we may not learn *how* to smile, but we learn *when*.

The source and observer of affect displays may or may not be aware of them. Obviously there are such things as polite smiles and studied frowns of which everyone is aware. However, some affect displays appear to be unwittingly transmitted and unknowingly received. Ekman has reported what he terms "micromomentary facial expressions," for example, which are expressions so fleeting (1/5 or 2/5 of a second) as to be consciously undetectable, imposed as they are on expressions of longer duration.[6] They serve the purpose of "emotional leakage," according to Ekman, and neither sender nor receiver appears to be aware of their existence. Dilation of the eyes appears to be similar. We are seldom aware of the dilation of our pupils, but there appears to be a close correlation between dilation and attention or interest. We are seldom aware of the dilation of the pupils of others, but there is evidence that we depend on such dilation as an index of the interest on the part of others.[7]

Regulators are devices by which we encourage or discourage the speaking of others; we nod if we want to encourage or look away if we want to discourage. They seem to be learned. We are generally not very aware of using them, but are usually quite aware when others use them. Of course, if we should place pupil dilation and micromomentary facial expressions into the class of regulators, which they may well be, they certainly do not operate at a high level of awareness.

Adaptors are nonfunctional behaviors, vestigial sublimations of more active behaviors that are not presently socially acceptable. Thus, foot shuffling and fidgeting may be vestiges of escape. They are probably learned, but we are not generally aware of them. We may be aware of them as we observe them in others, but are not usually totally aware of their meanings.

Birdwhistell has developed an elaborate classification system for body movement and facial expression.[8] It is beyond the scope of this book, although you may want to explore the subject further. I will be satisfied if you develop an increased sensitivity to cues you already understand in the channels of facial expression and body movement, so you can more readily judge the reliability of verbal messages.

Deception and control There appear to be three dimensions of feeling communicated nonverbally—that is, three kinds of information one looks for in nonverbal channels. One expects information about the direction of the other's interest or attention, his or her attitude or affect toward the object of his attention, and the level of his or her anxiety.

Ekman and Friesen distinguish among three general areas of the body from which emanate cues regarding these dimensions of feeling; the face, hands, and legs (including the feet). They hypothesize that the information capacity of a given channel depends upon the length of time required to transmit signals in that channel, the number of distinguishable stimulus patterns available in that channel, and the visibility of the channel.[9]

Thus, the face appears to have the greatest capacity for transmitting information since facial expressions change rapidly, there are a great many that are distinguishable, and the face is generally visible. The hands are not so facile nor so visible; therefore, they have a more limited capacity than does the face but have a greater capacity than do the legs and feet.

That order is not so clear in terms of capacity for deception or "emotional leakage." It appears that observers tend to watch most closely those channels that have the greatest information capacity. As a result, those who are attempting to deceive, send conflicting messages without detection, or "leak" strong but unacceptable feelings. They tend to use those channels that have the least information capacity and are least likely to be monitored by the observer. Consequently, the inadvertent expression of feelings one wishes to conceal might seem most likely to occur in the legs and feet, then the hands, and least likely to occur through the face.

As a general rule that is true. It is *entirely* true as long as the "facial" channels is restricted to relatively long-lasting facial expressions. However, there are a number of what might be termed "subliminal" facial channels that are heavily used for the disposal of emotions and that yearn for expression but are for one reason or another unacceptable.

One of these "subliminal" channels is pupil dilation, as I have mentioned. Another "subliminal" channel is the rate of speed at which one's eyes blink, with faster eye-blink rates indicating greater anxiety. A third is the muscular tension of the face, and a fourth is what Ekman terms "micromomentary" facial expressions, described earlier as an affect display.

A general increase in the level of activity of the hands and legs is indicative of increased overall physiological activation, usually nervousness, anxiety, or stress of some sort. The activity may be more specific, however. Many motions of the hands and legs are of the class labeled "adaptors," which I discussed earlier. These are vestiges of activities which under other circumstances would be useful, but they are for some reason socially unacceptable. Shuffling of the feet and shifting from one foot to another, for example, may be vestiges of walking, perhaps indicative of a desire to leave an uncomfortable situation.

Proxemics, Gaze, and Physical Orientation

Proxemics is the study of the space relationships maintained by persons in social interaction. People act so as to maintain between themselves and others distances that are physically and psychologically comfortable and appropriate to the limitations of whatever communication channel may be used, to the behavior in which they are engaged and, most importantly for our purposes, to the feelings they have about the others. In doing so, they may communicate a great deal, sometimes intentionally and sometimes quite unintentionally. However, the distance that will be judged comfortable and appropriate depends so heavily upon the gaze and body orientations of the participants that it is impossible to discuss the three separately.

It is customary to begin a discussion of personal space with Hall's description of the four categories of informal space: intimate, casual/personal, social/consultative, and public.[10] Intimate space, to which one admits intimate friends, ranges from actual physical contact to about 18 inches; casual/personal from there to about 4 feet; social/consultative (impersonal business) on up to about 12 feet; and public space from 12 feet to infinity. These figures were for a particular sample of white, professional Americans. Wide cultural variation has been observed; most of the examples in the literature indicate that most other cultures not only tolerate but expect closer physical proximity during conversation.

The dimensions of these protective buffer bubbles do not seem to be uniform; closer approach will be tolerated from the back and sides than will be tolerated from the front. This is probably due to the effect of seeing and being seen by the other individual. Research seems to lead to the conclusion that direct eye contact has the effect of reducing interpersonal distance, making both parties less comfortable than they would otherwise be at a given physical distance.[11]

The picture is actually more complex than that; perceived interpersonal distance depends also upon the body orientation to others as well as the angle of one's own body with respect to them. Thus, perceived interpersonal distance at a given physical distance is least when two people are directly facing one another, and it is greatest when they are back to back.

The intervention of physical objects such as furniture will generally increase perceived interpersonal distance, allowing closer physical proximity. Thus, a speaker may prefer to stand behind a desk in a small or crowded room when perceived distance would otherwise be uncomfortably close.

It seems clear that when a speaker attempts to decrease interpersonal distance, listeners generally interpret it as an indication that the speaker is interested and intent.[12] If the speaker provides additional cues, such as smiling and head nodding, one will perceive favorable attention; if he or she frowns and makes threatening gestures, one may make a sudden decision to leave the area. This appears true also when perceived interpersonal distance is decreased by a speaker who maintains a more direct gaze[13] a more direct body orientation.[14]

Spatial relationships also reflect status relationships. High-status persons generally occupy and are encouraged to occupy positions above and in front of others. High-status persons are also accorded greater personal space and approached less than low-status persons.

Practical proxemics   A knowledge of proxemics can be useful in at least three ways. First, it can be useful in planning the physical contexts in which public speeches are going to occur. Architects, interior decorators, conference planners, and teachers should be especially sensitive to the constraints imposed upon public speaking by the arrangement of physical objects. The person who has control of such arrangements can practically dictate the kind of communication that takes place. The teacher who seats students in straight rows facing a platform upon which he or she stands can be fairly assured that the students will be primarily engaged in listening and occasionally asking questions and that they will perceive him or her as expecting deference. If that is the goal, the teacher will be delighted with the outcome, but if the goal is to facilitate group discussion he or she will be disappointed.

Second, an understanding of proxemics can be useful in deciphering the verbal communication of another. *People communicate a great deal about the way they perceive a situation or the way they wish it to be by the way they use interpersonal space.* They indicate whether they are interested in another, whether they consider the other a friend, and what status they accord the other, among other things.

Finally, such knowledge is useful to speakers, who can use it to some extent to indicate interest and sincerity, and to focus and, indeed, almost force the attention of the listeners at vital points in the message. When they move toward the listeners, face them directly, and maintain maximum eye contact at a certain point in the speech, they can bring audience attention to a peak at that point. Needless to say, that part of the speech had best be worth all the fuss, and the less conscious and deliberate verbal cues had best reinforce the impression of sincerity, or a speaker may become an unwilling impromptu comedian.

Paralanguage

Mehrabian concludes from several of his studies comparing the effects of inconsistent messages transmitted by the verbal, vocal, and facial channels that listeners depend very little upon verbal cues, very heavily upon facial cues, and almost as heavily upon vocal cues.[15] That conclusion with respect to vocal cues must be considerably qualified, however, on the basis of other research. Variations in the physical characteristics of the voice (pitch, rate, volume, etc.) seem to produce reliable differences in listeners' perceptions of speakers and their emotional states, but these perceptions are not necessarily accurate. Furthermore, neither the variations in speakers' vocal characteristics nor the stereotyped perceptions they elicit from listeners seem to have any appreciable effect on listener comprehension or opinion change.

Vocal stereotypes   The clearest vocal stereotypes are those we term *inflections*, which obviously and usually quite intentionally modify verbal meanings. Actually, a discussion of inflections probably does not belong in a chapter on delivery, because inflections are really part of language, carrying both syntactic and semantic cues. Besides, it would be insulting to your intelligence for me to spend pages of expensive paper and ink explaining how inflection indicates a question, exclamation, emphasis, irony, sarcasm, and the like. So I won't.

Instead, suppose we consider some of the personal and personality characteristics that listeners stereotypically attribute to speakers on the basis of their vocal characteristics.

Perhaps not surprisingly, sex can be identified quite accurately on the basis of vocal characteristics alone, but race cannot.

The research dealing with the relation between vocal and personality characteristics has been plagued with methodological problems, most stemming from the extreme vagueness of the concepts involved in perceptions of both personality and voice. The general thrust of the studies seems to be toward the conclusion that people *reliably* associate certain personality stereotypes with certain vocal characteristics, but the associations are not very *accurate*.

Probably the most complete study in this area has been done by Addington, whose findings are summarized in Table 11-1.[16] There are a number of interesting suggestions to be derived from this table. The most obvious are that speakers can probably improve their image by increasing rate and pitch variety and guarding against nasality.

Listeners appear to judge the social status of speakers not only reliably but accurately on the basis of voice alone, even when speakers are attempting to fake status cues.[17] No one seems to be able to find what voice characteristics listeners are using as status cues, however. The finding also has to be qualified in cases when speakers having regional or national dialects are being judged, because such speakers are generally judged to be of somewhat lower status than those who speak standard American English.[18]

Studies in which listeners have been asked to judge emotions from voices alone have also suffered from methodological problems. The first of these is that such a test depends as much upon the speaker's ability to express emotion as it does on the listener's ability to identify it. A second is that the experimenter usually supplies the labels that the listeners use to identify the emotions, and there is a great deal of room for misunderstanding the meanings of those labels and the shades of meaning by which they are distinguished. Could you, for example, tell the difference between "fear" and "panic"? Still, there is considerable evidence that such judgments can be made with surprising reliability and accuracy.[18a] Table 11-2 represents one summary of the vocal cues that observers judge to be associated with certain emotional states.[19] The table should be interpreted cautiously, because the research findings on which it is based are scanty, sometimes contradictory, and indicate many differences among individuals.

Perceived credibility of a speaker and perceived "persuasiveness" of a message appear to suffer as a result of certain vocal characteristics. (This does not mean that voice characteristics actually make a difference in the effect of the message, however. That is discussed in the next section.) A

TABLE 11-1
Simulated vocal cues and personality stereotypes.*

Simulated vocal cues‡	Speakers	Stereotyped preceptions
Breathiness	Males	Younger; more artistic
	Females	More feminine; prettier; more petite; more effervescent; more highly strung and shallower
Thinness	Males	Did not alter listener's image of the speaker; no significant correlations
	Females	Increased social, physical, emotional, and mental immaturity; increased sense of humor and sensitivity
Flatness	Males	More masculine; more sluggish; colder; more withdrawn
	Females	More masculine; more sluggish; colder; more withdrawn
Nasality	Males	A wide array of socially undesirable characteristics
	Females	A wide array of socially undesirable characteristics
Tenseness	Males	Older; more unyielding; cantankerous
	Females	Younger; more emotional, feminine, high strung; less intelligent
Throatiness	Males	Older; more realistic, mature; sophisticated; and well adjusted
	Females	Less intelligent; more masculine; lazier; more boorish, unemotional, ugly, sickly, careless, inartistic, naive, humble, neurotic, quiet, uninteresting, apathetic. In short, "cloddish or oafish" (Addington)
Orotundity	Males	More energetic, healthy, artistic, sophisticated, proud, interesting, enthusiastic. In short, "hardy and aesthetically inclined" (Addington)
	Females	Increased liveliness, gregariousness, aesthetic sensitivity, and "increasingly proud and humorless" (Addington)
Increased rate	Males	More animated and extroverted
	Females	More animated and extroverted
Increased pitch variety	Males	More dynamic, feminine, aesthetically inclined
	Females	More dynamic and extroverted

*From *Nonverbal Communication in Human Interaction* by Mark L. Knapp. Copyright ©1972 by Holt, Rinehart and Winston. Reprinted by permission of Holt, Rinehart and Winston.

‡For description of these cues, see P. Heinberg, *Voice Training for Speaking and Reading Aloud* (New York: Ronald Press, 1974), pages 152-181.

Table 11-2
Characteristics of vocal expressions contained in the test of emotional sensitivity.*

Feeling	Loudness	Pitch	Timbre	Rate	Inflection	Rhythm	Enunciation
Affection	Soft	Low	Resonant	Slow	Steady and slight upward	Regular	Slurred
Anger	Loud	High	Blaring	Fast	Irregular up and down	Irregular	Clipped
Boredom	Moderate to low	Moderate to low	Moderately resonant	Moderately slow	Monotone or gradually falling	—	Somewhat slurred
Cheerfulness	Moderately high	Moderately high	Moderately blaring	Moderately fast	Up and down; overall upward	Regular	
Impatience	Normal	Normal to moderately high	Moderately blaring	Moderately fast	Slight upward	—	Somewhat clipped
Joy	Loud	High	Moderately blaring	Fast	Upward	Regular	
Sadness	Soft	Low	Resonant	Slow	Downward	Irregular pauses	Slurred
Satisfaction	Normal	Normal	Somewhat resonant	Normal	Slight upward	Regular	Somewhat slurred

*From *The Communication of Emotional Meaning* by J. R. Davitz et al., p. 63. Copyright © 1964 McGraw-Hill, Inc. Used with permission of McGraw-Hill Book Company.

study conducted by Mehrabian and Williams indicated that less pitch variety, lower volume, slower rate, and a greater number of nonfluencies resulted in less perceived "persuasiveness."[20] Studies by Sereno and Hawkins[21] and by Miller and Hewgill[22] concluded that vocal nonfluencies reduced listeners' perceptions of speakers' competence and dynamism, but not their trustworthiness. Studies by Pearce and Conklin[23] and by Pearce[24] concluded that two different styles of delivery produced differences in audience ratings of speaker's dynamism, likeableness, and trustworthiness, but had no effect on their ratings of speaker credibility. Unfortunately, these last two studies confounded quite an array of variables, making it impossible to tell which variables accounted for which effects.

Comprehension and attitude change   One would expect that *some* of these vocal stereotypes, especially those related to credibility, would also be related to audience comprehension or opinion change. Generally that is not true.

There is a little evidence that vocal *variety* of various types may increase comprehension,[25] and breathiness or nasality may decrease it.[26] Vocal characteristics in general, though, don't seem to have much effect on comprehension. Even very rapid rates of vocal delivery do not seem to reduce comprehension so long as the rate remains below the supernatural.

Results of research using opinion change present much the same picture. Sereno and Hawkins, Pearce and Conklin, and Pearce all failed to find any significant differences in opinion change due to the vocal characteristics they studied, which included nonfluencies, pitch, pitch variety, volume, volume variety, and inflection.

It is not too difficult to accept the fact that listeners may dislike certain vocal characteristics of a speaker and still comprehend his or her message. This may be especially true of college students, who have been carefully trained to comprehend under the most adverse conditions, including poor delivery on the part of the speaker. However, the fact that certain vocal characteristics affect perceived speaker *credibility* but have no detectable effect on opinion change seems really difficult to explain; it raises some basic questions about the acceptability of the operational definitions and/or the conceptualizations of credibility and opinion change.

What does all of this do for the advice most speech teachers and textbooks offer in the area of vocal delivery? Knapp lists them:

Typical prescriptions for the use of the voice in delivering a public speech include: (1) Use variety in volume, rate, pitch, and articulation. The probabilities of desirable outcomes are less when one uses a constant rate, volume, pitch, and articulation. Being consistently overprecise may be as ineffective as being overly sloppy in your articulation. Although it has not been formally studied, it is quite possible that when vocal variety is perceived as rhythmic or patterned, it is no longer variety and this decreases the probabilities of desirable outcomes. (2) Decisions concerning loud-soft, fast-slow, precise-sloppy, or high-low should be based on what is appropriate for a given audience in a given situation. (3) Excessive nonfluencies are to be avoided.[27]

Generally, the findings suggest that the speaker should follow these suggestions if he wants his audience to be comfortable, to like him, and to perceive him to be a high-status, credible person., There is little evidence, however, to lead the speaker to expect all of this to have much noticeable effect on audience comprehension or opinion change.

DELIVERY

Persons giving public speeches, like actors, have to be concerned with remembering what they are going to say, with the physical setting, and with their physical presence before an audience. However, the ways speakers handle those problems are frequently quite different from acting.

Speakers are not playing a role; they are real people operating in real situations shared by the audience. They are not creating an illusion of reality, they are actually trying to change some part of reality. They do not ask the listeners to willingly suspend disbelief and temporarily join them in a world they and the playwright and the director have created. Instead, they ask listeners to believe them because their perceptions are reliable and consistent with the listeners' own experiences. In a sense all the world's a stage on which everyone is playing a part, yes, but the actors are to some extent discovering and to some extent writing the script.

These differences make speakers' choices sometimes different from those of actors. Speakers' primary focus is upon their *ideas*, not upon appearances. Consequently, they do not choose to memorize a speech before delivering it, they avoid illusory costuming and stage settings, and they do not rehearse their movements and vocal inflections. Instead they make those choices that will produce the sort of delivery expected of public speakers: *delivery that (a) does not distract the listeners from what they have to say, (b) makes it clear that they are interested in the listeners, and (c) makes it clear that they believe their ideas are important to the listeners and want listeners to believe them, too. Their aim is a style of delivery that is direct, spontaneous, and not distracting.*

Prompting Your Memory

You have probably been wondering just how you are going to remember everything you have to say, and how you can use notes to help you remember. Suppose we apply these three general principles of good delivery to that question to see what sort of answers we can come up with.

Put plainly, you want to use enough notes to remind yourself of what you are going to say without allowing those notes to become distracting or to interfere with your attention to the audience or your attention to your ideas.

Your topic and the situation will have a great deal of bearing on the way you use notes. You can think of speeches as falling into four general categories: impromptu, manuscript, memorized, and extemporaneous. In an impromptu speech you won't have to be concerned with notes because you won't have time to prepare any. An impromptu speech is one given on the spur of the moment without any specific prior preparation. You may receive an award, for example, and be expected to give a response, or you may be involved in a public meeting and decide you want to express your opinion. In such cases you will have no notes. You can make an impromptu speech more coherent by deciding what major point you want to make, and what supporting points or major divisions you want to cover. Beyond that you will have to trust your memory.

A manuscript speech is a rather different sort of problem. There are some situations in which your specific wording is so important that you may have to write it out beforehand and read from a manuscript. The president of the United States, for example, almost always reads speeches from manuscript because his exact words are likely to be quoted and analyzed for subtle shades of meaning. Spokespersons for public figures and corporations frequently read their public statements, as do attorneys both in and out of court. Papers presented at scholarly conventions are usually read. You may write a paper for a college course, and the professor may ask you to read it for the class.

In such cases you will have extensive notes, obviously. The problem is to prevent the fact that you are reading from interfering with your communication. It is difficult to look at the audience and sound spontaneous when you are reading. Difficult, but not impossible.

First, you can write the speech in oral style. Imagine how you would *tell* someone orally, and then write it down. You could even go one step further by talking through the speech into a tape recorder, perhaps before one or two listeners, and then transcribing the recording onto paper. Then you can make whatever corrections are necesssary to clarify and amplify the crucial passages. Next you can become very familiar with the speech, familiar enough that you do not have to rely heavily on the manuscript. That will free you to look at your listeners frequently and to gesture and move around occasionally. Finally, you can underline important words and sentences, and make notes to yourself in the margins, so you can use vocal inflections and occasional side comments to give your reading an air of spontaneity.

Memorized speeches are very unusual outside of the theater. If for some reason you must give a speech word for word as you have written it, but for some reason you cannot use a manuscript, you have a very unusual problem. The best approach would probably be to write the speech using the suggestions for writing manuscript speeches. Then memorize it and practice delivering it. Your goal is to know it well enough that you don't have to worry about remembering the words and can concentrate on communicating with your listeners, looking and sounding spontaneous and direct. Too frequently speakers who have memorized their speeches look and sound as if they were desperately searching behind their eyeballs to recall the words they were supposed to say.

Because it is so difficult to read speeches from manuscript or to present them from memory, don't do it unless you have to. It may seem that a manuscript or a memorized speech will make you feel more secure, but what you gain in security will be more than lost in directness and spontaneity. This is why this book has concentrated on the extemporaneous speech, and why that is the type of speech you are usually assigned in this course. So suppose we consider the use of notes in such speeches.

Be sure to ask your professor what sort of notes he wants you to use. He may have specific reasons for limiting your use of notes, and you should know what those limitations are. Obviously a long speech will require more notes than a short one. The more notes you have, the more difficult it will be to keep them straight while you are trying to talk with your listeners.

I have already suggested that you take notes on fairly sturdy index cards so they are easier to handle. It is also a good idea to put all the information you will need on only one side of the card so you will not have to be flipping it over during the speech. That probably includes the name of the source, his or her qualifications, and the date and place the information was published.

To these informational notes you may want to add notes to yourself to indicate where your major divisions are and a brief sketch of your introductions, transitions, and conclusions. On one card you might want to put a condensed outline. This would be for a fairly long speech containing quite a bit of information from other sources. For a five-minute speech on a topic you know a great deal about, you can probably get by with a single card or no notes at all. For a demonstration speech or a speech with good visual aids, you may be able to use the visual aids or the steps in your demonstration as reminders so that you won't need notes.

Regardless of how many notes you use, don't depend on them too heavily and don't let them become distracting. Don't hestitate to gesture with the hand in which you hold the notes. If you don't have to depend too heavily on them you may be able to leave them on the lectern part of the time so your hands are completely free to gesture. Above all else, do not hold them up between yourself and your listeners and read from them. That will ruin your eye contact and physical directness.

Setting the Stage

Sometimes you can choose where you are going to speak, but that is not usually the case. More frequently the place is dictated, but you usually have some control over the physical arrangement. Your speeches in class will be given in a fairly standard classroom. There will probably be a desk and/or a lectern at the front of the room. The seats in the room may or may not be moveable. The brightness of the lights may be adjustable, and there are probably window shades. In some speech classrooms there are elevated platforms at the front of the room. These are the physical factors you have to work with. You don't have much leeway, but you do have some, and you do have decisions to make.

What should you do about the desk or lectern? By standing behind the lectern you will make the audience feel they are further from you than if you were to stand beside it or push it out of the way entirely. Usually you will want them to feel closer to you, so the less you have to use the desk or lectern the better.

The angle at which two people face one another also seems to decrease perceived interpersonal distance. Again, if you want your listeners to feel closer to you, you can ask them to pull their chairs into a semicircle so more of them will be facing you more directly.

If there is an elevated platform at the front of the room you will have to decide whether to stand up there or down in front of it. If you stand above your listeners they can see you better, but they will also perceive you as more isolated from them, less a part of their group. You may also *feel* more isolated. If you stand behind a lectern on an elevated platform, that effect will be further intensified. On the other hand, if the room is so crowded that the front row of seats is close to the edge of the platform, standing off the platform might put you *too* close. Speaking to a class such as this probably fits the category of situation Hall labels social/consultative, and the comfortably tolerated interpersonal distance in such situations ranges from four to twelve feet. If you move closer than four feet from your nearest listeners, you are violating their expectations, and probably you will all feel uncomfortable.

Notice that you can also decrease perceived interpersonal distance by looking more directly at your listeners.

Another consideration which may help you make these decisions is that these spatial relationships also reflect status relationships among communicators. High-status persons generally occupy and are encouraged to occupy positions above and in front of others. If you stand far from your listeners, on a raised platform, behind a lectern, like a king on a throne, they may get the impression you think pretty highly of yourself or not very highly of them. That would probably be a good impression to avoid.

I mentioned the lights and window shades primarily because, if you are going to use some sort of projector, you will need to make provisions for dimming the lights when you are using it and turning them back up when you are finished. Get someone else to do that for you. Sometimes—for some topics—you may want to create a more personal atmosphere, in which case you might think about turning the lights down or drawing the shades a little. If so, do it before class, not just before your speech. Otherwise it may look a little silly. The window shades may also be used to cut out competing events of interest outside. A hot volleyball game or an ROTC drill team just outside the window can be a formidable competitor for audience attention, as can something as simple as two amorous dogs on the lawn.

Doing It in Class

Chances are good you are nervous about actually standing in front of the class and having all that attention focused on you, right? Good. Your nervousness is going to create a state of physiological alertness that can help you look and sound more energetic, interested, and interesting.

Everyone, including the most experienced public speaker, is nervous before facing an audience. What's more, your listeners in this class are going to be especially understanding because they have been or are going to be standing in the same shoes. So relax. Stop worrying about how you look and how you sound, and think about what you are going to say. You chose this topic because it interests you and because some of the people in your class said it interested them. You have thought a lot about your audience and have talked to some of them. You have studied your topic thoroughly and organized your material carefully. You have given some thought to the language you are going to use. You have tested your speech on some listeners, so you know it is going to work. You may appear a little nervous at first, but your classmates certainly understand why, and besides that, nervousness is going to disappear very quickly once you get into the speech.

Now I just said to forget about how you look and sound, and here I am all ready to tell you to think about it. That is not really a contradiction, I hope. If you think about your delivery a great deal *before* the day of your speech you will be less likely to worry about it *during* your speech.

The best way to "think about" delivery is to practice it. When you first give your speech you may want to do it by yourself in your own room. But that shouldn't last very long. I've always found the most effective way to practice is to capture one or two people I can trust to give me an honest opinion and ask them to listen to me, preferably in the actual room where I'm going to speak or one very similar. So here is a scenario describing what might actually happen in such a session. The setting is a typical college classroom. Gary, the speaker, sits at one end of the front row of seats. Jo and Buford sit near the center of the room. Gary rises and shuffles, slouching, to the lectern.

Buford:	Hey, man, is that what you're going to wear when you give this speech?
Gary:	Well, yes, I thought . . . .
Jo:	Flashy slacks and a flowered silk sport shirt? A bead necklace? Do you usually dress like a fag when you go to this class?
Gary:	Hey, this is one of my favorite party outfits! Nobody got on me about it Friday night!
Buford:	Sure, Friday night! But this ain't gonna be Friday night! You don't wear stuff like that to class! People are gonna laugh and point! Use some common sense, man.
Gary:	You want I should take it off?
Jo:	Yes.
Buford:	God, no. But I'll tell you what I do want. I'd like to see you walk up there again, and this time look like you *want* to instead of like you're gonna get a beating if you don't.
	(Gary returns to his seat. He rises again, stands straight, walks briskly to the lectern, and begins his speech.)
Buford:	Hey, alright!!
	(Gary continues speaking.)

Jo: Gary, you're slouching again, and your're shifting from one foot to the other. You look like you're trying to rock yourself to sleep.
           (Gary straightens up again, puts his weight on both feet, and resumes speaking.)

Buford: Now you're swaying backward and forward. If you gotta go, we'll wait for you.

Gary: Hey, you turkeys! I asked for constructive criticism, not a put-down session!

Buford: We're just callin' 'em . . .

Gary: As you see 'em. O.K., where was I?
           (Resumes speaking.)

Jo: Ah . . . it it's O.K., I have a little constructive criticism to offer, if it won't offend you, your highness.

Gary: Sure, what?

Jo: *Get the hell away from the lectern!* You're hanging onto it like it's a life raft! Why don't you walk down here closer and talk *with* us instead of standing back there like a damn potentate and talking *at* us? And why don't you walk occasionally? Like between your introduction and your first main point would've been a good time to move a little.

Gary: O.K., O.K., I hope I don't ever get an *un*constructive criticism from you.
           (Walks up to about six feet from the first row of seats and resumes speaking.)

Buford: (Whispering to Jo) Just like Hall says in Chapter 12, socio/consulterive space, huh?

Jo: (Whispering back) "Social-consultative," Retard.

Buford: Could you take your hands out of your pockets? A minute ago you were playing with your key ring, now you look like you're playing . . . .

Jo: Never mind, Buford. Gary, why don't you relax and let yourself gesture sometimes? You do when you're just standing around talking, but now that you think you're giving a big formal speech you're all frozen up. Unlax. Pretend it's Show and Tell time, and show us a little, too. It'll give you something to do with your hands.

Buford: But don't get wild about it, like Nixon with his hands over his head and his big "V" sign. Or like Kennedy always chopping with his right hand like he was a hot karate expert.

Jo:	Gary doesn't do that, but he is always rubbing the side of his nose, at least when he doesn't have his hands in his pockets. I counted five time he rubbed his nose in about a minute a little while ago.
Buford:	At least he's rubbing the *outside* today. Usually . . . .
Gary:	Hey, could I break in for a minute and give a short speech I just happen to have brought along? I mean, if it wouldn't be too much of an interruption?
Buford:	Sure, go ahead, but make it short.
	(Gary resumes speaking.)
Buford:	Seriously, now, Gary, I think you're going to have to talk a lot louder than that when this room is full of people. And you're talking in sort of a monotone. Could you get some variety into your voice? Doesn't the textbook say something about people thinking a speaker is smarter if he has a lot of variety in his voice?
Jo:	It must say that in one of the cartoons if *you* read it.
Buford:	Buzz off, Fluff. The only reason you bought the book was to hide your Wonder Woman comics in. You were holding it upside down in class the other day.
Jo:	You were probably too stoned to know. Hey, while you're stopped, Gary, you were pacing back and forth a lot, too. Moving once in awhile is good, but you were pacing like a fox in a cage.
Gary:	Well, you'd pace too if you had two people on your back all the time.
Buford:	Paranoid.
Gary:	I wouldn't be so paranoid if people weren't always picking on me.
	(Resumes speech, which he finishes without further interruption. He says his last sentence as he walks back to his seat.)
Buford:	You aren't going to do that when you really give the speech, are you? I mean, walk back to your seat while you're still talking?
Jo:	Yeah, it looked like you couldn't wait to get it over with. If you aren't any more interested than that, you can't expect anyone else to be.
Gary:	O.K., that's true. But what did you think about it in general?
Buford:	Well, I thought Jo and I gave pretty good speeches, but you kept interrupting us.
Jo:	Really, Gary, I thought it was good. It was well organized and it sounded like you knew a lot about it.

Buford: Seriously, I thought so too. But there is one more thing I think you could do. You know, when you come to an important point you talk a lot louder, like you're trying to blast it at us, pound it into us to make us remember it. I think it'd get attention better if you dropped your voice a little when you came to those places, and maybe walk toward us and lean forward a little and look right at us and hold your hands out like this. You know, make it real intense and direct instead of loud. Ten-four?

Gary: Ten-four. Where to now?

Buford: The Graduate. I'm *de*hydrated. Buy you one, Jo?

Jo: Let's let Gary buy. He owes us at least a pitcher for what he put us through.

Gary: Put *you* through! Man, I haven't been so thoroughly stomped since the day my mother threw me in the pigpen!

Jo: So *that's* why they call you Pigpen.
(All exit.)

I could not add much to that, and I would second everything Jo and Buford said. I *could* suggest that if your friends find some problem with your voice—if it is monotonous, has a repetitive pattern, or is too high, for example—that you record your speech on audiotape so you can hear it for yourself. Then you can work on it, using the tape recorder, until you get rid of the problem. If you're really lucky and have access to a videotape recorder, you can have a friend record your speech so you can also *see* yourself, which should be quite an advantage. You might be able to borrow a videotape recorder from your speech or mass communication department or from the educational television center, the audio-visual center, or the teaching resources center. Ask your professor. He or she might be able to videotape one of the speeches for the entire class.

SUMMARY

Extraverbal communication is especially likely to contain messages of which speakers are not fully aware, but messages they nevertheless use in making decisions. Some types of extraverbal communication that are especially important are *general appearance, kinesics* (posture, gesture, and facial expression), *proxemics* (interpersonal distance and spatial arrangement), and *paralanguage* (extraverbal elements of voice).

People frequently judge others erroneously on the basis of physical appearance, which cannot be changed, or on the basis of dress and grooming, which may be irrelevant to the judgment.

Although it is difficult for speakers to prevent their true feelings from being revealed in posture, gesture, or facial expression, knowledgeable observers can still enhance their chances of detecting deception by learning to watch for those physical mannerisms that most often serve as means of "emotional leakage."

Interpersonal distance frequently affects interpersonal communication in subtle ways, and the ways people manipulate interpersonal distance can serve as cues to their perceptions of themselves, others, and the communication events in which they are involved.

Finally, extraverbal characteristics of speakers' voices are likely to be misleading, in that listeners show high agreement in their judgments of others' voices even though those stereotyped judgments are frequently inaccurate. Variety in vocal volume, pitch, and rate, as well as a moderate amount of fluency and careful articulation, all seem to make a speaker's image more favorable with listeners even though, paradoxically, there is little evidence that such vocal characteristics contribute much to listener comprehension or opinion change.

The delivery expected of public speakers (1) does not distract their listeners from what they have to say, (2) makes it clear that they are interested in their listeners, and (3) makes it clear that they believe their ideas are important to the listeners and that they want them to believe it, too. Speakers aim for a style of delivery that is direct, spontaneous, and not distracting.

Therefore, speakers must (1) use enough notes to remind themselves of what they are going to say without allowing the notes to become distracting to the listeners or to interfere with their attention to the listeners or their ideas, (2) arrange and use the area in which the speech is to be delivered so as to focus audience attention without making themselves or their listeners uncomfortable, and (3) use physical activity (walking, gestures, and facial expression) in ways that clarify and call attention to the ideas rather than to themselves.

References

a   See, for example: R. Bridwhistell, *Kinesics and Context* (Philadelphia: University of Pennsylvania, 1970); and A. Mehrabian and S. R. Ferris, "Inference of Attitudes from Nonverbal Communication in Two Channels," *Journal of Consulting Psychology* 31 (1967): 248-252.

b   Judson Mills and Elliot Aronson, "Opinion Change as a Function of the Communicator's Attractiveness and Desire to Influence," *Journal of Personality and Social Psychology* 1 (1965): 73-77.

1   R. N. Widgery and B. Webster, "The Effects of Physical Attractiveness Upon Perceived Initial Credibility," *Michigan Speech Journal* 4 (1969): 9-15.

2   Mills and Aronson, *op. cit.*

3   P. Ekman, "Body Position, Facial Expression, and Verbal Behavior During Interviews," *Journal of Abnormal and Social Psychology* 68

(1964): 295-301; and P. Ekman and W. Friesen, "Head and Body Cues in the Judgment of Emotion: A Reformulation," *Perceptual and Motor Skills* 24 (1967): 711-724.

4   E. T. Hall, *The Silent Language* (Garden City, N.Y.: Doubleday, 1959).

5   P. Ekman and W. Friesen, "The Repertoire of Nonverbal Behavior: Categories, Origins, Usage, and Coding," *Semiotica* 1 (1969): 49-98.

6   P. Ekman and W. Friesen, "Nonverbal Leakage and Clues to Deception," *Psychiatry* 32 (1969): 88-106.

7   Eckhart H. Hess, "Attitude and Pupil Size," *Scientific American* (1965): 46-65.

8   Birdwhistell, *op. cit.*

9   Ekman and Friesen, "Nonverbal Leakage and Clues to Deception."

10 E. T. Hall, *The Hidden Dimension* (Garden City, N.Y.: Doubleday, 1966)

11 M. Argyle and J. Dean, "Eye Contact, Distance, and Affiliation," *Sociometry* 28 (1965): 289-304.

12 See: A. Mehrabian and S. R. Ferris, *op. cit.*; and A. Mehrabian and M. Wiener, "Decoding of Inconsistent Communication," *Journal of Personality and Social Psychology* 6 (1967): 109-114.

13 Argyle and Dean, *op. cit.*; and M. Argyle and A. Kendon, "The Experimental Analysis of Social Performance," in *Advances in Experimental Social Psychology*, ed. L. Berkowitz (New York: Academic Press, 1967), 55-98.

14 A. Mehrabian, "Orientation Behavior and Nonverbal Attitude in Communication," *Journal of Communication* 17 (1967): 324-332; and A. Mehrabian, "Relationship of Attitude to Seated Posture, Orientation, and Distance" *Journal of Personality and Social Psychology* 10 (1968): 26-30.

15 Mehrabian and Wiener, *op. cit.*; and Mehrabian and Ferris, *op. cit.*

16 D. W. Addington, "The Relationship of Selected Vocal Characteristics to Personality Perception," *Speech Monographs* 35 (1967): 492-503.

17 D. S. Ellis, "Speech and Social Status in America," *Social Forces* 45 (1967): 431-451.

18 W. Wilke and J. Snyder, "Attitudes Toward American Dialects," *Journal of Social Psychology* 14 (1941): 349-362.

18a See: J. A. Starkweather, "Vocal Communication of Personality and Human Feelings," *Journal of Communication* 11 (1961): 69; and J. R. Davitz, *The Communication of Emotional Meaning* (New York: McGraw-Hill, 1964), 23.

19 Davitz, *op. cit.*, 63.

20 A. Mehrabian and M. Williams, "Nonverbal Concomitants of Perceived and Intended Persuasiveness," *Journal of Personality and Social Psychology* 13 (1969): 37-58.

21 Kenneth Sereno and G. J. Hawkins, "The Effect of Variations in Speakers' Nonfluence Upon Audience Ratings of Attitude Toward the Speech Topic and Speakers' Credibility," *Speech Monographs* 34 (1967): 58-64.

22 Gerald R. Miller and M. A. Hewgill, "The Effect of Variations in Nonfluency on Audience Rating of Source Credibility," *Quarterly Journal of Speech* 50 (1964): 36-44.

23 W. B. Pearce and F. Conklin, "Nonverbal Vocalic Communication and Perceptions of a Speaker," *Speech Monographs* 38 (1971): 235-241.

24 W. B. Pearce, "The Effect of Vocal Cues on Credibility and Attitude Change," *Western Speech* 35 (1971): 176-184.

25 Charles Woolbert, "The Effects of Various Modes of Public Reading," *Journal of Applied Psychology* 4 (1920): 162-185; and G. M. Glasgow, "A Semantic Index of Vocal Pitch," *Speech Monographs* 19 (1952): 64-68. One study reports failure to detect a relationship: C. F. Diehl, R. C. White, and P. H. Saltz, "Pitch Change and Comprehension," *Speech Monographs* 28 (1961): 65-68.

26 C. F. Diehl and E. T. McDonald, "Effect of Voice Quality on Communication," *Journal of Speech and Hearing Disorders* 21 (1956): 223-237.

27 Mark L. Knapp, *Nonverbal Communication in Human Interaction* (New York: Holt, Rinehart and Winston, 1972): 165.

PART THREE
QUESTIONS FOR SELF-EVALUATION

Speaking Objectives

Language
1. Is your language fluent?
2. Is your language clear, avoiding unfamiliar words and awkward or unnecessarily complex sentence structure?
3. Is your language concise?
4. Is your language varied in word choice and sentence structure?
5. Is your language active and interesting?
6. Is your language intensity appropriate to your personality, to your listeners, to your purpose, and to the occasion?
7. Is your language stylistically pleasing?
8. Is your language grammatical, maintaining standard usage?
9. Does your language maintain oral style, or does it sound as if you had written it?

Appearance
10. Do you appear poised?
11. Are you speaking in a direct, friendly, conversational manner?
12. Are you looking at your listeners and talking with them?
13. Is your delivery spontaneous, or does it appear you are reading or have memorized your speech?
14. Do you appear lively and animated, using meaningful movement, including occasional walking and gestures, without pacing, shifting, swaying, or swinging?
15. Is your posture erect, with your weight comfortably distributed on both feet?
16. Are you avoiding distracting and repetitive mannerisms?
17. Are your notes unobtrusive and not distracting?
18. Are your audiovisual materials and demonstrations well planned, visible or audible, and not distracting?

Voice and articulation
19. Are you speaking loudly enough to be heard by everyone?
20. Is your voice lively, not monotonous; that is, is it adequately varied in pitch, volume, rate, and quality?
21. Is your voice free of distracting, repetitive patterns?
22. Is your pronunciation of words correct?
23. Do you have clear articulation, avoiding omissions, additions, substitutions, and distortions of sounds?

Listening Objectives

Reacting to language
1. Does the speaker's language conform to semantic rules, or is he or she bending the semantic rules to make room for pragmatic strategies? In particular, is he or she using devious language or language that is unfairly "loaded" or biased in his or her favor?
2. If the speaker is using devious or biased language, are you capable of recognizing that and still evaluating the proposal objectively?
3. If the speaker is violating phonemic and syntactic rules, or using phonemic and syntactic rules that differ from your own, are you capable of overlooking that so it does not adversely affect your attention or objectivity?
4. If the speaker is using language that is for one reason or another unclear, are you capable of clarifying it without allowing it to adversely affect your attention or objectivity?
5. If the speaker is using language that seems inappropriate in one way or another, are you capable of overlooking that so it does not adversely affect your attention or objectivity?
6. If the speaker is using language that is either too dynamic or inadequately dynamic, are you capable of overlooking that so it does not adversely affect your attention or objectivity?
7. Are you capable of disregarding the speaker's ability or inability to use language that is aesthetically pleasing, at least insofar as your attention and objectivity are concerned?

Reacting to nonverbal communication
8. Are you able to maintain sensitivity to anything the speaker's attire and grooming may communicate about his or her perception of you, of himself or herself and of your relationship without allowing irrelevant elements of general appearance, especially physical attractiveness or lack of it, distract your attention or cause you to accept or reject the proposal uncritically?
9. Can you detect any elements of the speaker's nonverbal communication that seem to contradict the verbal message?
10. If so, do the contradictions form a pattern that seems to indicate insincerity or attempted deception, or might they be merely unfortunate habits and/or reflections of speech anxiety?
11. Do the speaker's choice of speaking environment, arrangement of that environment, and use of space offer any clues as to his or her perceptions of his/her self and role, of you and your role, or of the relationship between you?
12. If so, are those clues relevant or irrelevant to your decision about the speaker's proposal?

13. Is there anything about the environment that makes it more difficult for you to keep your attention focused on the speaker or to give him or her a fair hearing?
14. Can you prevent the nonverbal reactions of other listeners from distracting your attention or unduly influencing your own reaction to the speaker?

CONCLUSION

BECOMING AWARE OF YOUR EDUCATION

As I mentioned earlier in this book, public deliberation plays an unusually important role in the evolution of ideas, because decisions made in public contexts generally influence far more people than do decisions made in other contexts. Thus, your role when speaking in public is also unusually important. Therfore, it might be a good plan to think a little beyond means of increasing your *proficiency* as a speaker to consider your *functions* in that role.

I emphasized that a speaker usually assists listeners in gathering information or in acting cooperatively, and occasionally assists them in self-actualization. Now the problem is that you as a speaker cannot be expected to *know* at all times what information is most reliable and useful to your listeners; you cannot be expected to *know* at all times what cooperative plans will be best for them; and you cannot be expected to *know* what their self-concepts "should" be. Plato took the line that, in order to be ethical, a speaker *must* know such things.[1] His reasoning led him to the conclusion that essentially there is no such thing as an ethical public speaker, or at least the requirements he set for speakers were so high that no one is ever likely to achieve them.

I take a very different position. I do not believe anyone "knows" what ideas will be "best" for the immediate audience or for humanity in general. In fact, people presuming they *know* what is "right" are, in my view, the most serious threat to ethical communication.

I definitely do not mean that you should hesitate to stand up for what you *believe* is right. What is dangerous is to discount the possibility that you may be wrong. Speakers who believe too strongly that they cannot be wrong are too likely to begin to resort to *any* available means to get their listeners to accept their ideas. They may lie; they may conceal information; they may appeal subtly to motives of which their listeners are unaware; or they may use faulty reasoning with the faults cleverly concealed. Then they may justify those actions by saying they knew what was best for their listeners.

I think that is a dangerous conceit, impossible to distinguish from deceit. Early chapters described how easily we can deceive ourselves, and speakers frequently deceive themselves into thinking ideas are good for their listeners when, in fact, the ideas are only good for the speakers themselves. As speakers we are not infallible. We are not saviors, or popes, or even priests. Arguing that a speaker must know what is right is not only holding up an impossible standard, it is encouraging a dangerous and potentially unethical presumption.

No, as a speaker you will do better to respect your listeners' right to decide for themselves what is best for them, just as you expect speakers to respect that right when you are a listener. Individuals make their own decisions and suffer the consequences. Therefore, they have a right to be fully aware of the bases for their decisions, and no speaker should presume to deny them that right.

Thus, as a public speaker, you have a function to serve in the process of ideological evolution that is even more basic than disseminating information, facilitating cooperation, or facilitating self-actualization. That function is to promote your listeners' awareness of their available alternatives and the bases on which they are making their choices.

Suppose we return to thinking about your function in terms of those three basic concepts of ideological evolution: variety, selection, and retention. Sometimes you will be presenting new ideas and information, contributing to the *variety* your listeners have available. Sometimes you will be arguing that, in view of what is known about the available alternatives and in view of their motives, your listeners should *select* one alternative rather than the others. Sometimes you will be trying to get your listeners to take some action to *retain* or preserve an alternative already selected.

Now if we assume that a speaker's basic function is to maximize the listeners' awareness, it is fairly easy to see what kinds of behaviors would undermine that function in each case. A speaker presenting new ideas and information would undermine that basic function if he or she were to conceal alternative ideas and information. He or she would be decreasing listeners' awareness of the variety of available alternatives. A speaker arguing for the selection of one alternative would undermine that basic function if he or she were to conceal favorable consequences of other alternatives or appeal to unconscious motives. Finally, a speaker trying to get listeners to take some action to retain an alternative already selected would undermine that basic function if the action he or she urged would restrict their ability to adopt other alternatives to adapt to future situations.

Frankly, I thought a long time before writing this book. I have been concerned because I believe teachers of communication have spent too much time teaching speakers how to manipulate others instead of teaching listeners how to avoid being manipulated. I am still concerned, because I realize many of the techniques described here can be used to decrease instead of increase listeners' awareness. I hope by presenting the techniques in a context that has emphasized the importance of communication awareness, the misuse of those techniques will be avoided, and my concerns will prove groundless. But that is now entirely up to you. I have described the alternatives available to you as clearly as possible because I respect your right to make your own choices as to how to use those techniques. I hope you choose wisely.

You will probably occupy the role of listener in public deliberation more frequently than you serve as speaker. You have important functions to serve in that role as well. As a listener you will *choose* certain speakers to whom you will give your attention; you will choose to encourage certain speakers and certain of their explanations and arguments and discourage other speakers, explanations, and arguments; and you will choose to retain, accept, and act on some of the information and arguments you encounter. As you do so, you will help to shape the future course of public deliberation and ideological evolution.

Many of us bemoan the present poor quality of advertising because it seldom gives us hard information about the products, so we have difficulty making critical decisions about what to buy. Too frequently advertising strives to be "cute" or to offer listeners ready-made self-images of which the product is a part. We also bewail the pathetic level of political campaigning because it provides little data on the abilities and qualifications of candidates or on the probable consequences of voting for or against ballot propositions. Instead it concentrates too often on image-building and "sloganizing."

But advertisers and politicians take great pains to find out what kinds of persuasion work most effectively, which means that *listeners choose* the kinds of advertising and political propaganda to which they are subjected. If they encourage the use of devices that conceal the true bases for decisions, they cannot escape responsiblity for diluting the quality of public deliberation and the evolution of ideas.

QUESTIONS FOR SELF-EVALUATION

Chapter One Speaking Objectives

Topic analysis

1. Do have a clear purpose in mind; that is, do you know specifically what you want your listeners to learn, or be able to do, or to believe, or what actions you want them to take?
2. Do you have a clear, unified central idea (thesis) which is adapted to that purpose?
3. Is your central idea narrowed so that you can do it justice in the time you have available?
4. Is your central idea important, significant, and interesting to your listeners?
5. Is your central idea adapted to this assignment or occasion?
6. Is your central idea adapted to your own knowledge and interests?
7. Is adequate information available to explain or support your central idea?
8. Have you analyzed your central idea into divisions that are appropriate to the material, significant to you and your listeners, and roughly proportionate to one another?

Part One Speaking Objectives

Audience analysis

9. Have you considered what motives your listeners have that are relevant to your topic in this situation?
10. Have you considered what interests your listeners have and the ways those interests will make them attentive or inattentive to your speech?
11. Have you considered how the opinions and policies of your listeners relate to your speech?
12. Have you considered how the reference groups of your listeners will shape their responses to your speech?
13. Have you considered what people or organizations your listeners are most likely to believe on this topic?
14. Have you considered what images your listeners might be trying to maintain?
15. Have you thought about what beliefs, values, and plans your listeners hold?
16. Have you thought about external (objective) data and internal (subjective) characteristics that your audience is sensitive to?
17. Have you considered what social rewards or punishments your listeners are sensitive to?

18. Have you thought about consistency in your arguments and presentation of data?
19. Have you thought about the role of your ego and that of your listeners in overcoming barriers to good communication?
20. Are you sincerely and respectfully attempting to empathize with your listeners and their demographic, personality, and belief differences and similarities?
21. Have you considered which model best fits your needs—Johari window, Stewart, MYLAR, Image: Belief-Value-Plan?

Part Two Speaking Objectives

Organization

22. Does your speech begin with an introduction suited to your purpose?
23. Does your introduction make provision for getting the initial attention of your listeners?
24. Will your introduction help your listeners like and respect you?
25. Does your introduction contain a clear statement of purpose? If not, do you have a good reason for omitting it?
26. Does your introduction contain a clear statement of your central idea or thesis? If not, do you have good reason for omitting it?
27. Does your introduction contain a clear organizational statement (statement of major divisions or arguments)? If not, do you have good reason for omitting it?
28. Does your introduction include all the definitions of terms and background information your listeners will need to understand your speech?
29. Is the sequence of your divisions logically planned?
30. Are your transitions clear and effective?
31. Do you have a conclusion?
32. Does your conclusion adequately summarize your speech?
33. Does your conclusion provide a climax which will bring your listeners to a peak of attention and interest and get them to take some specific action if that is your purpose?

Amplification and information

34. Is your information specific and concrete?
35. Is all your information relevant to your purpose and central idea?
36. Do you have enough information?
37. Is your information attributed to qualified sources or otherwise adequately tested for reliability?
38. Is your explanation clear?
39. Is your reasoning sound?

40. Is your material interesting?
41. Is your audiovisual material adequate to clarify your explanation?

Part Three Speaking Objectives

Language
42. Is your language fluent?
43. Is your language clear, avoiding unfamiliar words and awkward or unnecessarily complex sentence structure?
44. Is your language concise?
45. Is your language varied in word choice and sentence structure?
46. Is your language active and interesting?
47. Is your language intensity appropriate to your personality, to your listeners, to your purpose, and to the occasion?
48. Is your language stylistically pleasing?
49. Is your language grammatical, maintaining standard usage?
50. Does your language maintain oral style, or does it sound as if you had written it?

Appearance
51. Do you appear poised?
52. Are you speaking in a direct, friendly, conversational manner?
53. Are you looking at your listeners and talking with them?
54. Is your delivery spontaneous, or does it appear you are reading or have memorized your speech?
55. Do you appear lively and animated, using meaningful movement, including occasional walking and gestures, without pacing, shifting, swaying, or swinging?
56. Is your posture erect, with your weight comfortably distributed on both feet?
57. Are you avoiding distracting and repetitive mannerisms?
58. Are your notes unobtrusive and not distracting?
59. Are your audiovisual materials and demonstrations well planned, visible or audible, and not distracting?

Voice and articulation
60. Are you speaking loudly enough to be heard by everyone?
61. Is your voice lively, not monotonous; that is, is it adequately varied in pitch, volume, rate, and quality?
62. Is your voice free of distracting, repetitive patterns?
63. Is your pronunciation of words correct?
64. Do you have clear articulation —avoiding omissions, additions, substitutions, and distortions of sounds?

Chapter One Listening Objectives

Preparing for reception and retention

1. Are you sitting where you can clearly see and hear the speaker?
2. Are you physically comfortable, mentally relaxed, and yet alert?
3. Are you ready to concentrate on the speech rather than reminisce, daydream, or plan future activities?
4. Are there distractions in the physical environment which you can eliminate or minimize?
5. Is there anything about the speech topic or about the speaker's prior reputation or immediate appearance which might cause you to prematurely dismiss the topic and/or speaker?
6. Are your prepared to temporarily suspend your own preconceptions or counterarguments until you have given the speaker a fair hearing?

Part One Listening Objectives

Analysis of self and speaker

7. Are you actively trying to empathize with the speaker to determine what motivates him or her to present this speech?
8. Are you earnestly working to minimize or at least recognize the effects of any differences between yourself and the speaker?
9. Do you have any demographic characteristics, personality characteristics, reference persons, reference groups, beliefs, values, plans, or policies that might hinder your attention or comprehension or cause you to *reject* uncritically this speaker or the speech?
10. Do you have any such characteristics (as in item #9) which might cause you to *accept* uncritically this speaker or the speech?
11. Have you considered the age, sex, race, socioeconomic status, education of the speaker and how similar or different they are from your own background?
12. Have you thought about the cultural assumptions that are being made by the speaker and by yourself?
13. Is the speaker dogmatic or open-minded? Which are you?
14. Is the speaker high in self-esteem, need to influence, trusting, and other personality characteristics? How similar are you in these areas?
15. What authorities is the speaker citing and do they meet the reliability tests:
    a) in a position to observe the facts?
    b) capable of observing the facts?
    c) objective or subjective?

     d) reliable in the past?

     e) accountable?

16. What beliefs, plans, or policies is the speaker asking you to understand or change?

17. What rewards are possible from this speaker? Is he or she delivering them?

18. Is the speaker appealing to any consistencies or inconsistencies in your image? What about the speaker's image?

19. Is the speaker ego-defensive or ego-involved? How defensive are you and how ego-involved?

Part Two Listening Objectives

Understanding and evaluating content and structure

20. Does the speaker's purpose appear to be only to inform or also to persuade?

21. If the speaker's thesis, central idea, purpose, and major divisions or arguments are stated in the introduction, does your initial agreement or disagreement make you want to prematurely, uncritically accept or reject the speech?

22. If the speaker's introduction does *not* contain such statements, are there any indications he or she may be deliberately concealing them?

23. If the speaker's introduction does *not* contain such explicit statements, can you provide them on the basis of transitions or your overall analysis of the speech?

24. If the speaker's purpose appears to be only to inform, which type of informative speech is it?

25. What methods of explanation and amplification is the speaker using?

26. Is the speaker's material or its structure and sequencing threatening your attention, comprehension, or retention?

27. If the material is creating such problems, can you help by relating the explanation and amplification to other information or experiences you have encountered?

28. If the speech structure and sequencing are causing problems, are there ways you can rearrange it which will aid your comprehension and retention?

29. If the speaker's purpose appears to be to persuade as well as inform, which of your beliefs, values, plans, and policies is he or she trying to change?

30. If the speaker is trying to persuade you, what *specifically* is he or she trying to get you to do?

31. What physical, social, or internal consequences is the speaker explicitly claiming will ensue if you accept or reject the proposal?

32. Is the speaker suggesting implicitly that any other physical, social, or internal consequences will ensue? If so, does this reflect his or her unwillingness to state those implicit suggestions as explicit claims?

33. Are these consequences ones on which you want to base your decision?

34. Are there any consequences in addition to those the speaker mentions? If so, are there any reasons to believe the omissions are intentional?

35. Are the speaker's data related to the claims by adequate warrants; that is, does the reasoning used relating the evidence to the claims meet the applicable tests for such reasoning?

36. Does the speaker leave unsupported any data or warrants you believe require further support?

37. Are the speaker's data or items of evidence attributed to reliable sources or, if not, do you know them to be accurate?

38. To what extent is the speaker depending on the likeablenss or general prestige of his or her sources rather than upon their qualifications to offer expert testimony on the specific matter in question?

39. Are there any other data or lines of reasoning you know of that are relevant to the speaker's claims? If so, do they hurt his or her cause? If so, are there reasons to believe the omissions are intentional?

40. Which type of persuasive speech structure is the speaker using?

41. Is there anything about that structure that might lead you to accept or reject the speaker's proposal uncritically?

42. If the structure is one that might produce uncritical acceptance, are there reasons to believe the speaker might have chosen the structure for that reason?

43. Does the speaker at any point attempt to get you to commit yourself to the proposal in ways which might prevent you from objectively evaluating future information?

44. Does the speaker at any point appeal for immediate action when it seems more beneficial to postpone action pending further investigation?

45. Does the speaker fairly describe and adequately refute important opposing arguments, or does he or she describe those arguments unfairly and/or try to prepare you to uncritically reject opposing arguments you may encounter in the future?

46. Have you previously encountered messages from this speaker or other speakers that are relevant to the present proposal?

47. If so, is there anything about those previous messages that might cause you to uncritically accept or reject the present proposal?

48. Is there anything about this present speech that might prevent you from objectively evaluating future messages from this speaker or future messages on this topic?

49. Has the feedback you have provided this speaker reinforced his or her speech behavior in ways that will be beneficial to his or her future listeners?

Part Three Listening Objectives

Reacting to language

50. Does the speaker's language conform to semantic rules, or is he or she bending the semantic rules to make room for pragmatic strategies? In particular, is he or she using devious language or language that is unfairly "loaded" or biased in his or her favor?

51. If the speaker is using devious or biased language, are you capable of recognizing that and still evaluating the proposal objectively?

52. If the speaker is violating phonemic and syntactic rules, or using phonemic and syntactic rules that differ from your own, are you capable of overlooking that so it does not adversely affect your attention or objectivity?

53. If the speaker is using language that is for one reason or another unclear, are you capable of clarifying it without allowing it to adversely affect your attention or objectivity?

54. If the speaker is using language that seems inappropriate in one way or another, are you capable of overlooking that so it does not adversely affect your attention or objectivity?

55. If the speaker is using language that is either too dynamic or inadequately dynamic, are you capable of overlooking that so it does not adversely affect your attention or objectivity?

56. Are you capable of disregarding the speaker's ability or inability to use language that is aesthetically pleasing, at least insofar as your attention and objectivity are concerned?

Reacting to nonverbal communication

57. Are you able to maintain sensitivity to anything the speaker's attire and grooming may communicate about his or her perception of you, of himself or herself and of your relationship without allowing irrelevant elements of general appearance, especially physical attractiveness or lack of it, to distract your attention or cause you to accept or reject the proposal uncritically?

58. Can you detect any elements of the speaker's nonverbal communication that seem to contradict the verbal message?

59. If so, do the contradictions form a pattern that seems to indicate insincerity or attempted deception, or might they be merely unfortunate habits and/or reflections of speech anxiety?

60. Do the speaker's choice of a speaking environment, arrangement of that environment, and use of space offer any clues as to his or her perceptions of his/her self and role, or you and your role, or of the relationship between you?

61. If so, are those clues relevant or irrelevant to your decision about the speaker's proposal?

62. Is there anything about the environment that makes it more difficult for you to keep your attention focused on the speaker or to give him or her a fair hearing?

63. Can you prevent the nonverbal reactions of other listeners from distracting your attention or unduly influencing your own reaction to the speaker?

64. If there are aspects of the speaker's posture, gestures, facial expressions, articulation, or voice which are distracting and/or unpleasant, can you prevent them from interfering with your attention or from causing you to reject the proposal uncritically?

65. If the speaker's physical activity, articulation, and voice are unusually smooth and pleasant, can you prevent them from causing you to accept the proposal uncritically?

66. Is your own nonverbal communication helping or hindering the speaker and other listeners?

Conclusion Reference

1 Plato, *Gorgias*, tr. W. C. Helmbold (Indianapolis: Bobbs-Merrill, 1952).

Speech Rating Scale

Speaker _____

Audience analysis   Considered relevant motives, interests, opinions and policies, reference groups, and credibility of sources?

Topic analysis   Clear purpose? Clear, unified, narrowed, important, significant, interesting central idea? Adapted to assignment or occasion, own knowledge and interests? Adequate information available? Major divisions appropriate, significant, and proportionate?

Organization   Introduction suited to purpose; attention-getting; conducive to liking and respect; containing statement of purpose, central idea, major divisions, definitions of terms, and background information as appropriate? Sequence of divisions logical? Transitions clear and effective? Conclusion with summary, climax, and action appeal (if appropriate)?

Amplification and information   Specific, concrete, relevant, adequate quantity? Attributed to qualified sources or otherwise reliable? Clear explanation? Sound reasoning? Material interesting? Audiovisual material contributes to understanding?

Language   Fluent, clear, concise, varied, active, interesting, of appropriate intensity, stylistically pleasing, grammatical, maintaining oral style?

Appearance   Poised, direct, friendly, conversational? Looking at and talking with listeners? Spontaneous, not read or memorized? Lively, animated, with meaningful nondistracting movement? Posture erect, comfortable, balanced? No distracting and repetitive mannerisms? Notes unobtrusive? Audiovisual materials and demonstrations well-planned, visible or audible, not distracting?

Voice and articulation   Adequate volume? Voice lively, not monotonous, comprehensible rate, free of distracting, repetitive patterns? Pronunciation correct? Articulation clear?

Total

NAME INDEX

SUBJECT INDEX